Critical Theo
Then and Now

# Critical Theories of Mass Media: Then and Now

Paul A. Taylor and Jan Ll. Harris

McGraw Hill

Open University Press

Open University Press
McGraw-Hill Education
McGraw-Hill House
Shoppenhangers Road
Maidenhead
Berkshire
England
SL6 2QL

email: enquiries@openup.co.uk
world wide web: www.openup.co.uk

and Two Penn Plaza, New York, NY 10121—2289, USA


First published 2008

Copyright © Paul A. Taylor and Jan LI. Harris 2008

A catalogue record of this book is available from the British Library

ISBN: 13: 9780 335218110 (pb) 9780 335218127 (hb)
      10: 03335 218113 (pb) 0335218121 (hb)




Typeset by Kerrypress Ltd, Luton, Bedfordshire
Printed in Poland by OZGraf S.A.
www.polskabook.pl

It comes as a shock to that first audience.
The street they walked in off just moments before
hangs pale on the wall ...
*and their hairs stand on end to a shimmer of leaves*
*or the movement of clouds, and the way the tense*
*has been thrown like a switch, where the land turns to dreams,*
*and where,*
*sad to say, we have been living since.*
(Paul Farley, '*Electricity*', from *The Boy from the Chemist is Here to See*
*You*

I was witnessing a time when most things, including hard cash and
our perception of reality itself, were about to be turned into an idea
of themselves ... I began to notice the insistence of image over
substance and this insistence began to pester me, like a bad radio
station that you can't afford to turn off.

   ... we were just that bit too old to buy into the rumble of a world
described by advertising and products ...That was the world where
everything had turned into an idea of itself, where life no longer
had an inner life ... It's a process which just seems to have built up,
like an accumulation of fat around the heart's weary muscle.

(Michael Bracewell, *Perfect Tense*)

# Contents

# Acknowledgements

Paul: warmest regards to the stalwart, and justifiably cynical, fellow barrel-dwellers from The Eldon Club branch of the Diogenes Society (past and present) – Kishore Budha, Allison Cavanagh, Richard Howells, Azeez Lukumann, Diane Myers, and Nicholas Ray – diamonds in the midden.

Jan: for Maisie R.I.P.

# Chapter outlines

## Introduction

The need for more critical engagement with the cultural consequences of the mass media is asserted. It is suggested that contemporary theorists have been too willing to overlook the various
alienating and inauthentic aspects of mediated culture in their
enthusiasm to detect evidence of proactive interpretive activity within
mass audiences. Excessively optimistic faith in such interpretive
activities are discussed using the umbrella term *cultural populism*. A
brief critique of cultural populism is provided in preparation for this
book's corrective presentation of an alternative perspective based
upon both a historical and a contemporary account of such central
critical theory tenets as *the culture industry thesis* – the argument that
mass media culture is disproportionately commodified and systematized.

## Part 1    *Then*

### Chapter 1    *Walter Benjamin's 'The work of art' essay*

Walter Benjamin's essay, '*The work of art in the age of mechanical
reproduction*' (henceforth referred to as the Essay), is presented as a
seminal piece from which to better understand the 'hinge point' in
the development of the mass media. Despite its generally optimistic
tenor, Benjamin's examination of photography and early cinema is
shown to contain the roots of a much more pessimistic interpretation of the harmful cultural effects of mass media. We argue that
Benjamin's Essay reveals how technological reproduction is intrinsically aligned with commodity values at the expense of non-
commodified culture.

### Chapter 2    *Siegfried Kracauer's Mass Ornament*

A contemporary of Benjamin, Siegfried Kracauer shared some of the
former's optimism regarding the potentially emancipatory qualities
the mass media held for their audiences. However, there is a need to
reassess the more critical aspects of Kracauer that lie close to the

surface of his treatment of popular culture, particularly his concepts of *Ratio*, the *cult of distraction* and the *mass ornament*. It is argued that the negative implications of these notions remain highly relevant to a critical understanding of today's media.

## Chapter 3    Theodor Adorno and the culture industry

Adorno's *culture industry thesis* is defended as a key intellectual resource with which to approach contemporary media. Sharing both Benjamin and Kracauer's interest in the theme of *distraction* as a new mode of audience reception in the age of mass media, Adorno's work is explored for the ways in which it highlights the links to be found between media technologies and the fundamental philosophical underpinnings of Western capitalist culture. It is argued that, far from being unduly cynical and elitist as critics often suggest, Adorno's *culture industry thesis* actually underestimated the sophistication and reach of today's mediascape.

## Chapter 4    Marshall McLuhan's understanding of the media

Despite the apparent optimism with which he analysed media technologies, McLuhan's work is shown to contain the seeds of a deeply critical portrayal of the media's social impact. He consistently emphasizes the various ways in which the media profoundly rearrange and disorientate the human sensorium. McLuhan shows how the media promote essentially reactive, adaptive responses to *their* needs rather than those of the societies they increasingly dominate.

## Chapter 5    Guy Debord's Society of the Spectacle

Part 1 concludes with an account of Guy Debord's *Society of the Spectacle*. This brings together the key themes of the previous chapters with Debord's conception of a mass media society whose cultural frame of reference is dominated by the ubiquitous and defining presence of the spectacle. In conjunction with the previous examination of McLuhan, Debord's theory is shown to provide a key transition point between the theorists of the *then* who wrote in the relatively early days of mass media society and Part 2's treatment of the *now* and more recent forms of the *society of the spectacle*.

## Part 2    Now

## Chapter 6    The culture of celebrity

The origins and current prevalence of celebrity values in mass culture are examined in direct relation to Part 1's themes of the decline of aura and the culture industry thesis. New forms of celebrity are defined and examined in the context of a critical account of their cultural effects. The tautological nature of contemporary fame in which people are frequently famous merely for being famous, irrespective of any other identifiable talent, is analysed as an aspect of industrial production processes that are now applied to culture in an unprecedentedly sophisticated fashion. It is suggested that, from a critical perspective, celebrity *now* serves to undermine the positive role Benjamin foresaw for distraction *then*.

## Chapter 7 *Banality TV: the democratization of celebrity*

Part 1's critique of cultural populism is continued with a critical assessment of theories that find empowering possibilities within the pervasive phenomenon of celebrity. The counter argument is put forward that, as the human embodiment of commodity values, contemporary forms of celebrity represent a further disturbing expansion of the culture industry's harmful effects. *Banality TV* is the term used to describe celebrity's widespread democratization within the increasing conflated genres of lifestyle programmes, Reality TV[1] and chat shows. These formats consist of predominantly unscripted presentations of everyday life but the idea that this fosters increased audience involvement and empowerment is critically offset against the conception of *Banality TV* as an ultimately disempowering phenomenon intimately related to the media's promotion of contingent, superficial detail over substantive thought.

## Chapter 8 *The politics of banality: the obscene as the mis-en-scène*

The final chapter argues that instead of being an exclusively cultural phenomenon, *Banality TV* has profound political consequences. World events such as 9/11, the Gulf conflicts and the Abu Ghraib controversy are used in conjunction with Jean Baudrillard's conception of the *obscene* to demonstrate critical media theories' continued importance for a fuller understanding of popular culture's ideological qualities.

# Introduction: Cultural populism and Critical theory

## The new Plato's Cave

> I want you to go on to picture the enlightenment or ignorance of our human condition somewhat as follows. Imagine an underground chamber like a cave, with a long entrance open to the daylight and as wide as the cave. In this chamber are men who have been prisoners there since they were children, their legs and necks being so fastened that they can only look straight ahead of them and cannot turn their heads. Some way off, behind and higher up, a fire is burning, and between the fire and the prisoners and above them runs a road, in front of which a curtain-wall has been built, like the screen at puppet shows between the operators and their audience, above which they show their puppets ...
>
> (Plato 1955: 317)

Plato's allegory of prisoners in a cave is contained within *The Republic* (approx 375 BC). It was originally used to describe the philosophical difficulty of uncovering truth in a human world that is inevitably error-strewn. From our contemporary perspective we can easily imagine the shadows projected onto the cave wall as a primitive form of cinema projection and thus Plato's image becomes highly resonant with our own media-saturated society. Citing Plato from the very beginning of this book underlines the key *now* and *then* theme of its subtitle. Any novelty in the following analysis stems paradoxically from the relatively unfashionable insistence that the central tenets of critical theories of mass media are still highly relevant despite their relatively marginal position in mainstream cultural/ communication studies and the sociology of the media. This book aims to give these critical theories of the past a fresh impetus from more recent theoretical developments. It is hoped that this will provide an antidote to the present dominance within academic discourse of excessively uncritical theories of mass-media culture that contribute to our staying bound within a new Plato's Cave – albeit an unprecedentedly comfortable one replete with high-definition plasma screens.

The lack of a critical edge to much discussion of the mass media has profoundly dangerous political implications for two main reasons.

1   The inhabitants of Plato's Cave lacked the physical freedom to
    see the unmediated reality beyond the cave entrance that was
    causing the shadows on the wall. In the new mass-media cave the
    constraints are all the more insidiously effective for their pre-
    dominantly immaterial and frequently voluntary nature[1]. To
    paraphrase Marx – mankind is free yet everywhere he is in
    chainstores.

We shall see in the following chapters that our mass-media
environment is permeated by ideological components that are
overlooked – not because they don't exist, but rather because they
are an innate part of how the media functions. Familiarity not only
breeds contempt – it also sometimes makes it difficult to spot what is
under our noses so that:

2   Even when the mass media's deeply ideological aspects are
    recognized, instead of being seen as a source for concern,
    uncritical theories of the media have a perverse tendency to
    celebrate such ideological processes as evidence of the rude
    health of cultural life and agency within mass media society.

In the following pages it is repeatedly pointed out how this
tendency constitutes a particularly disturbing variation upon Plato's
allegory of the Cave. At least the original dwellers could claim the
mitigating circumstance of enforced imprisonment: frequently, their
counterparts in the contemporary media cave (and their apologist
theorists) appear to connive actively at their own oppression.

## The trouble with being critical: in defence of pessimism

To complement the above two main political dangers, there are also
two basic problems faced by critical theories of mass media.

1   It is difficult to gain the necessary analytical distance to properly
    understand the social implications of the mass media.

Marshall McLuhan compared the difficulty of seeking an objective
perspective upon the media to explaining the notion of water to a
fish, while Friedrich Kittler (1990, 1997, 1999) argues that we can
only begin to understand media configurations from a suitably long
historical perspective, thus questioning the possibility of meaningful
contemporaneous analysis. In *Plato's Cave* (1991), John O'Neil
describes the additional problem of developing a *critical* perspective
in relation to the media:

One is either a player, a committed commentator, or a fan –
but hardly ever is a place kept for the contemplative mind. To

claim to know more than what is going on in the media than
the media allow for, however, is to be out of joint with the form
and content of the media. Critics of the media are exiles, or
else they are allowed to strut their brief moment among life's
killjoys, as a reminder of those higher things for which we have
neither the time nor the taste.

(O'Neil 1991: 21)

Implicit in O'Neil's complaint is a sense of the overwhelming
immediacy of the media environment that successfully displaces any
attempt to obtain a more considered vantage point. But, rather than
producing critical engagement with this situation, difficult as that
may be, the dominant response from current media theorists tends
to be one of excessively optimistic celebration. They laud the
media's powerful ability to produce environments predicated upon
the untrammelled pervasion of immanent flows of information[2] and
images but fail to consider how much *genuine* empowerment can be
gained from engagement with such heavily pre-processed content, no
matter how imaginative and proactive that engagement attempts to
be. This book's assessment of the possibilities for empowerment is
much more straightforwardly pessimistic.

2  Critics of mass culture are often accused of being conservative,
   out-of-touch elitists.

In relation to the vexed question of optimism versus pessimism,
this book seeks to:

- rectify the situation whereby critical theory has been unfairly
  neglected simply because of its downbeat tone – there seems little
  intellectual basis for the common tendency to automatically prize
  positive interpretations over more negative ones, especially if the
  Old Testament (a foundational cultural text of *then* if ever there
  was one) is correct in claiming: 'For in much wisdom is much
  vexation; and he that increaseth knowledge increaseth sorrow'
  (Ecclesiastes 1:18).
- suggest that even amid theories generally accepted as optimistic,
  there is frequently ample evidence for a more critical rereading.

Consistently, valid grounds for critical engagement with the media
seem to be unduly passed over in preference for Panglossian
analyses. At certain crucial points, commentators wilfully either step
around, or even over, those negative elements that early theorists did
in fact identify but which they thought could be overcome. Such
optimism is more understandable in the early days of the mass
media but our benefit of historical hindsight makes uncritical
repetitions of these interpretations, at best, untenable, and at worst,

disingenuous. This book explores past thinkers who are explicitly critical thinkers (Adorno and Debord) but also those we label critical based upon our against-the-grain reading of their underlying critical credentials (Benjamin and McLuhan). A common quality that unites both optimistic and pessimistic sets of thinkers is their shared belief that the media is deeply disruptive to prior forms of social organization. There is a surprising amount of agreement on the basic social processes of the mass media but radically different conclusions as to their ultimate cultural consequences.

## Cultural populism: the paradox of conservatism

Past and present critical media theories emphasize the negative consequences that stem from the innately commodified nature of such mass cultural phenomenon as Reality TV (for example, Andrejevic 2004) and lifestyle Television (Palmer 2004, 2005, 2006, 2007). *New audience theory, reception studies* and *cultural populism* are, among others, all terms used to describe those studies of the media that tend to emphasize the empowerment enjoyed by mass audiences. In relation to the media's content, they focus upon audiences' productive emotional investments, imaginative interpretations, and the generally active, non-passive nature of their counter-hegemonic reading strategies. Although the relevant literature in this field is rich and diverse[3], the term *cultural populism*[4] is used in this book as an umbrella term to create a dichotomy between these approaches and much more obviously negative critical theories. While producing a dichotomy risks simplifying matters for the sake of a clear contrast, there are obvious characteristics that do distinguish the two approaches.

Contemporary rejection of critical media theory is largely based upon varying degrees of post-structuralist sensitivity to the ways in which the audience can re-appropriate the meanings imposed upon them by the owners and producers of media content. Rather than seeing media audiences or commodity consumers as simply passive consumers of the products of an overarching culture industry, cultural populists (broadly defined) prefer to emphasize the way in which audiences actively reinterpret or 'read' programmes or products using alternative meanings better suited to their own particular, localized environments (McLaughlin 1996). Fiske (1987, 1989a, 1989b, 1993, 1996), is a particularly radical proponent of the notion that rather than being passive dupes of the culture industry, mass-media audiences are in fact skilled interpreters of media content. He forcefully argues against the culture industry's focus upon the manipulation of audiences and uses concepts such as *polysemy* and *heteroglossia* to discuss how audiences apply a large and

adaptable range of interpretations to the media content they consume. Other typical features of cultural populism include an emphasis upon the *performative* (Abercrombie and Longhurst 1998) and the
*participatory* (Livingstone and Lunt 1994) aspects of audiences. More
recently, while some recognition has been given to its underlying
commodity values, the notion of the *ordinary* in media content has
been presented as a site of potentially empowering interpretive
contestations for equally ordinary audiences (Brundson et al. 2001;
Giles 2002; Taylor 2002; Kompare 2004; Bonner 2003).

In recent years there have also been various critical accounts of
lifestyle and Reality TV programmes (brought together in this book
under the term *Banality TV*) that allude to the relationship between
media *form* and *content* but which mostly concentrate upon the
discursive and persuasive aspects of the latter. For example, Lorenzo-
Dus (2006) examines the manipulative aspects encoded within
British property shows, Dunn (2006) adopts a similar approach to
the personalized voyeurism of holiday programmes that concentrate
more upon presenters and particular participants than the destina-
tions themselves, and Banet-Weiser and Portwood-Stacer (2006)
explore the ideological components of a new spate of make-over
shows (involving a range of targets from participants' property to
their bodies). This book concentrates more upon those critical
thinkers who see the negative cultural effects of the media as an
*innate* part of their mode of operation. The fact that their theories
are consequently pessimistic about the possibilities for *any* media
content being significantly re-appropriated and reinterpreted in a
particularly empowering fashion, often results in the charge that
they are traditional conservatives or 'elitists'.

This is a charge typically levelled at the Frankfurt School, who laid
much of the groundwork for contemporary critical theories. This is
an accusation misapplied to those who are actually criticizing the
ultimately conservative consequences of the pervasively and invasively
commodified nature of mass-mediated social life despite its often
superficial presentation as 'edgy' and counter-cultural. Ironically, a
*paradox of conservatism* arises from the fact that the real conservatives
are those cultural populists who act, either openly or inadvertently,
as apologists for the deeply alienating and reactionary qualities of
the mass media's output. Critical theories of media do not so much
flatly deny the basic findings of cultural populism as argue that
specific evidence of audience interpretive activity needs to be judged
in terms of the deeper political significance of that activity. The
brief, illustrative, examples below suggest that the desire of cultural
populism to find evidence of audience empowerment risks, at best,
gilding the evidentiary lily and, at worst, actually producing its own
form of conservative and elitist values. A patronization of the masses

in a theoretical form of *noblesse oblige* occurs if the content consumed in mass culture tautologically becomes evidence of audience empowerment irrespective of its quality.

With due respect to O'Neil, only killjoys would object to cultural pleasure in and of itself, but a failure of intellectual duty takes place when theorists fail to point out when such pleasure becomes its own justification and vulnerable to excessive manipulation for profit and ideological ends – in the process excluding *any* other social considerations. The *critical* aspect of this book's account of various media theories is repeatedly emphasized. It highlights and sympathetically reassesses those theories that are conventionally labelled and (unfairly) dismissed as somehow elitist for their stubborn insistence that popularity does not prove culture's ultimate worth. Less obviously critical authors are reread for their generally under-acknowledged negative attributes. For example, Benjamin, Kracauer and McLuhan have all been viewed as predominantly optimistic interpreters of the positive cultural potential of mass-media technologies but there are strong reasons to re-evaluate this reputation.

The main difference between proponents of the culture industry thesis and cultural populists is their contrasting view of the framing function of the media. The Frankfurt School are accused of investing media with a malign agency, in other words, fetishizing the frame into an oppressive monolithic structure. The weakness of cultural populism, however, rests in the various theoretical over-compensations it makes in order to find examples of audience empowerment. These compensations take three main forms of argument:

1  The media frame is at worst neutral, and at best, positive
2  Inadvertently counterproductive evidence
3  The content of the frame is open to radical reinterpretation.

## 1   *The media frame is at worst neutral, and at best, positive*

In contrast to the culture industry's perspective of the media frame as a negative circumscription of the public sphere, Scannell (1996) sees it as a predominantly neutral or even positive constitutive part of contemporary life. In a misleadingly selective reading of Heidegger that ignores his specific analyses of technology, the media's pervasive and durable presence in the lives of the audience is claimed to provide a 'world-disclosing' function. In a similar vein, Couldry presents a neo-Durkheimian interpretation of media rituals (2003) and an enthusiastic account of the role of *visiting pilgrims* that soap fans adopt at the set of Coronation Street (2000). He non-ironically states that the programme has over its nearly forty year life span, 'offered a continuous fictional reality, operating in parallel to viewers' lives. For some, it may serve as mnemonic system for events in their own life ... For such visitors ... visiting the set has a temporal depth connected not just with the programme's history, but with their own lives' (Couldry 2000: 76). In such readings, it is claimed that the media provides *mediation* for the inevitably large amount of para-social relations that exist in contemporary society and helps to ground them in the audience's lived experience.

This process is viewed by cultural populists as predominantly positive – despite poor supporting evidence. The media's construction of a whole realm of social discourse that provides much needed sense and orientation in the disorientating flux of mass-media society is, in terms of this book's argument, part of the problem rather than a comforting solution. The central point made throughout this book is that à la Heidegger, Ellul, McLuhan et al., *technological form is itself content* and this form/content hybrid has disturbing *not* reassuringly constitutive powers. As Couldry himself acknowledges, 'the media process does not merely interact with the rest of society; it has a major impact on how the rest of society understands and imagines itself' (Couldry 2000: 54). Critical theory throws into sharp relief such concepts of empowerment as *media-pilgrims*, drawing as they do upon group-models that are more obeisant, gullible and pliable than meaningfully empowered.

## 2   *Inadvertently counterproductive evidence*

The misplaced optimism of uncritical media theorists is repeatedly revealed in the use of evidence that is frequently counterproductive and which critical theorists such as Adorno would be hard put to better as illlustrative material for their own much darker critiques. Couldry (2000), for example, seeks to show how pilgrims to the actual site of media production sets are freshly empowered by the fillip a physical 'seeing it with their own eyes' provides for their deconstructive abilities. In making this argument, however, Couldry's rich fieldwork material provides strong evidence of stubbornly disempowering attitudes. For example, there is the bathos/banality, of a mother and daughter's dialogue subsequent to a purportedly enlightening tour of Granada Studios Coronation Street set:

Mother:      ... I just wish I could have met a star [...] or if I'd gone round a studio.

Daughter:   It'd be nice if somebody came up the Street and wandered around, one an hour, one an hour, one an hour, a different one every hour.

Mother:      Oh, it would have been lovely.

Daughter:    Just to see different people, probably not to talk to
them, just to see them, walking up the Street, or
around wherever we've been, yeah.
Mother:    Yeah, it would've been lovely.

Daughter:    Just to see one.

(Couldry 2000: 97)

Similarly, in an otherwise critically aware text, Inglis (1990) support-
ively cites Morley's attempt to document the empowering aspects of
television in his work *Family Television* (1986). From a critical
perspective, however, this attempt meets with limited success. Morley
portrays a working-class patriarch who watches certain programmes
to a tight regimen and assiduously videotapes any other programmes
that clash. This is a man loathe to leave the private realm of his
living room. He appears *avant la lettre* (ahead of his time) remarkably similar to the character Jim from the BBC series *The Royle
Family*. Morley describes: 'the bottomless pit of this man's desire for
programmes to watch' (Morley 1986: 71). Inglis, nevertheless, refers
to him as 'a fascinating folk-figure' and claims that 'His unstoppable
soliloquy must do here to suggest just how various are the needs and
purposes working themselves out in audiences' (Inglis 1990: 154). In
such misguidedly optimistic evaluations, we can see clear illustrations
of a widespread risk that theorists bend over backwards not to see
personifications of the culture industry thesis in their own subjects
of enquiry. Indeed, ironically, it is likely that if material of the same
tone was found in the work of culture industry theorists it would in
all likelihood be rejected for its overly selective, exaggeratedly
patronizing, and generally unrealistic depiction of alienated consumption. Inglis claims that Morley 'speaks up for and documents
the sociable and sociable uses of television' (Inglis 1990: 153). This
is an aim that is consistent with the cultural populism approach, but
which in fact fails to take us far from a contemporary manifestation
of Plato's Cave to the extent that: 'in going out to a public place this
man experiences a loss of the total power which he has established
within the walls of his own home' (Morley, cited in Inglis 1990: 153).
Emblematic of cultural populism's lack of critical edge, borderline
agoraphobia is represented as personal empowerment.

Further illustrations of counterproductive evidence of audience
empowerment are evident in the work of Radway (1984) and Barker
and Brooks (in Dickinson et al. 1998) and more recently Poster
(2006) and Jenkins (2006a, 2006b). Radway's much cited study
explored the purportedly empowering way in which women read
Harlequin series romances. She argued that the act of carving out
personal time to do this reading amongst the otherwise pressing
demands of their families meant that the women were effectively
resisting the patriarchally imposed, gendered roles conventionally

assigned to them. Barker and Brooks, meanwhile, attempt to find evidence of empowerment in the way fans consume the comics and 1995 film of *Judge Dredd*. Such approaches tend to overemphasize the extent to which such activities constitute 'empowerment' in any deeper sense as understood by critical theory. Little, if any, evidence is provided that cultural populism's version of empowerment involves the ability of the audience/media pilgrim to challenge or even question the fundamental nature of the media's structuring of their social conditions. Greater access to the sites of media production (Couldry 2000, 2003) or more *regulated pluralism* (Thompson 1995) in the ownership of the means of media production, will not solve the innately alienating features of the media framework itself. For example, Barker and Brooks fail to see the irony in their choice of the term *investment* to 'summarize all the ways in which audiences demonstrate strength of involvement to a social ideal of cinema' (Dickinson et al. 1998: 225). Although they openly acknowledge that: 'This concept of "investment" is a key one for us' (1998: 225), it appears much better suited to describing the deep overlapping of cultural values with a pervasively commodified cultural setting as set out in the culture industry thesis than it is to representing 'a social ideal'. Similarly, Jenkins and Poster's accounts focus upon the immersion of consumers within a commodity life-world with little recognition that this could be anything other than an ultimately liberating experience.

There may be a sense in which culture industry advocates and their opponents are arguing in parallel monologues. Those seeking to emphasize audience empowerment concentrate upon the ways in which a cultural commodity is consumed with various degrees of gusto, whereas culture industry theorists question that very gusto. For the Frankfurt School et al., the very consumption of a commodity is part of the underlying problem rather than a possible solution. Summarizing this debate Alasuutari suggests that active audience notions of consumption represent: 'a move away from the sphere of aesthetics to the political, or one could say that it politicizes the aesthetics of everyday life' (Alasuutari 1999: 11). This represents a *now* version of the similar *then* argument that, using very similar language, Benjamin makes for the positive potential of mass culture explored in detail in the next chapter. A perennial caricature of critical theory's position is that it represents an elitist defence of highbrow against lowbrow art. This is a misrepresentation that leads to the further misleading implication that the culture industry thesis is rooted in the aesthetic (rather than the political) because arguments against the cultural industry thesis are purported to represent 'a move away from' the aesthetic sphere. In fact, the opposite of Alasuutari's conclusion can be argued because the very juxtaposition of the term *industry* next to *culture* in the Frankfurt School's term makes it an already politically rooted statement. Critical theory argues that attempts to see political meaning in acts of consumption actually serve to aestheticize the everyday further rather than politicize it. The deeply conservative properties of uncritical consumption are glossed over. Aesthetic appreciations of commodity culture are fuelled by often impressively imaginative interpretations – but they frequently fail to recognize the true political implications of its *essentially* commodified nature.

According to Ang (1985), it is misguided to debate whether cultural products are inherently progressive or conservative because this approach fails to appreciate fully the independently important nature of pleasure as a distinct, politically neutral entity. In relation to the US television series *Dallas,* Ang argues that, 'pleasure is first and foremost connected with the *fictional* nature of the position and solutions which the tragic structure of feeling constructs, not with their ideological content' (cited in Alasuutari 1999: 11; emphasis in original). Again, this represents a fundamental point of departure from the culture industry thesis which is not anti-pleasure per se but which highlights the manufactured, manipulative ways such pleasure is produced in *commodity form.* Ang's argument is premised upon the possibility of separating out the enjoyment of fictional forms from their underlying commodity form. What she fails to address in her claim that appreciating fictional forms is politically neutral is the depth and complexity of the links between the culture industry's deliberate commodification of the fiction process itself. Thus, in terms of celebrity culture:

> The entertainment-celebrity model takes over because it is a rational one, one that meets professional and commercial needs. The blurring of fact and fiction is not a conspiracy but a practicality; the uncoupling of merit and notoriety, hardly new or complete but certainly very advanced, is the result of the routine pursuit of profit.
>
> (Gamson 1994: 191)

Against Ang, Part 2 of this book explores the political consequences of this blurring of fact and fiction and we show that such pleasure in fiction can indeed still be ideological because it serves to embed the consumer further within the commodified matrix of celebrity production.

## 3    *The content of the frame is open to radical reinterpretation*

central to the Post-structuralist approach is the notion that star images are inflected and modified by the mass-media and the productive assimilation of the audience. Thus a dispersed view of power is articulated in which celebrity is examined as a developing field of intertextual representation in which meaning is variously assembled. Variation derives from the different constructions and inflections vested in the celebrity by the participants in the field, including agents, press officers, gossip columnists, producers and friends.

(Rojek 2001: 44)

Cultural populism tends to underplay the extent to which nominally independent readings are inevitably shaped, a priori, by the pervasively manufactured nature of the content being interpreted. Rojek's (2001) notion of *a dispersed view of power*, for example, while seeking to assert audience agency actually concedes a significant degree of circularity: variations in the interpretation of celebrity are constructed by various participants, but they are all still intrinsically part of the industry that produced the celebrity they are interpreting. When the content itself is looked at for evidence of material that can be used to undermine the dominant meaning system, the effort can seem forced, producing extremely tenuous results. Hermes, for example, sees radical potential in *The Sound of Music*: 'At its most abstract, The Sound of Music is about the dialectic between freedom and order. Andrews embodies the two in her singing and her acting: while her singing is unparalleled, her acting is stilted' (Hermes, in Alasuutari 1999). Similarly, in their paper exploring the behaviour of *Judge Dredd* fans, Barker and Brooks claim that. 'In giving scope for imaging the future, even a dark and fearful one, the comic made a space within which they could keep social and political hopes alive' (Barker and Brooks, in Dickinson et al. 1998: 229).[5] This tendency to find grounds for optimism in otherwise dispiriting examples of commodified culture has continued with the rise of Reality TV.

Brundson et al. point out that the trade magazine *Broadcast* has three prize categories for Reality TV programming – *documentary programme, documentary series*, and *popular factual.* They recognize the growing conflation of entertainment and documentary modes but choose to see it as an opportunity for fresh interpretations rather than a worrying sign of dumbing down:

distinctions between such categories have become increasingly difficult to ascertain. Factual is no longer synonymous with 'serious', issue-based programming, but now forms a strong and central part of the entertainment schedules. What these programmes invite, therefore, is a reconsideration of the terms under which we evaluate both 'entertainment' and 'documentary', rather than being dismissed out of hand as examples of the debasement of factual television.

(Brundson et al. 2001: 44)

Bratich also applies this perspective of optimistic opportunism to Reality TV:

> Ultimately, I argue that RTV [Reality TV] is about power as it is configured in the new society of control and communication. Thinking of this as reality programming, we can dislodge reality from its status as authoritative source of representation. This milieu of transmutation (not stability) can be harnessed for various purposes and interests; it is bound to the historical changes in power and sovereignty. By understanding this, we can envision the potentials these changes offer.
>
> (Bratich 2006: 66)

Finally, still in this optimistic vein, Lisa Taylor makes positive claims for the cultural effects of lifestyle programming:

> Analysis of lifestyle programming undoubtedly reveals that lifestyle ideas hold a measure of educational value for citizens. They might also offer people the opportunity, within the context of the commonplace routines of their everyday lives, to mould the strategies and sites of lifestyle in ways which help them to navigate their own relationship to social change.
>
> (Taylor 2002: 491)

The rest of this book pursues a critical response to these types of arguments, but at this point it is sufficient to point out how such examples illustrate the risk of promoting the act of interpretation while excluding considerations of what constitutes meaningful empowerment. Purportedly radical interpretations may leave the media's conservative effects largely unchallenged, if not ultimately reinforced. Hermes, for example, seeks to use even the naturally conservative personality-based coverage of the British Royal Family as evidence of counter-hegemonic potential. Previously, the audience's appreciation of news coverage was hindered by its unduly 'abstract' nature. Personality-based news such as reporting on Princess Diana, according to Hermes, can literally put a face on the issues of the day. He conceptualizes the role of the celebrity as an embodiment of abstraction as an empowering development towards the creation of 'a wider world of cultural citizenship' (Hermes, in Alasuutari 1999: 83). Finding the personal in the abstract becomes, not a negative development, but a positive means of breaking open 'the modernist discourse of quality news'. Hermes cites the media coverage of Charles and Diana's marital breakdown as an example of this breaking open, but it is interesting to note what replaces modernist discourse in this model: 'the breakdown of their marriage has spawned many a discussion of infidelity, personal freedom and anorexia' (in Alusuutari 1999: 83).

Only the second of these categories can easily be construed in radical political terms likely to challenge the dominant meaning system. Even the 'personal freedom' issues embodied in Charles and Diana's failed relationship needs some further translation before it can be used to illuminate the social conditions of those markedly less privileged. Indeed, despite attempts to represent the audience's response to media coverage of Diana's death as a challenge to the Royal Family, the sum total of its political effects was a temporary disturbance to Royal protocol with two unprecedented (but hardly revolutionary) events: the lowering of the flag to half-mast at Buckingham Palace and a round of applause during Diana's funeral service both outside and inside Westminster Abbey. The media's personalization of the Charles and Diana saga can be viewed more cynically than Hermes as a good example of Baudrillard's (1983a) notion that media coverage of the superficial rupture of hegemonic structures (for example, Watergate), in practice, reinforces the status quo. In actuality, such apparent ruptures serve only to simulate the presence of real accountability and provide an opportunity to display equally superficial responses from those in power.

## Conclusion

Illustrating O'Neil's previously cited claim that contemplative thought is disproportionately excluded from discussions of the mass media, critics tend to beach themselves on the rocks of either the Scylla of excessively celebratory cultural populism or the Charybdis[6] of reactionary conservatism. The former approach tends to overcompensate for the weak quality of the mass-media's content by praising the inherent worth of *any* content that requires *any* interpretation, while the latter promotes cultural exclusivity for its own sake. *Critical Theories of Mass Culture* attempts to steer a middle ground. It argues that the mass media need to be engaged with on a much more critical and less accommodative basis. It should be noted that those least willing to adopt a critical perspective and most willing to lay the charge of cultural elitism on others are frequently those whose work exacerbates rather than ameliorates the disenfranchised condition of large sections of the mass-media audience – an audience that frequently does not share the same levels of access to cultural capital enjoyed by their purported champions. Cultural populists thus risk celebrating the nature of the life of the enchained prisoners in the Cave while their intellectual capital at least gives them the opportunity to leave it.

There is a distinct possibility of an inverse relationship between the enthusiasm with which the arguments of cultural populism are put forward and the likelihood of improvements to the cultural

conditions of those upon whose behalf those arguments are prof-
fered. Unable to envisage a genuinely empowering mass culture,
cultural populists tend to disingenuously find virtue in the culture
industry that does exist. The consistently *critical* aspect of this book is
its stubborn rejection of this uncritical accommodation. It repeatedly
emphasizes how a more oppositional response to the culture industry should be based upon an informed recognition of the continuing
importance of those critical theorists unfairly dismissed as elitist for
desiring a more nuanced and sophisticated mass culture. Having
provided a short critique of cultural populism, it is now time to
introduce the critical corrective.

# Part 1

Then

# 1

# Walter Benjamin's 'Work of art' essay[1]

## Introduction: the politics of aura

Walter Benjamin's (1892–1940) 'Das Kunstwerk im Zeitalter seiner technischen Reproduzierbarkeit', written in 1936 and known in English as 'The work of art in the age of mechanical reproduction' (referred to in subsequent pages as the Essay) is one of the most important texts in media theory. In the space of a few pages it provides perhaps the first systematic account of the mass cultural effects of the media technologies that emerged in the first decades of the twentieth century. It is particularly significant within the context of this book's analysis of critical media theory because it relates directly to the themes of Kracauer and Adorno's writings and lays much of the theoretical groundwork for later thinkers such as Debord and Baudrillard. The Essay focuses upon the way in which the nature of a work of art is irretrievably altered with the advent of the mass media and it concerns itself with the wider social effects of this fundamental development. Earlier writers failed to address the full nature of this change because they limited themselves to exploring the implications of individual media technologies on particular art forms and so failed to consider the broader implications for the whole cultural environment of a mass-mediated communicational infrastructure. In contrast, Benjamin attempted to identify the general underlying structural conditions of aesthetic production in the opening decades of the twentieth century. He takes the whole of society as his target and seeks to understand the lived-in experience of a mediated world.

Of critical importance for Benjamin's reading of art and its mediatization is the physical component resident in all forms of aesthetic production. This physicality is traditionally regarded as mere matter – material to be moulded in accordance with wishes of the artist. Benjamin's Essay is a seminal piece of work for the way it prefigures McLuhan's *the medium is the message*. It fundamentally questions this assumption that the physical manner in which media content is transmitted is essentially neutral – to be determined by the artist. In Benjamin's Essay we encounter the radical (and we suggest essentially *critical*) notion that a particular medium has a specific *grammar*, a way of structuring meaning and this occurs *irrespective* of the artist's intentions. Perhaps the best way to express this conceptualization of the non-neutral nature of new media technologies can be found in the Essay itself when Benjamin claims that, instead of arguing whether photography is an art form or not, the real question to be asked is the extent to which art itself has been fundamentally transformed: 'Earlier much futile thought had been devoted to the question of whether photography is an art. The primary question – whether the very invention of photography had not transformed the entire nature of art – was not raised' (Section VII). Thus, it is not physical matter that must serve art, but art that must be transformed in keeping with the new nature of im/materiality in an age of industrial (re)production[2]. As Valéry points out in the epigraph to the Essay, 'neither matter nor space nor time has been what it was from time immemorial'. This is how Benjamin sees mass-media technology – as a fundamental, revolutionary force. He seeks to develop a Marxist interpretation with which to make best use of such tradition-shattering power. His analysis is therefore much more than merely a matter of aesthetic theory – it relates directly to political action.

His analysis is political because, writing at the time of German fascism, he opposes the way in which reactionary social forces misuse and subvert the traditional artistic notions of creativity, individual genius and the timeless mystery of the artwork. According to Benjamin, the drive by fascism to uphold these traditional concepts occurs in the face of technological developments that should actually undermine that tradition. By contrast, he sought to establish principles in the Essay that, fully sensitive to the social implications of these technological developments, could lead to a politics of emancipation. This new strategy is to be found within the account Benjamin provides of the historical formation and function of the work of art. In particular, the radical political potential to be found in his key notion that traditional *aura* is evacuated by the media to be replaced by a new, more empowering, relationship of the masses to an unprecedentedly mediated reality. In its most general definition, aura is understood in terms of singularity, uniqueness – all that is that is irreproducible:

> What is aura, actually? A strange weave of space and time: the unique appearance or semblance of distance, no matter how close the object might be. While resting on a summer's noon, to trace a range of mountains on the horizon, or a branch that throws its shadow on the observer, until the moment or hour

become part of their appearance – that is what it means to breath the aura of those mountains, that branch.

(Benjamin 1985b: 250)

While the experience of aura in Nature is identified with the singularity of the instant and directly experienced moment of reality, within the more restricted context of the artwork, aura refers to the elements that comprise the unique history of a given artefact – its production at a particular moment in time, its occupation of specific space, its provenance, and the manner in which these are woven into the very fabric of the object itself.

Benjamin states that the 'uniqueness of a work of art arises from its being embedded in the fabric of tradition'. In this manner the work of art and the traditions of society are involved in a dialectical relationship – an ongoing process of mutual modification and reformulation of which aura is an index. For Benjamin the contemporary form of this ongoing interrelationship or 'dialectic' consists of the steady decline of traditional forms of cultural power. Owing to the mass mediation of society, the social significance of aura decreases. He suggests that this situation gives rise to another dialectic; a positive, empowering, socialist dialectic. The rise of *mass-media* technologies necessarily and intrinsically coincides with the rise of the *masses*. For Benjamin, the dialectical consequence of a new mode of artistic production was the emergence of new social relations. From the critical perspective of this book, however, Benjamin's optimistic interpretation of this close alignment between the mass and the media is deeply problematic. The following chapters demonstrate how he correctly identified the central social processes at work, but he failed to foresee their profoundly negative cultural consequences – he did not adequately envisage how the masses would become the malleable target of the culture industry rather than a self-empowering new social body. Benjamin wrote the Essay in the historical context of the rise of Nazism; the loss of art's traditional aura thus provided a welcome antidote to the fascists' fetishistic use of images. In relation to contemporary media, however, subsequent chapters suggest that this fascistic form of fetishism has merely been replaced by the sophisticated re-creation of fetishism in the much more subtle form of a pervasively commodified mediascape – a *friendly fascism* of unthinking consumption (akin to Marcuse's notion of *surplus repression* [1964] 2002). In the sections that follow the aspects of the media technologies that inspired Benjamin's hopes are considered in more detail, before turning to the reason why 'the phoney spell of the commodity' (that even the optimistically minded Benjamin recognized as a downside to the loss of aura) has not been broken, but instead, has tightened its hold over the masses.

## From ritual to mechanical reproduction

Different values are subscribed to the artwork at different periods throughout history. Benjamin identifies three major stages:

1  Art as ritual
2  Art as exhibition
3  Art in the age of mechanical reproduction.

### 1   Art as ritual

Some of the earliest known art (for example, the cave painting) is deliberately located inaccessibly. Benjamin thus asserts that the primordial value of art was its *ritual value* – not how many people could see it. The act of creation itself was paramount and carried out for the gaze of the gods rather than other humans: 'the elk portrayed by the man of the Stone Age was an instrument of magic. He did not expose it to his fellow men ... it was meant for the spirits' (Section V).

### 2   Art as exhibition

The ancient origins of *art as ritual* continued in the Western tradition of organized religion but there is shift from the act of creation to the artefact itself. The artwork begins to assume a new value of exhibition. Thus, within Renaissance churches, although the artwork is tied to its location within a place of worship it is designed to be seen by the congregation. Artworks also become objects of veneration and pilgrimage, initially in their role as religious artefacts, but increasingly in their own right as objects to be admired for their artistry (for example, the ceiling of the Sistine Chapel). The secular cult of beauty in today's art world inherits many of these religious functions – the artist as saint, the critic as priest and the gallery as temple.

### 3   Art in the age of mechanical reproduction

Benjamin argues that the ability to mechanically replicate a work of art has historically been limited. In the art of classical Rome and Greece, for example, the only means of reproduction were casting and stamping, and thus only a small class of artefacts were reproducible. Later, woodcuts and lithography, in combination with the printing press, extended the domain of reproducibility. Nevertheless, they left the auratic function of art largely unaffected since the relative crudity of the copies confirmed the apparent distance between profanely reproducible and sublimely singular art. The artwork's ritual function bequeaths its aura. Tradition animates the work of art such that 'to perceive the aura of an object we look at means to invest it with the ability to look at us in return' (Benjamin 1973: 187). But the age of mechanical reproduction announced by the photograph, profoundly alters this ability of the artwork to dominate its viewer. For the first time, art is liberated from its 'parasitical relation' to ritual and a radically new social atmosphere is created by an unprecedented wealth of easily reproduced media content. This release involves a major revaluation of art and its very nature and function.

## The cultural implications of mechanical reproduction

Benjamin's Essay lends itself to a critical reading that cuts directly across its own optimistic tone. It can be argued that Benjamin seriously underestimated the negative implications of the way in which the exhibition quality of art is fundamentally altered by the rise of mechanical reproduction. The quantitative increase of artistic reproductions creates an environment in which the whole act of exhibition becomes irrevocably devalued, diluted – whichever critical term one wishes to use. The roots of this process of devaluation can be seen in Benjamin's own description of the evolution of art from highly symbolic religious and ritualistic sites to the more functional art galleries that accompanied the early rise of capitalism. Formerly, there was an intimate and inextricable link between an artefact and its symbolic relationship to its particular location (an aspect of Benjamin's aura) such as a Bible and its placement upon a church altar. Thus, in distinguishing between mediated signs and more culturally grounded symbols, Baudrillard refers to the latter's bonds of *unbreakable reciprocity with their social setting* (Baudrillard 1983a: 85). With the advent of mechanical reproduction, this intrinsic connection an artwork formerly held to a particular site of religious veneration (the cave wall, the cathedral ceiling) is broken in favour of its ability to circulate freely beyond a physical home.

The rise in importance of the quality of exhibition over and above these previously *unbreakable bonds of reciprocity* threatens the symbolic, ritualistic quality of artwork. The simple act of viewing becomes more important than its much deeper original religious purpose. In the early historical stages of this process, however, even this diluted form of consuming an artwork still required some substantial effort of consumption. For example, one does not need to be a devout Catholic to view the Sistine Chapel but, even as merely an art aficionado, one still needs to make a significant physical effort to see it in person. In the move from ritual to exhibition status and the dislocation and dilution of symbolic grounding so implied, the rise of mechanical reproduction takes the process a major stage further. The domain of reproducibility swamps traditional aura-based society so that accessibility strips out all symbolic freight from the act of consumption. This is what Valéry meant when he observed: 'Just as water, gas, and electricity are brought into our homes from far off to satisfy our needs in response to a minimal effort, so we shall be supplied with visual or auditory images, which will appear and disappear at a simple movement of the hand, hardly more than a sign' (Essay: Section I).

First-time readers of the Essay may feel somewhat confused because Benjamin's account of aura seems to emphasize its decline and fall and it is not immediately obvious why this is a development to be welcomed. Indeed, this book is devoted to arguing that the optimism Benjamin attempts to bolt onto his critical analysis of aura's decline was unfounded in the light of the subsequent history of mass-media society. Benjamin's hopes for this technologically sponsored process lay in the new opportunities that arise once aura is deposed. Thus, Benjamin describes quite literally the ruin of traditional artistic aura: 'Then came the film and burst this prison-world asunder by the dynamite of the tenth of a second, so that now, in the midst of its far-flung ruins and debris, we calmly and adventurously go travelling' (Section XIII). Aura is inextricably bound to a unique position in time and space. The sophisticated form of reproduction that arises with the mechanization of images, however, liberates the object from these physical/temporal constraints. The camera frees reproduction from being merely derivative or subordinate to an original artwork. The quasi-independent gaze of the auratic artwork (it almost appears to look at the viewer rather than just being the passive recipient of the gaze of the person viewing it), is a condensation or personification of its history. As such it is a form of inadvertent memory and consequently it is diminished in the face of reproductive media that can preserve and return a representation at any chosen moment – with mechanical reproduction, it is no longer tied down to a unique point in space and time. This alone represents a profound shift in human experience. The age-old role of human memory is significantly undermined (a theme pursued by Kracauer in the next chapter) with the arrival of media technologies that effectively become prostheses for not just our physical abilities, but also our consciousness (McLuhan's notion of media technologies as an electronic nervous system for humankind is dealt with in Chapter 4). Time itself is no longer the same. As with time, so with space, the artwork as a reproducible object has no proper location; its place is wherever a reproduction is encountered.

Although Benjamin hoped for empowering freedom from the inhibiting qualities of tradition, critical readings of the mass media stem from this dislocation of the artwork from its previously unique point in space and time. While the artwork and its public are now freed from a dependence upon location, a reduction in the particularity of the artwork occurs as it loses part of this singular location-specific context. It is now usurped by a simulacral copy that can never encompass the totality of the original. In the subsequent chapters, we examine the full consequences of a society in which the simulacral increasingly contributes to a *society of the spectacle* manifested in various forms of *pseudo-events* (Chapter 5) and simulated cultural categories (Chapter 6 – the democratization of celebrity forms; Chapter 7 – Reality TV; and in both Chapters 7 and 8 we see the decline of aura revisited in the form of a decline in the discourse of sobriety and a corresponding rise in pseudo-news – the *Other News*). Benjamin believed the *quantitative* shift in the amount of mechanically reproducible artworks newly available for consumption by the masses was an opportunity of momentous *qualitative* importance. It represented the subordination of all previous dimensions of art to the value of exhibition – art after mechanical reproduction becomes, first and foremost, what is exhibited. New media of reproduction de-localize art, and place it directly in front of the masses, thus 'today, by the absolute emphasis on its exhibition value the work of art becomes a creation with entirely new functions, among which ... the artistic function, later may be recognized as incidental' (Section V). However, in subsequent pages, the betrayal of Benjamin's hopes is demonstrated as the process he analysed in its early stages has proceeded beyond his optimistic projections to produce the commodified disempowerment of the masses. In Part 2 we analyse in detail how the decline of aura has tended to evolve closely with ever more sophisticated commodity forms. The freeing of the masses from their dependence upon aura is shown to have broken through the previously *unbreakable bonds of reciprocity* Baudrillard saw in symbolically grounded cultural practices. The decline of aura gives free rein for the commodity form to create its own ersatz aura based upon the inevitably shallow, made-for-manipulation, and therefore ultimately disempowering/alienating, social bonds of commodity culture – *the culture industry.*

## Benjamin and McLuhan

With the different methods of technical reproduction of a work of art, its fitness for exhibition increased to such an extent that the quantitative shift between its two poles turned into a qualitative transformation of its nature.

(Essay: Section V)

Benjamin's analysis of aura prefigures certain elements of McLuhan's thinking. Although Benjamin does not read media history as a grand narrative of the human body's externalization in quite the same way, his thesis that mechanical reproduction results in fundamental and traumatic derangement of the senses anticipates certain aspects of McLuhan's idea that media technologies constitute new extensions of the sensory organs of man – *outerings* of the body. In addition, Benjamin's emphasis upon *qualitative* social changes stemming from technologically inspired *quantitative* increases prefigures a crucial aspect of McLuhan's work – his argument that the major effects of a medium are 'the change of scale or pace or pattern that it introduces into human affairs' (McLuhan [1964] 1995: 8). From Benjamin's earlier perspective, the human sensorium is not a trans-historical, unchanging structure but, rather, it is historically determined and delimited by a combination of social and technical constraints that are also subject to radical overhaul when new innovations arise. In keeping with his Essay's opening exhortation, Benjamin builds upon Marx's observation that 'the forming of the five senses is a labour of the entire history of the world down to the present' (Marx 1988: 108) by considering the contribution of his particular historical moment to this ongoing project of the senses and their development. Benjamin shows that it is in photography that the nature of a profound shift in our mediated sense of the world around us finds its first expression, before its yet further and fuller realization with the advent of cinema. Photography initiates a radical alteration in the scale of perception, it reveals a new realm of novel images, previously too fleeting, above or below the spectrum of a perception unaided by artificial means, a new realm that Benjamin terms the *optical unconscious.*

The *optical unconscious* describes those aspects of the natural world inaccessible to the naked eye and which the camera allows us to see for the first time. Examples include the corona of drops that can be seen rising up from the surface of a liquid that is broken and filmed in slow motion, the exact manner in which a horse's hooves move over the ground when it is running at full speed, bird's-eye views of cities, and so on: 'photography, and later film, revealed an entire realm, thus the latter destroyed the world of ordinary perception with 'the dynamite of the tenth of a second' (Section XIII). It parallels Freud's discoveries about the mind's unconscious nature to the extent that:

Fifty years ago, a slip of the tongue passed more or less unnoticed. Only exceptionally may such a slip have revealed dimensions of depth in a conversation which had seemed to be taking its course on the surface. Since the *Psychopathology of Everyday Life* things have changed. This book isolated and made analyzable things which had heretofore floated along unnoticed in the broad stream of perception.

(Section XIII)

This terrain is not simply a source of aesthetic novelty but also one of shock, assault, and radical de-familiarization. A life-world previously self-contained and familiar has now become threatening. In this respect it partakes of a wider process of perceptual disruption that accompanies the historical shift from the countryside into the industrial metropolis. The optical unconscious revealed by film and photography represent the most visible expression of this much broader alteration in the nature of perception.

Of the countless movements of switching, inserting, pressing and the like, the 'snapping' of the photographer has had the greatest consequences. A touch of the finger now sufficed to fix for an unlimited period of time. The camera gave the moment a posthumous shock, as it were. Haptic experiences were joined by optic ones, such as are supplied by the advertising pages of a newspaper or the traffic of the big city. Moving through this traffic involves the individual in a series of shocks and collisions. At dangerous intersections, nervous impulses flow throughout him in rapid succession, like energy from a battery.

(Benjamin 1973: 177)

This is a critical (in both senses of the word) feature of Benjamin's analysis – the notion that media technology serves to acclimatize people for life within a heavily technologized society can be read in much more negative fashion than he chooses. For example, in the next chapter Kracauer exhibits more sensitivity than Benjamin manages in relation to the negative social impact of these perceptual shocks. He describes how they are caused by the sheer proliferation and contiguity of images stemming from the combination of media technologies and the rise of urban centres. Thus, Kracauer talks in terms of 'a strike against understanding' and describes the disempowering, alienating features of such shock effects. Similarly, Adorno's extremely critical account of the culture industry is largely premised upon his perception of how the values and needs of advanced industrialization colonize and undermine competing social and cultural values. Unlike Benjamin, the fact that the media serve to prepare people for the similar perceptual shocks of industrialized life can be seen as evidence of the damagingly pervasive nature of the culture industry's influence upon peoples' lives. Benjamin is only able to see new media as empowering by being unduly reluctant to ask – *empowerment in terms of what and in whose ultimate interest?*

The alteration in the pace and scale of perception is *imposed* upon the masses as the condition of their emergence as a new political force. The masses do indeed arise as a force but one that is born into a heavily commodified and rationalized world. Benjamin's new 'haptic experiences' result from increased levels of technological mediation and contain within them a major element of disempowerment despite his best hopes. For example, prefiguring later active audience studies approaches, the audience for Benjamin is active but often in the form of the self-controlling behaviour required to suit the needs of industrial society:

> technology has subjected the human sensorium to a complex kind of training. There came a day when a new and urgent need for stimuli was met by the film. In a film, perception in the form of shocks was established as a formal principle. That which determines the rhythm of production on a conveyor belt is the basis of the rhythm of reception in the film.
>
> (Benjamin 1973: 177)

> The film is the art that is in keeping with the increased threat to his life which modern man has to face. Man's need to expose himself to shock effects is his adjustment to the dangers threatening him. The film corresponds to profound changes in the apperceptive apparatus – changes that are ... experienced by the man in the street in big-city traffic ...
>
> (Essay: note 19)

The 'shock' of the modern urban environment is figured in terms of a welter of new micro-perceptions, disorientating cuts and contingent images – a realm of experience that also characterizes the cinematic experience. Cinema thus trains the sensorium and helps the subject adapt to this new technological social reality. Below the surface-level optimism of Benjamin's account, is the basis of a critical analysis very similar to Adorno's scathing observation that the culture industry uses even leisure time to prepare workers more efficiently for their work lives.

One reason for Benjamin's stubborn optimism resides in the fact that while photography and film extend 'our comprehension of the necessities which rule our lives' (Section XIII), at the same time, they also expose the manner in which modernity creates the masses, and transforms them into labouring bodies. This is a sentiment shared by Kracauer for whom the camera, despite its alienating effects, at least forces humankind to consider the mediated nature of its relationship to a heavily technologized world. Benjamin's interpretation suggests that the dialectical nature of this relationship between media technology and the mass audiences it produces serves to create the possibility for an empowered, non-passive mass –

a self-determining body, fully adapted to the environment capital has imposed on them and thereby capable of making its own changes to that environment. The camera requires both a complex education of the sensorium, and at the same time provides a means of anatomizing, revealing and deconstructing the specific training involved in that education. The problem with this argument, however, is contained within Adorno's basic insight that knowledge of the culture industry's workings is not sufficient guarantee of empowerment. In fact, as Goldman and Papson (1996, 1998) point out in their detailed studies of contemporary advertising, the culture industry often builds into its content deliberate signposts to its manipulations of consumers for whom compensation is to be found in recognizing the 'knowing wink' and thereby feeling part of a sophisticated joke. A major element of Part 2 is its updated account of Adorno's notion that consumers tend to connive at their own oppression – *they work the magic of commodities upon themselves*. As Žižek (1989) has put it much more recently, the problem with the ideology of the contemporary mediascape is not Marx's notion of *false consciousness* in which the masses do not realize what they are doing, but, rather, the way in which ideology now resides in various forms of ideological manipulation that are readily apparent to the masses – *but they continue to do what they are doing anyway* (a notion we return to in our conclusion). Benjamin foresaw the revelatory properties of the media technologies but failed to see how ideological manipulation can still occur despite (and often *because of*) such a realm of apparent openness.

## The political implications of the decline in aura

for the first time in world history, mechanical reproduction emancipates the work of art from its parasitical dependence upon ritual ... the instant the criterion of authenticity ceases to be applicable to artistic production, the total function of art is reversed. Instead of being based on ritual, it begins to be based on another practice – politics.

(Essay: Section IV)

From Benjamin's perspective, conditions of aesthetic production and reception are of great political significance. In the Essay's epilogue Benjamin maintains that the failure of society to accommodate the productive forces of technology results in the latter's distorted expression in the form of war:

Imperialistic war is a rebellion of technology which collects, in the form of 'human material,' the claims to which society has denied its natural material. Instead of draining rivers, society directs a human stream into a bed of trenches; instead of dropping seeds from airplanes it drops incendiary bombs over cities; and through gas warfare the aura is abolished in a new way.

(Essay: Epilogue)

Industrialized warfare is for Benjamin the inevitable result of a failure to culturally align technology and the masses. It furnishes 'proof that society has not been mature enough to incorporate technology as its organ, [and] that technology has not been sufficiently developed to cope with the elemental forces of society' (Essay: Epilogue). Benjamin saw the First World War and the increasing dominance of fascism in European politics as a direct result of this arrested development, and thus defined fascism as a strategy for organizing the masses born of industrial capitalism into a collectivity while leaving untouched the traditional distribution of resources and power so that: 'only war makes it possible to mobilize all of today's technical resources while maintaining the property system' (Essay: Epilogue). This accounts for the peculiar mix within fascism of traditional stereotypes and mythical figures and the very latest in technological developments. Fascism's political project calls both for an active exploitation of mechanical reproduction, but simultaneously, the firm repression of its emancipatory potential – fascism seeks to use today's tools to perform yesterday's work.

Fascism clings to, and accentuates the auratic function of art. The concentration and contemplation required for traditional aesthetic forms, in conjunction with its ritualistic elements, is a powerful tool for recruiting the masses. The early twentieth-century artistic movement of *Futurism* prefigured fascism's reactionary aestheticism in relation to industrial technology. Futurism declared:

> War is beautiful because it establishes man's dominion over the subjugated machinery by means of gas masks, terrifying megaphones, flame throwers, and small tanks. War is beautiful because it initiates the dreamt-of metalization of the human body. War is beautiful because it enriches a flowering meadow with the fiery orchids of machine guns. War is beautiful because it combines the gunfire, the cannonades, the cease-fire, the scents, and the stench of putrefaction into a symphony.
>
> (Essay: Epilogue)

Futurism thus embraced and celebrated the qualitative shift in perception brought about by new media, while refusing the political changes that Benjamin saw as the natural outgrowth of their interaction with the masses they helped create. The Futurist mentality ushered in an era in which the destruction of humanity became a pure spectacle staged for the predilection of humanity. In Benjamin's estimation this was not an unavoidable consequence of media technology but the product of their fascistic misapplication. His Essay aims to expose the true character of aura whose 'uncontrolled (and at present almost uncontrollable) application ... lead[s] to a processing of data in a fascist sense' (Essay: Epilogue). Benjamin is motivated by a profound belief in socialism's ability to realize the productive power of new technologies and the masses through authentic cultural forms, thus avoiding Futurism's reactionary nihilism. Like the proletariat's role for Marx, Benjamin saw the masses as at once both the product of industrial technology and the only force capable of truly realizing technology's true potential. As we have already seen, however, his analysis contains the seeds of its own critique.

The role played by the masses in the new appreciation of art, in addition to being interpreted as a politically enabling phenomenon, can also be seen as containing the roots of art's total envelopment in a commodity culture that re-creates a new, but still reactionary, aesthetic. This new aesthetic based upon the decline of aura is less overtly horrific than the Futurists' worship of war, but it still undermines the radical political values Benjamin hoped to find within the masses. While fascism, and its hideous manipulation of aura for political purposes, was defeated, critical theory would suggest that the Futurist mentality has reappeared within the contemporary mediascape – the life-world is no longer regimented by military oppression but by commodified affluence (again, Marcuse's *surplus repression*). The current relevance of the unacknowledged criticality within Benjamin's Essay is aptly indicated by his description of the extent of the Futurists' nihilism in which: 'Mankind, which in Homer's time was an object of contemplation for the Olympian gods, now is one for itself. Its self-alienation has reached such a degree that it can experience its own destruction as an aesthetic pleasure of the first order' (Essay: Epilogue). This evocative quotation is repeatedly highlighted in Part 2 as a disturbingly accurate summary of the latest developments in our contemporary *society of the spectacle*. 'Destruction as an aesthetic pleasure of the first order' is evident both in terms of the physical carnage of war presented for passive viewing (the heavily televised Gulf conflicts) and the socially pervasive phenomena that exhibit the same basic processes of self-alienation and reactionary aesthetics that Benjamin was perceptive enough to fear, but did not live to see – *Banality TV*.

The *optical unconscious* that accompanies the advent of technological reproducibility marks a qualitative change not only in the way society views the physical world, but also in the way it views its own cultural products. The spread of technical values now extends into the realm of culture and its representations. Photography and particularly cinema's obliteration of aura represents a highly effective vehicle for the seamless integration of technological thinking into ever deeper levels of society. In the next chapter, Kracauer argues that traditional artistic expression and modes of its reception are premised on the production of objects 'permeated by cognition' – a contemplative form of artistic appreciation. This type of relationship to art is fatally undermined and displaced by mechanical reproduction's creation of a largely autonomous realm of standardized objects pre-designed for mass consumption. For Benjamin who saw the roots of fascism's aesthetic manipulations in the contemplative attitude, this was a good thing. It meant that the masses now had a much better access to art beyond the control traditional elites. In Benjamin's eyes, the potential of film as a means of awakening the masses resides in the receptiveness it encourages towards contingency. The traditional work of art was completely overdetermined, every detail and element assembled with a view to its reception through applied contemplation. As such it dictated its own conditions of appreciation, it imposed its terms upon its audience. For Benjamin, art after the advent of its technological reproduction contains elements that escape the control of its creators. This results in its capacity to make the masses confront their historical condition – ideology is to be unveiled by the stresses the new media create in the traditional forms of communication used to maintain that ideology: 'Film is the first art form capable of showing how matter interferes with people's lives. Hence, film can be a means of materialist representation' (Hansen 1987: 203). This exposure of the material conditions of mass existence takes place outside of the media's explicit content, it is part of the medium's essential mode of operation – the manner with which it highlights the contingent.

## The contingency of media

each former fragment of a narrative, that was once incomprehensible without the narrative context as a whole, has now become capable of emitting a complete narrative message in its own right. It has become autonomous ... in its newly acquired capacity to soak up content and to project it in a kind of instant reflex.

(Jameson 1998: 160)

In their analyses of photography, Benjamin, Kracauer, and later Barthes, emphasize the manner in which the internal logic of the media privileges contingency – the rise to prominence of incidental detail. Thus in Benjamin's account the optical unconscious designates an inexhaustible ream of random features: 'No matter how artful the photographer, no matter how carefully posed his subject, the beholder feels an irresistible urge to search such a picture for the tiny spark of contingency, of the Here and Now, with which reality has so to speak seared the subject' (Benjamin 1985a: 243). Likewise, in Kracauer the genius particular to photography is to be found in the 'tiny spark of accident' that captures a 'moment of futurity responding to the retrospective gaze' (Kracauer, cited in Hansen 1987: 209). Barthes ([1957] 1973) describes this quality of photography using the terms *punctum* and *studium*. The *studium* designates the general environment portrayed in a photograph – a family scene, the military associations immediately understood from the picture of a soldier and so on. The *punctum* is the contingent, inessential detail whose particularity overspills the bounds of the *studium*'s more general message – the fact the soldier may have a large ear lobe and so on. Benjamin viewed this interruption of the traditional processing of meaning through cultural associations and contemplation as a liberating political development. According to the culture industry thesis, it has proved to be the exact opposite. As Jameson points out above, the rise of the punctum in the age of mechanical reproduction creates an *instant reflex* that undermines sustained thought. The state of distraction that underwrote Benjamin's revolutionary faith in the new media of his time appears deeply naive in the face of a current mediascape that prides itself upon the generation and clever manipulation of such instant reflexes.

Koch suggests that Benjamin's assertion that film offers the audience the chance to become active in relation to what they are witnessing: 'is dubious because it excludes the possibility that the apparatus itself might be perceived to be a naturalized fetish with which the audience identifies – less on the level of an instrument with which to test the actor than on the narcissistic level of an enormous extension of the perceptual apparatus' (Koch 2000: 207–8). In other words, the ability of media technologies to act as an extension of our senses (as explored by McLuhan in Chapter 4) becomes an end in itself – it creates a culture of *greedy eyes*. It is in such a scenario that the actual content of programmes diminishes in importance and not only are images mechanically reproduced, but so too is their subject matter:

Take the truly awful Dallas-Dynasty family of programmes ... They are etherealized characters whose simple binary opposi- tions – family/non-family, men/women, sex-power/money- power – may be the vehicles for any fantastic perambulation. And their circle is closed: each opposition complements the other and resists the other. There is no synthesis, and therefore no exit (and therefore as we've found no end to the series).

(Inglis 1990: 152)

This type of criticism is frequently dismissed (along with many of the Frankfurt School's insights) as 'elitist'. What such a refutation misses, however, is the extent to which these banal formats embody the true message of the medium rather than its nominal content. This is the negative, critical alternative to Benjamin's faith in the social possibilities created by mechanical reproduction – the basis of Part 2's analysis of *Banality TV*.

Inglis's key insight here relates to the role programmes like soap operas play in fostering a general social climate amenable to commodity values. They create a closed, tautological circle of interpretation: like commodities they are made for circulation. In terms of the culture industry thesis their complete lack of artistic merit stems from the fact that they inherently lack any potential for provoking ideas that transcend the dominant social value of consumption, as Inglis puts it, they are incapable of providing a synthesis upon which non-commodified meanings can be constructed. Whereas Benjamin saw radical possibilities in the endless reproducibility of representations, in practice, the commodified format of contemporary television actually extinguishes them. Inglis proceeds to argue that this repetitive content actually constitutes a form of psychosis. The cultural danger it poses stems from the fact that, just as the Frankfurt School (and theorists such as Mellencamp[3]) argued, consumer culture fosters an arrested emotional development at the level of either the infantile or the adolescent according to the severity of the critical judgement. For Inglis the cultural harm results from a:

> return to the mechanical rhythms of the libido, with no help from the alter ego. Psychosis designates a rhythm of compulsion and gratification of a regular but unregulable kind in which the play of fantasy upon experience is such as to preclude rational reflection or the direction of action towards diverse ends. In countless narratives on American film and television, the circuit of action is closed to reflection in this way.
>
> (Inglis 1990: 152)

Benjamin's positive notion of distraction as habit (see next section), albeit in a much revised, more pessimistic form, is pertinent to Inglis's concerns. The habit of distraction in contemporary media now relates to an unthinking familiarity with inherently uncritical, emotion-based forms of expression – explored in Part 2 as *the emo*. A wealth of substantive issues become 'naturally' excluded by editorial standards driven by either overt celebrity values or closely related libidinal requirements for personality-driven features. In addition to these forms of censorship by exclusion can be added the preponderance of material whose suitability is defined in strictly pictorial terms. Over-reliance upon the charge of elitism by the critics of the culture industry thesis, means that, despite often being left-leaning commentators, they frequently fail to engage critically with the full extent of the political implications of the conceptual banality produced by the media (a failure examined in Chapter 8). To this extent they often risk patronizing the working class they seek to represent with ill-conceived notions of empowerment. The negative aspects of mass reproduction insufficiently developed by Benjamin are the basis of the much more critical accounts of the subsequent chapters. The true dialectic is one in which disempowerment of the masses is produced by industrialized distraction.

In this more critical context, Jameson (1998) identifies the Enlightenment's forces of secularization and realism as the first stage of an ongoing historical evacuation of aura in a process he distinguishes from Benjamin's notion of empowerment. Jameson prefers to talk of a *dialectic of reification* which:

> seizes on the properties and the subjectivities, the institutions and the forms, of an older pre-capitalist world, in order to strip them of their hierarchical or religious content ... what is dialectical about it comes as something like a leap and an overturn from quantity into quality. With the intensification of the forces of reification and their suffusion through ever greater zones of social life (including individual subjectivity), it is as though the force that generated the first realism now turns against it and devours it in its turn.
>
> (Jameson 1998: 148)

This identification of a transformation from quantity into quality recalls Benjamin's similar description of the quantity/quality transition induced by the mechanical reproduction of images. Jameson argues that this process, which drives modernity's liquidation of traditional hierarchical society, results in its own demise in the form of a postmodern undermining of modernist values. The quantitative increase in mechanical production is achieved only at the price of the implicit and widespread acceptance of cultural outputs in overwhelming commercial terms. It is at this point of cultural alignment between media technologies and commodity values that previous barriers between the cultural and economic spheres dissolve (in Marx and Engel's words 'all that is solid melts into air[4]') on an unprecedented scale – the commodity's social role significantly expands as it simultaneously becomes an economic and culture-defining concept.

From this perspective, the transformation of art's reception from one of contemplation to a 'state of distraction' is important, but for reasons directly counter to those offered by Benjamin. Mechanical reproduction does not so much destroy tradition as ossify it in the constant repetition of the individualized commodity form aimed at the socially alienated consumer:

> The culture industry consists of repetition. That its characteristic innovations are never anything more than the improvements of mass reproduction is not external to the system. It is with good reason that the interest of innumerable consumers is directed to the technique, and not to the contents – which are stubbornly repeated, outworn, and by now half-discredited. The social power which the spectators worship shows itself more effectively in the omnipresence of the stereotype imposed by technical skill than in the stale ideologies for which the ephemeral contents stand in.
>
> (Adorno, in Duttmann 2000: 40)

Repetition for the purposes of consumption becomes its own raison d'être. This may seem quite an abstract issue at this early point in the book but the remaining chapters explore the various forms such repetition takes and the profound cultural harm it causes. In Part 2, for example, we see how Adorno's blanket statement 'the culture industry consists of repetition' can be seen at both a micro and macro level. From the former perspective, the increasing prevalence of pseudo-pornographic modes of representation is shown to utilize the innately repetitive voyeuristic tendencies of the camera (see Chapter 7's analysis of the gastroporn of the US television's *Food Network*). At a macro level, Chapter 8 shows how the media's coverage of global politics has become fatally infected by repetitive and uncritical modes of expression and representation (for example, the endlessly repetitious showing of the 9/11 plane crash and the toppling of the Saddam statue in Baghdad in the second Gulf conflict).

## Benjamin and distraction

While Benjamin's Essay is perhaps the most significant early statement on the emancipatory potential of modern media, it suffers from a dearth of evidence as to how such emancipation might occur in practice. For example, towards the end of the Essay, Benjamin presents the concept of *distraction* as positive force that emerges in the wake of the liquidation of aura that he has detailed, however he remains reticent as to the precise relation between distraction and emancipation. Gilloch has argued that Benjamin's identification of film as an intrinsically emancipatory medium, resides in the medium's instantiation of two closely related aspects of distraction – *habit* and *non-contemplation*:

1  The media user can learn from the unconscious effort of habit which is, 'not forgetfulness as such, but rather a form of accomplishment amidst amnesia'.
2  Distraction is 'not to be understood as simple inattention. Distraction involves *paying attention elsewhere*'. (Gilloch 2002: 191; emphasis in original)

In Benjamin's account the person experiencing traditional auratic art is invited to contemplate the piece in a highly structured fashion and a controlled environment. This is true whether it be in the ritualistic forms of early religious art or the later secular, but still essentially ritualistic, form of an art gallery. According to Benjamin this leads to the viewer's absorption by the work. In contrast, with the advent of media such as film, the critical appreciation of the work takes a much more natural and enjoyable form – the masses absorb the artwork. For Benjamin this shift from auratic concentration to reproductive distraction can be illustrated by considering the different processes involved in the reception of a painting and a building. The individual artwork in a gallery or church is removed from the stream of common life, contemplating it represents a suspension of ordinary physical and mental processes and their conscious redirection. Its removal from daily life means that access to it is strictly limited, the space/time restrictions that characterize the auratic artwork are such that (historically) it can never be fully present before the mass. In this manner the singularity of aura is controlled by those who regulate access to the artwork and aura incorporates within itself the distinction of the class that possesses it (think of the stereotypically goateed and pony-tailed gatekeepers of the contemporary art market).

For Benjamin, architecture provides the model for a radically different and more empowering mode of appreciation, it is by its very nature a public art (or at least the clearest prototype of an art of the masses). Architecture is not subject to the same short-term cultural fads that determine the rise and fall of other cultural forms, rather it is (like the poor) always with us (and as the proletariat slumbers within the poor so within architecture there resides a hidden potentiality). The historical and environmental presence of architecture's buildings results in quite a different means of appreciation from that of traditional art. Architecture is absorbed through use and perception, by a process of 'tactile appropriation'. Unlike the total but circumscribed contemplation of the artwork, a building becomes known through everyday use that slowly and almost unconsciously leads to an understanding of the whole. Like the media of reproduction, and in distinct contrast to the auratic work of art, architecture constitutes an environment. When media become 'environments' immediately accessible to all, it thus follows that their characteristic mode of apprehension would display a proximity to the existing environmental apperception already to be found in architecture. In this manner, the tactile appropriation encountered by the masses and their buildings anticipates the state of distraction that exemplifies the consciousness of the masses in the age of media technologies. For Benjamin this new mode of consciousness is no mere somnambulism, but a form of sensory instruction. It bypasses the conscious mind and acts directly on the sensorium. But why should tactile appropriation in the guise of distraction assume such importance? Because, we are told, there are 'tasks that face the human apparatus of perception ... that cannot be solved by ... contemplation alone (Essay: Section XV). The task is that of adjusting to these novel affects, the new realm of the senses generated by reproductive media.

Film is exemplary in this respect since the 'characteristics of the film lie not only in the manner in which man presents himself to mechanical equipment but also in the manner in which, by means of this apparatus, man can represent his environment' (Section XIII). This re-presentation of man, media and environment is what defines Benjamin's *distraction*. The external environment is figured in terms of 'shock', the previously cited welter of new micro-perceptions, disorientating cuts and contingent images that characterizes both the built environment and the cinematic encounter. In this situation, 'film is the art that is in keeping with the increased threat to his life which modern man has to face. Man's need to expose himself to shock effects is his adjustment to the dangers threatening him. The film corresponds to profound changes in the apperceptive apparatus – changes that are ... experienced by the man in the street in big-city traffic' (Essay: note 19). The kind of distraction that commentators such as Duhammel had seen in terms of a theft of thought 'I can no longer think what I want to think. My thoughts have been replaced by moving images' (a sentiment cited in Section XIV of the Essay and also present in Kracauer's notion, explored in the next chapter, that the 'image-idea drives away the idea'), is perversely the source of Benjamin's optimism. Distraction's emancipatory potential allegedly resides in its ability to educate humanity en masse – bypassing the hierarchies encoded in traditional knowledge. Cinema imposes shock, but in training the sensorium of viewers it provides them with the means to deal with the wider social environment of shock, and thus provides the foundations for an authentic mass culture.

## Conclusion: Benjamin today

ideology is intrinsic to the mechanical reproduction of art, to destruction, and not only to the tradition or what remains of it.

In the age of the mechanical reproduction of the work of art, ideology is never simply that which remains of a tradition which is being progressively destroyed, nor does it simply exhaust itself in the reanimation of a tradition in the midst of destruction. Ideology is also that destruction itself, but as that which remains, as pure innovation, even as pure repetition without content.

(Duttmann 2000: 39)

Rather than the empowered distraction Benjamin sensed, 'pure repetition without content' is a good description of the endless circulation of commodified fragments that characterize the contemporary mediascape. Benjamin's previously cited observation that mankind is now an object of contemplation for itself fits well with the current cultural climate of Reality TV shows, celebrity trivia, and the mechanically reproduced emotion that accompanies such large-scale media events as the funeral of the Princess of Wales, *Live 8*, and so on. In opposition to the fascists' deliberate misappropriation of aesthetics, Benjamin called for the politicization of art. For Benjamin, fascism represented a systematic aestheticization of politics that necessitated suppressing the intrinsic tendencies of new media, however, he failed to grasp capitalism's flexibility – its apparently uncanny ability to co-opt and exploit the potentialities in which he had such faith. Quoting Benjamin's description of life in the Weimar Republic, Gilloch could equally be providing a concise summary of the social atmosphere that has resulted as a failure of Benjamin's hopes for the media: 'the most selfish narrowest private interests combine with the dullest instincts of the mass … The radical potential of the optical unconscious is reduced to the situation where: 'everyone is committed to the optical illusions of his isolated standpoint' (Gilloch 2002: 97).

Despite his good intentions and hopeful analysis, Benjamin's analysis has proved an inadvertent, albeit important, guide to our understanding of aura's decline and its negative cultural consequences. In television coverage of mediated events that Benjamin did not live to see (such as the Gulf conflicts) we have witnessed how Benjamin's desire for a media-radicalized mass with which to confront fascist tendencies has been co-opted by the corporate, CNN model. Fascism on a mass scale has been transformed into the 'thrill of technomastery' by the individual viewer as a 'fascistic subject' (Meek 1998: n.p.). Society now has a hollow core due to the superficially neutral, but in reality deeply ideological, nature of the media technologies themselves. Benjamin hoped that media such as film would explode like dynamite our 'prison-world', 'so that now, in the midst of its far-flung ruins and debris, we calmly and adventurously go travelling' (Section XIII). In practice, the wide-eyed ramble has become a ghoulishly voyeuristic trip manifested in a diverse range of examples including the surreal game-show video-clip element of some of the US military briefings in the Gulf conflicts and the outpourings of public emotion at the death of Princess Diana, for whom (to all but a tiny minority of the mourners) she was just a screen image[5]. At present it seems that the most likely impact of the media's explosive properties is that its ruins and debris will block our exit from Plato's Cave.

# 2
# Siegfried Kracauer's *mass ornament*

## Introduction

Using Benjamin's Essay as a theoretical focal point, in the previous chapter it was suggested that mass media society involves a process of cultural fragmentation. This is caused by a decline in traditional aura and a matching rise in media representations that do not depend upon aura's ties to a unique point in space and time. This decline in aura is fostered by an alignment between capitalist commodity values and mechanically reproduced images. The social fabric becomes permeated by this complex mix of the social and the technological. Although seeking to argue that media technologies empower the masses, Benjamin's analysis of aura's decline is more insightful about the camera's profound contribution to a historically unprecedented way of seeing than it is able to persuade how this may actually produce empowerment. This chapter addresses more explicitly the exact nature of this relationship between media technologies and their wider social environment using as its key text a collection of Siegfried Kracauer's essays *The Mass Ornament: The Weimar Essays*.

Although less well known than Benjamin in media and cultural studies, Kracauer (1889–1966) played a formative role (he had been Adorno's tutor, and regularly corresponded with Benjamin) in the analyses of culture and media carried out by various members of the Frankfurt School, to the extent that Benjamin and Adorno's accounts of the mass media can be seen as direct response to Kracauer's path-breaking readings. Until fairly recently, Kracauer's best-known work in the English-speaking world was *From Caligari to Hitler: A Psychological History of the German Cinema* ([1947] 2000), which presented a history of German cinema in the inter-war years, arguing that its themes reflected the psycho-social conditions that led to fascism. His influence on Adorno and Benjamin's media theory, however, was the result of a series of articles published in the 1920s (and collected together as *The Mass Ornament*). Since these articles were pieces of journalism aimed at a relatively wide audience, their ideas are adumbrated rather than systematically developed. Nevertheless, Kracauer's essays are still highly suggestive for critical theory and manage in a few pages to anticipate a number of important concepts, for instance, Adorno and Horkheimer's *dialectic of enlightenment* and Benjamin's notion of *distraction*. Moreover, their value is not simply one of anticipation – they offer (albeit in embryo) a unique, critical perspective upon mass-media culture.

## The alienation of the spectacle

The need to lay in supplies for Sunday brings together a crowd that would appear to astronomers as nebulae. It jams together into dense clumps in which the tightly packed individuals wait, until at some point they are again unpacked. *Between purchases they savor the spectacle of the constant disintegration of the complexes to which they belong, a sight that keeps them at the peripheries of life.*
(Kracauer 1995: 41; emphasis added)

The above quotation from Kracauer's essay, 'Analysis of a city map' (first published in 1926), provides a prescient description of the process of *cultural disenchantment*[1] that forms an important theme of this book. Kracauer describes here how a new environment is created by rapid urbanization – an environment that envelops the masses (in contrast to Benjamin's previously explored hope that the masses would actively absorb new cultural content rather than passively being absorbed by it). This new urban atmosphere seamlessly blends widespread commodification with the increasingly powerful social role played by the spectacle (prefiguring Chapter 5's analysis of Debord's *society of the spectacle*). While Kracauer describes the physical act of shopping, the self-reflexivity of the consumers as they watch their own formation – their 'complexes' – can be seen as an early forerunner of the mass-media audience. For example, watching commercial television now represents a more technologically mediated and sophisticated example of the experience Kracauer encountered here in its much earlier and vestigial manifestation as people physically shopping. 'Between purchases' (or in contemporary television terms – advertisements for future purchases), Kracauer provides us with a cogent summary of the current television viewing experience and its complex imbrication of commodity values and Reality formats. '[T]hey savor the constant disintegration of the complexes to which they belong' becomes an encapsulation of our contemporary refashioning of communal life not into the empowered masses Benjamin portrayed but, rather, a body of consumers kept at the periphery of life and for whom culture has become merely an alienating spectacle to be viewed rather than lived.

Kracauer is thus a key critical thinker of the *then* for the way in which he draws out the more negative implications of the destruction of aura and provides insights into the way in which new media technologies have fostered the development of negative social consequences. Such negativity is partially acknowledged by Benjamin himself in the concluding lines of his Essay to which this book repeatedly returns, where he describes how: 'Mankind, which in Homer's time was an object of contemplation for the Olympian gods, now is one for itself. Its self-alienation has reached such a degree that it can experience its own destruction as an aesthetic pleasure of the first order' (Essay: Epilogue). Implicit in Benjamin's Essay, but more explicitly developed by Kracauer and authors in subsequent chapters of this book, is a particularly disturbing feature of the alienation created by the media. In an iterative fashion, alienation itself risks becoming fodder for the yet further alienating processes of a society for which disintegration and destruction are reduced to the status of aesthetic pleasure – the content of yet more media representations. In Kracauer's description of shoppers, the analysis is limited to the physical act of consumption in a modern urban environment but it nevertheless manages to recognize the seeds of a process that has led to the media-saturated *hyperreal* of global capitalism (the focus of Part 2).

Like Benjamin, Kracauer saw a complex interrelationship existing between the modern urban environment and media technologies. He saw a symbiosis between the masses as a social concept and the technologies of reproduction that facilitate their existence[2]. But unlike Benjamin's image of an adventurous wanderer walking in the debris of exploded traditional cultural forms, Kracauer also emphasizes the potentially negative changes wrought upon the social landscape by media technologies. Accordingly, his account of the effects of the newly mediatized urban environment consists of a significantly more downbeat notion of distraction than that found in Benjamin's Essay:

> In the centers of night life the illumination is so harsh that one has to hold one's hands over one's ears. Meanwhile the lights have gathered for their own pleasure, instead of shining for man. Their glowing traces want to illuminate the night but succeed only in chasing it away. Their advertisements sink into the mind without allowing one to decipher them. The reddish gleam that lingers settles like a cloak over one's thoughts.
>
> (Kracauer 1995: 43)

Both the prescience of Kracauer's analysis and an example of the vastly different conclusions to be drawn from similar descriptions of mediated culture (the difference between critical theory and cultural populism) can be judged by the marked similarity between his above description of Parisian nightlife in the relatively early days of electricity and, 74 years later, Seabrook's panegyric to a central New York suffused with the neon glow of the information revolution:

> The air was fuzzy with the weird yellow tornado light of Times Square by day, a blend of sunlight and wattage, the real and the mediated – the color of Buzz. Buzz is the collective stream of consciousness. William James's 'buzzing confusion,' objectified, a shapeless substance into which politics and gossip, art and pornography, virtue and money, the fame of heroes and the celebrity of murderers, all bleed. In Times Square you could see the Buzz that you felt going through your mind. I found it soothing just to stand there on my way to and from work and let the yellow light run into my synapses. In that moment the worlds outside and inside my skull became one.
>
> (Seabrook 2000: 5)

Whereas Benjamin saw the evacuation of traditional auratic meaning as a good thing which could free the masses from any tendency to fall into fascism, and Seabrook, similarly praises rather than finds fault with 'the buzz', it is Kracauer's belief that modernity represents 'an evacuation of meaning, a bifurcation of being and truth' (Levin, in Kracauer 1995: 13).

Unlike Benjamin, Kracauer describes how the rise of the mediated masses is accompanied by this 'evacuation' of meaning – an evacuation that is fostered by capitalist values that compete with and undermine non-commodified forms of mass empowerment. A major aspect of this book's critical interpretations of the *now* is based upon updating this central insight from *then*. Instead of empowering the masses, media technologies reinforce their subordination to commodity forms that are no longer limited to just physical objects that can be bought and sold, but also a much more intangible (yet profoundly effective/affective) series of images. Kracauer's early analysis of mediated culture, is thus an important precursor of Debord (Chapter 5) and Baudrillard's (Chapter 8) later identifications of *the society of the spectacle* defined as a cultural environment in which the spectacle becomes the dominant social category. Baudrillard, in particular, argues that traditional symbolic societal processes increasingly succumb to shallower, mediated forms of cultural interaction.

## Kracauer's photography: signs and symbols

In his essay 'Photography' (first published in 1927) Kracauer's analysis of this medium encapsulates some of the key links to be made between the growth of capitalist society and the advent of media technologies. He approaches the photograph as an artificial form of memory. Like memory, the photograph preserves the past, but what the photograph preserves is not defined by its meaning in terms of conceptual significance but solely by the spatial organization and contiguity of the photograph's material content. As its name implies, the snapshot offers an instant slice of space and time and according to Kracauer is what makes its meaning contingent and arbitrary. For example, he distinguishes between human memory and the quality of a photographic image by considering an old photograph of a relative. Whereas a family's memory would have preserved this person in the context of a range of memories to form a sense of their unique character over a long period of time – a collection of impressions that gives their memory human, familial meaning – the photograph merely preserves the relative in the representation of an instant. A problem arises when, as this unique moment in space and time passes, so that the particular features of the person recorded in that instant are increasingly removed from the living memory that would animate them. They are represented in the photograph as discrete, individual features that are technically very precise but which are taken out of the more general context by which we normally remember people.

In terms of Benjamin's notion of aura, what we have in the photograph are those details that appear at the moment that preservation and 'substantive duration ceases to matter'. Thus, in a process that Part 2's cultural focus represents on a much larger scale, in the individual photograph, the most irrelevant and fleeting details (for Barthes – the *punctum*) increasingly become the photograph's substance. They override its larger context (for Barthes – the *studium*) so that specific things like the particular clothes worn, the furnishings that surround the subject, begin to obscure the living individual. In time, the photograph becomes a mere index of the particular cultural moment in which it was taken. This occurs in spite of other attempts to control and determine the meaning of the image, to manage its contents and thus its semiotic value. This attests to the power of the media's form over its content (the import of McLuhan's aphorism – *the medium is the message*).

Kracauer makes an explicit distinction between human and photographic memory. He argues that when meaning is presented to us in a technological medium it assumes a markedly different quality to non-mediated experience:

> Photography grasps what is given as a spatial (or temporal) continuum; memory images retain what is given only in so far as it has significance. Since what is significant is not reducible to either merely spatial or merely temporal terms, memory

images are at odds with photographic representation ... from the perspective of memory, photography appears as a jumble that consists partly of garbage.

(Kracauer 1995: 50–1)

He contrasts the characteristics peculiar to a conceptualization of history premised upon non-mediated memory and the substantive meaning found in a 'liberated consciousness' with the much more arbitrary information presented by the technological mediation of the photograph: 'This history omits all characteristics and determinations that do not relate in a significant sense to the truth intended by a liberated consciousness ... In a photograph, a person's history is buried as if under a layer of snow' (1995: 51; emphasis added). Unlike Benjamin's underdeveloped and rather vague notion of *distraction*, Kracauer is unambiguous in the implications photography has for human cognition. He talks of how 'the flood of photos sweeps away the dams of memory' (1995: 58) a process accelerated *now* by their seamless integration with other media formats and platforms (computers, mobile phones, and so on).

Working in a journalistic environment in the relatively early days of mass-media technologies, Kracauer was particularly sensitive to the implications of introducing images to the predominantly textual format of the newspaper.

The aim of the illustrated newspapers is the complete reproduction of the world accessible to the photographic apparatus ... never before has an age been so informed about itself, if being informed means having an image of objects that resembles them in a photographic sense ... In reality, however, the weekly photographic ratio does not at all mean to refer to these objects or ur-images.

(Kracauer 1995: 58)

Here he identifies a central paradox that we revisit in Chapter 8 – the irony that in an age of unprecedented visuality and ease of image production, media technologies actually tend to alienate us more, not less, from our surroundings. In the above excerpt, Kracauer problematizes the word *informed*. He is pointing out that photographs only inform us to the extent that they provide us with images of objects that resemble rather than equate to the objects they are portraying. Because a photograph is an objectively recorded, mechanized/chemical capturing of a moment in space and time, the realism of its content's presentation tends to be taken for granted. What Kracauer's analysis highlights, however, is that 'the weekly photographic ratio' (the increase in the number of images made available to us) creates its own cognitive impact. There is an aggregative effect in experiencing hitherto unprecedented numbers of images. Kracauer thus identified at an early historical stage the negative aspects of a trend whose true significance is more fully apparent today.

Benjamin was able to conceptualize the way in which traditional aura is replaced by a new realm more accessible to manipulation by the masses but, constrained by his particular historical perspective, he could not trace the process far enough to realize the extent of its negative implications. In the mass-media capitalism of the contemporary mediascape, our conception of an underlying reality behind media representations has become increasingly distorted by the exponential circulation of signs. This has created a semi-autonomous realm of *pseudo-events* and the *hyperreal* (see Chapter 5 and 8's treatment of Debord/Boorstin and Baudrillard respectively). With great foresight, Kracauer identified the combined social and technological origins of this simulated environment – a culture in which the notion of the original is consistently and profoundly undermined by the rise of mediated copies and representations. For Kracauer, these reproductions which appear to place the world in front of the reader/viewer, are nothing more than 'signs ... of the original object', as such they neither inform nor represent. The word *signs* is crucial here because it marks the technologically sponsored move away from the location-dependent symbols based upon aura's previously discussed dependency upon location and physical grounding. Signs are decontextualized and freed from the otherwise *unbreakable bonds of reciprocity* that Baudrillard claims are a basic property of symbols and their innate dependence upon a physical context – aura as a unique point in space and time. Thus, the qualitative effect of 'the flood of photos' is so great that it threatens to destroy the original object.

Prefiguring Benjamin's description of aura's decline and Baudrillard's much later theorizing of the simulacral/*hyperreal*, Kracauer observes that 'the resemblance between the image and the object effaces the contours of the object's "history"' (1995: 58). Photography creates an explosion in the amount of visual information that can be circulated independently of any physical origins. This causes social experience to become increasingly fragmentary because such ungrounded image-signs create a knowledge of the world that is increasingly disembedded. Taken out of its original auratic context a new mode of sensory experience is indeed created as Benjamin argued, but for Kracauer: 'the contiguity of these images systematically excludes their contextual framework available to consciousness. *The "image idea" drives away the idea*' (Kracauer 1995: 58; emphasis added). Rather than empowering the masses, Kracauer describes how the magazines and techniques they employed provided a new means of control so that: 'In the hands of the ruling society, the invention of the illustrated magazines, is one of the most powerful means of organizing a strike against reality' (Kracauer 1995: 58). Paradoxically, explicit images prevent true observation and understanding. The net result of photography's qualitatively new impact is thus a profound transition in our experience of the world around us – a transition, both Benjamin and, in parts of his work, Kracauer attempted to be optimistic about, but which provides much food for critical thought. A highly useful summary of the negative implications of Kracauer's analysis can be found by forming an aphoristic contradiction by joining two phrases from his 'Photography' essay, otherwise separated by half a page, 'Never before has an age been so informed about itself... Never before has a period known so little about itself' (Kracauer 1995: 58).

Kracauer's analysis directly rejects the temptation to see photography as a technical but ultimately neutral, scientifically accurate representation of the world. He argues that photography *re*-presents the world. The new technological medium brings the world into conformity with its mediated image rather than the other way around: 'the world itself has taken on a "photographic" face; it can be photographed because it strives to be absorbed into the spatial continuum that yields to snapshots' (Kracauer 1995: 59). This is very close to Sontag's later assertion that: 'There is an aggression implicit in every use of the camera ... technology made possible an ever-increasing spread of that mentality which looks at the world as a set of potential photographs' (Sontag 1979: 7).[3] Cinema, too, contributes to this process:

> Film patches together shot after shot and from these successively unfurling images mechanically recomposes the world – a mute world ... in which the incomplete speech of optical impressions is the only language. The more the represented object can be rendered in the succession of mere images, the more it corresponds to the filmic technique of association.
>
> (Kracauer, in Hansen 1991: 50)

Part 2 explores the development of these trends in the *now* and the full extent to which the succession of mere images and the technique of association have created a strike against understanding to such an extent that, although working on the right theoretical lines, even Kracauer's critical perspective could not adequately account for its harmful cultural effects.

The question of the status of the photograph as a unit of representation is a crucial one for Kracauer. He defines the photograph as the 'last stage of the symbol' (Kracauer 1995: 59). This statement must be understood within its wider theoretical context: Kracauer conceived history in terms of human consciousness's progress from an immediate sensory immersion in nature to an increasingly independent and abstract realm of thought. Following Weber's notion of *disenchantment,* Kracauer's history of thought in its broadest sense thus becomes a kind of escape from mythology, and in this regard is a direct precursor to Horkheimer and Adorno's *Dialectic of Enlightenment* described in the next chapter. Kracauer argues that, historically, images have been closely associated with the physical environments in which they have arisen. This relation to the physical environment is an essential aspect of what constitutes a symbol. It is understood as an expression of the human mind but one that is intimately intertwined with the nature that surrounds it. By contrast, a technologized, mediated society increasingly liberates itself from nature and tends to lose more and more of this symbolic quality. For Kracauer, this results in the growing dominance of allegorical signs over grounded symbols. Freed from their immediate grounding in a physical environment, symbols begin to encompass and articulate a more abstract, wider range of relationships and are thereby transformed into signs.

This process represents a further development of Marx's economy-based conceptualization of the way in which capitalism promotes a move away from the social importance of use-value of objects to exchange-value. The physical properties of objects become less important than their position in relation to the abstraction of money. Similarly, in a culture dominated by media technologies, symbols come to circulate more abstractly as signs. On the one hand, this move away from the symbolic is empowering. It allows culture to free itself from falsely *concrete* myths, that is, beliefs it misguidedly (from the purely rationalist point of view) places in material objects – for example, the fetishes and totems (as in the totem pole of Native American culture) of non-technological societies. On the other hand, the new realm of abstraction opened up by the mediation of culture (the *falsely abstract*) can be an even more alienating environment. It is divorced from the strong links more traditional and symbolically rich societies have with their immediate surroundings no matter how irrational or superstitious those links might appear to the Western mind. In terms of the *now,* this rather abstract discussion of abstraction can be understood in terms of the globalization debate. The whole purpose of a Starbucks coffee shop (and any other international franchise) is that its product should appear largely the same no matter what city in the world you are buying it. In this case, a form of coffee overladen with milk produces a taste that is as homogenized as possible (both literally and more figuratively). Specific, grounded taste (the notion that coffee might taste different in different countries) is replaced by the more geographically independent and hence more easily circulated concept – internationally standardized coffee.

Kracauer's argument clearly matches the changing function of the work of art in Benjamin's Essay where it emerges from a strictly ritual function to assume a religious or latter exhibition value, and then as a result of mechanical reproduction, becomes independent of any material context/unique point in space and time. Benjamin, and to a lesser extent, Kracauer, believed that there was a positive potential to this ability of technology to disembed by removing aura and promoting processes of increasing abstraction. This is because it presents opportunities for the newly emerging masses to free themselves from the aura of tradition. However, to be upheld, the optimism of both writers requires that the alienating consequences of the decline of aura are adequately recognized and then compensated for by providing a convincing account of empowering new alternatives – but in both writers little direct evidence is in fact given of likely alternatives. Benjamin assumed as his post-mediated cultural horizon, a world of fragments, mere detritus left by the dynamite of one-tenth of a second. With the benefit of historical hindsight it is still unclear to contemporary eyes whether wandering adventurously among the rubble can provide meaningful empowerment beyond the dubious value to be found in Benjamin's notion of *distraction*. Amid his occasional optimism, Kracauer's analysis tends to provide a more realistic assessment of the negative consequences of a de-symbolized culture. He describes how the technologized removal of symbols is replaced by a systematized, industrialized perversion of human reason that he calls *Ratio* and which he discusses in relation to his *mass ornament* – a notion that prefigures both Adorno's *culture industry* and Debord's *society of the spectacle*.

## The mass ornament

> The position that an epoch occupies in the historical process can be determined more strikingly from an analysis of its inconspicuous surface-level expressions than from that epoch's judgments about itself ... The surface level expressions ... by virtue of their unconscious nature, provide unmediated access to the fundamental substance of the state of the things ... knowledge of this state of things depends on the interpretation of these surface-level expressions.
>
> (Kracauer 1995: 75)

Among his Weimar essays, Kracauer's 'The mass ornament' (first published in 1927) is a cogent summary of his guiding analytical principles and is perhaps the most significant of his early writings. In it he identified the principle of *Gleichzeitigkeit* or 'simultaneity' – the idea that the spheres of production and leisure had begun to fuse under the capitalist phase of production. Faced with this fusion, and

in keeping with Benjamin's previously cited linkage of the simultaneous rise of the optical unconscious and the Freudian unconscious,
Kracauer asserts his belief in the above quotation that mundane
cultural phenomena can reveal significant underlying analytical
truths. In this spirit, Kracauer turns his attention to the 'Tiller Girls'
– an American dance troupe specializing in the kind of choreo-
graphed geometric spectacle that Busby Berkeley was to turn into an
art form in the Hollywood musicals of the 1930s. Kracauer
approaches this seemingly frivolous and ephemeral production of a
nascent culture industry, as emblematic of the entire system of
production:

> Not only were they American products: at the same time they
> celebrated the greatness of American production … When they
> formed an undulating snake, they radiantly illustrated the
> virtues of the conveyor belt; when they tapped their feet in fast
> tempo, it sounded like business, business; when they kicked
> their legs high with mathematical precision, they joyously
> affirmed the progress of rationalization; and when they kept
> repeating the same movements without interrupting their rou-
> tine, one envisioned an uninterrupted chain of autos gliding
> from the factories into the world, and believed that the
> blessings of prosperity have no end.
>
> (Kracauer, cited in Witte 1975: 64)

This description clearly demonstrates how the quality of simultaneity
– an apparently harmless entertainment   actually replicates and
celebrates the logic of the capitalist production. Kracauer sees the
Tiller Girls as a literal embodiment of the disembedding or
de-territorializing effects of capital: the women who make up the
spectacle are de-individualized. They become interchangeable mannequins, doubles of a generic white-toothed, firm-bodied, long-
limbed humanity. This process does not respect the body as an
organic whole, its members are themselves disarticulated and recombined; not 'fully preserved bodies' but 'arms, thighs and other
segments are the smallest component parts of the composition'
(Kracauer 1995: 78). The fate of the individual body serves as a
microcosm of the fate of the body politic. Capitalism disarticulates
the latter's natural organs (understood as various forms of community) and recombines them in accordance with the dictates of
production even when apparently in the service of art or entertainment (hence Adorno's use of the oxymoronic phrase *culture industry*).

Although a high-kicking dance troupe of the 1920s might seem
somewhat anachronistic to a modern readership, Kracauer's analysis
demonstrates how, at the very beginnings of mass-mediated culture,
apparently rational (but ultimately disempowering) systems and

processes had insinuated themselves into cultural forms. The cultural and the industrial were now subtly intertwined when once they were separate areas of human activity. To help highlight this point, Kracauer attaches great significance to that very apparent superfluity of the Tiller Girls' formations. In apparent contradistinction to the system they reflect, these formations are unproductive and purely aesthetic. Their geometric formations are merely ornamental both in terms of form and function – a clear expression of what he calls *the mass ornament*. This is a crucial concept and therefore warrants close attention. *Mass ornament* describes the manner in which the Tiller Girls are at once de-individualized, reduced to a common mass, and then recomposed as components in a larger geometric spectacle, they are the mass assuming ornamental form. At the same time this mass ornament acts as a 'seed' that draws the much larger audience viewing the formation of dancers into a formation itself, thus the regularity of the Tiller Girls' patterns are 'cheered by the masses, themselves arranged by the stands in tier upon ordered tier' (Kraucer 1995: 76). While Kracauer refers here to the physically present audience for live performances, in the following chapters we shall see how this formative, regimented impact upon the audience also applies to the amorphous mass of the de-auraticized (not present at the unique point in space and time but distanced by mechanical reproduction) audience viewing in the comfort of their own homes.

The pattern that the troupe, and to a lesser degree their spectators, forms is something they themselves cannot appreciate, it is an activity whose overriding purpose it is structurally impossible for the individual participant to observe:

> although the masses give rise to ornament, they are not involved in thinking it through. As linear as it may be, there is no line that extends from the small sections to the entire figure. The ornament resembles aerial photographs of land-scapes in that it does not emerge out of the interior of the given conditions, *but rather appears above them.*
> (Kracauer 1995: 77; emphasis added)

The key point to note here is how the process required to convert a group of women into a geometrical spectacle involves a degree of rational abstraction, an abstraction that 'appears above' the heads of the participants, in other words, an alienating intrusion from the outside rather than 'the interior of the given conditions', or what we have previously repeatedly referred to in terms of Baudrillard's phrase 'the *unbreakable bonds of reciprocity*'. The ornament, divorced as it is from its constituent parts, resembles the pure lines of 'Euclidean geometry' or the simple forms of physics. It is an inorganic, abstract order and as such 'the structure of the mass ornament reflects that of the entire capitalist situation' (Kracauer 1995: 78). As in our previous discussion of signs and symbols, the mass ornament stems from capitalism's destruction of pre-existing forms and their specific physical groundedness. Component parts are recombined in conformity with an alien, abstracted order – in what could be seen as a motto for the culture industry, 'community and personality perish when what is demanded is calculability' (Kracauer 1995: 78). It is this process of abstraction that Kracauer calls *Ratio*. It may be intangible but its influence is felt deeply within and widely across commodity culture. It is not just the actual performers who experience their own performance as something external, imposed upon them from the outside (what we shall soon see Adorno discuss in terms of *heteronomy*); viewers too now consume culture that comes to them, above their heads, in a pre-packaged non-spontaneously created form.

*Ratio* can be seen as further developing the distinction between signs and symbols. It is part of the capitalist tendency to supplant a symbolism grounded in spatial proximity to physical objects. Kracauer thus distinguishes between nature's symbolic power and the distortedly allegorical form of reason that flourishes when objects derive their meaning from their relationship to an overarching, standardizing frame of reference. According to Kracauer, reason involves a process of abstraction from the natural world, a retreat from sensory immediacy in favour of the general concept. A process that in turn facilitates the exploitation of the natural world – 'reason speaks wherever it disintegrates organic unity and rips open the natural surface' (Kracauer 1995: 84). When the 'natural surface' is ripped open (in a similar fashion to Benjamin's notion of the optical unconscious) there arises the possibility that the masses can see more clearly than ever before the nature of the reality that surrounds them and hence be empowered with that insight. But Kracauer sees *Ratio* as the stalling of reason, a perverted reason because it serves to obscure such insight: '*Ratio* flees from reason and takes refuge in the abstract' (1995: 84). In the next chapter we explore Adorno's account of the way in which the culture industry abolishes the natural tension between the general (in this context, the abstract) and the particular (in this case the grounded symbolic) that fuels great art. The removal of this tension and the promotion of abstraction produces an uncritical friction-free cultural experience (Seabrook's *buzz*). It is this insight that provides the basis for understanding the banal predictability of a diverse range of culture industry experiences such as fast food and soap operas – and demonstrates the roots (the *then*) of a contemporary society dominated by abstraction (the banal *now* of Part 2).

The mass ornament as the aesthetic reflex of capitalism is closely tied to the essentially self-referential nature of the commodity form, neither have any substantial meaning beyond their own self-generation: 'Like the mass ornament, the capitalist production process is an end in itself. The commodities that it spews forth are not actually produced to be possessed; rather, they are made for the sake of a profit that knows no limit' (Kracauer 1995: 78). Both share a rationale but they are not truly rational in terms of having an ultimate justification:

> Value is not produced for the sake of value. Though labor may well have once served to produce and consume values up to a certain point, these have now become side effects in the service of the production process. The activities subsumed by that process have divested themselves of their substantial contents. The production process runs its secret course in public. Every-one does his or her task on the conveyor belt, performing a partial function without grasping the totality.
>
> (Kracauer 1995: 78)

The only purpose of both capitalist production and its aesthetic reflection of the mass ornament is self-augmentation. Their overriding purpose is to generate a surplus but whether one thinks of the actual contributors to the productive process (the workers on the assembly line or the Tiller Girls in formation) or consumers who consume for the sake of consumption – all such groups suffer alienation because they are participating in a process that is without an autonomously rational end. To the extent that a rationale exists it is the externally imposed (above their heads) requirements of profit-driven *Ratio*.

The concept of *Ratio* is an inversion of the *false concreteness* that characterizes traditional mythology. It represents a new form of myth for highly technologized culture – the *false abstractness* of the commodity fetish in the form of mediated signs to be circulated. As previously mentioned, traditional myth is *falsely concrete* in the sense that it plays an excessively determinative role within a society in which people impute unwarranted beliefs into inanimate objects. From the standard of *ratio*nal analysis, such mythic thinking prevents a true relationship with the real. Non-technological societies are prevented from developing technologically and rationally because they are bound by their groundedness to their richly symbolic environments. Rationality involves a departure from this mythic mode of thought. However, in the capitalist stage of production, a mode of *false abstractness* predominates and becomes the new mythic way of thinking. The mass ornament as an aborted form of reason 'reveals itself as a *mythological cult* that is masquerading in the garb of abstraction' (Kracauer 1995: 83; emphasis in original). In opposition to *Ratio*, Kracauer privileges *Vernunft* (true reason) as an oppositional factor to the forces of nature in a similar manner to the way Benjamin seeks the socialist power of the masses to be a corrective to the aura of tradition. But like Benjamin, he provides little detail as to how *Vernunft* will overcome *Ratio* beyond wishing it so.

Kracauer sees cinema as a possible solution to the alienating warehousing of the world that photography has brought about. In particular, the cinematic technique of montage provides opportunities by which the fragments of modernity can be recomposed in pursuit of a new and truly rational and humane order. However, just as from a critical perspective Benjamin's notion of empowering distraction provides an apparently weak basis from which to oppose the alienating cultural features of media, Kracauer explicitly acknowledges the difficulty of the path he espouses. The *Ratio* of *mass ornament* is powerful in its role as a new mediated form of myth. He speaks of it as a 'mythology of an order so great that one can hardly imagine its being exceeded' (1995: 84) and suggests that: 'Reason can gain entrance only with difficulty' (1995: 85). *Ratio*'s social purpose is likened to the circus games of the Roman Empire and in Part 2 we see how much more sophisticated and insidiously pervasive this new mythical cult of *Ratio* has become with the spread of *Banality TV* into realms previously protected by 'discourses of sobriety'. Kracauer's invocation of a mythological cult brings to mind Benjamin's characterization of fascism as *the aesthecization of politics*. The more critical import of Kracauer's analysis, however, stems from the way in which his notions of *Ratio* and *mass ornament* demonstrate the manner in which Benjamin's corresponding desire to see *the politicization of aesthetics* has been frustrated by the temptations of *false abstraction*. In his essay '*The hotel lobby*' (first published 1922–25) to which we now turn, Kracauer argues it is false because it does not attain the full abstraction of genuine reason, rather: 'The desolation of *Ratio* is complete only when it removes its mask and hurls itself into the void of random abstractions that no longer mimic higher determinations, and when it renounces seductive consonances and desires itself even as a concept' (Kracauer 1995: 180).

## The hotel lobby

Kracauer believed that the apparently insignificant, if not tawdry, products of the mass media are, if carefully examined, capable of yielding up the secrets of the whole. Unlike many cultural populists, this does not mean that he is some sort of cultural relativist, who believes that all culture is of equal value and that any attempt to erect hierarchies of taste are necessarily spurious. Neither does this imply some faith in a consciously subversive or critical dimension to mass cultural products. What it does indicate is that the truth of an era can be uncovered from the particular cultural forms to which it gives birth. Thus, in a similar fashion to our focus in Part 2 on *Banality TV*, Kracauer reads the rise of the detective novel around the beginning of the twentieth century in terms of the growing hegemony of *Ratio*. This is reflected not in the explicit themes or characterization of individual texts, but rather in the genre's narrative structure in which a fragmented world (made up of disparate clues) is deciphered. A society that exists 'only as a concept ... is fully realized in actions and figures'. In exploring such a society by constructing 'a whole out of the blindly scattered elements of a disintegrated world' the crime novel 'transforms an ungraspable life into a translatable analogue of actual reality' (Kracauer 1995: 174). Noting that hotel lobbies frequently appear in detective fiction, Kracauer examines them in terms of their illustration of some of the spatial experiences of a society ruled by *Ratio*. In order to accentuate their particular features and the distance of these from earlier spatial forms he uses the comparison of a church and its congregation. Both are indexes of particular forms of community, and the contrast they provide serves to illuminate the stakes involved in the transition from one to the other. Kracauer sees a church as a spatial expression of a certain form of community, whose members are present to themselves and others in their gathering in the presence of God.

The hotel lobby represents a kind of 'negative church'; like the church it is a place of waiting, like a church it is a site preserved from the currents of everyday life, and into both one enters as a guest. However, unlike a church whose 'gathering is a *collectedness* and a unification of this directed life of the community' (Kracauer 1995: 176; emphasis in original) in the lobby people gather alone, its 'detachment does not lead the community to assure itself of its existence as a congregation ... people find themselves *vis-à-vis de rien*' (Kracauer 1995: 176). The hotel lobby thus embodies for Kracauer the essential emptiness of what we begin to explore in the next chapter as the culture industry and then in later chapters as the *society of the spectacle*/simulation. In the lobby the social is encountered as a spectacle so that 'the person sitting is ... overcome by a disinterested satisfaction in the contemplation of a world creating itself, whose *purposiveness is felt without being associated with any representation of a purpose*' (Kracauer 1995: 177; emphasis added). This notion of purposiveness without purpose is borrowed by both Kracauer and Adorno from the German philosopher Immanuel Kant's *Critique of Pure Reason*. Here, Kant famously defined beauty as 'purposiveness without any representation of a purpose' (*Critique of Judgment* 1.18) or as the German mystic-poet Angelus Silesius (1624–

1677) put it 'Die Rose ist ohne warum; Sie blühet, weil Sie blühet' ('The Rose is without an explanation; She blooms, because She blooms').

The Kantian perspective that Kracauer draws upon, suggests that in great art or a religious congregation, the ineffably sublime nature of the form's ability to express its content provides its justificatory purpose. By contrast, in a culture produced in a systematic fashion, or the emblematic space of the hotel lobby – the externally generated guarantee of sublime beauty's ultimate purpose is lacking. This is because the content is pre-packaged and innately limited since it is generated from within a self-contained framework. This has a profound impact upon the aesthetic experience of systematized culture so that its: 'aesthetic ... is presented without any regard for these upward-striving intentions and the formula "purposiveness without purpose" also exhausts its content' (Kracauer 1995: 177). The sublime nature of what critical theorists (in opposition to their less judgemental cultural populist counterparts) stubbornly insist upon as a *truly* aesthetic experience resides in its lack of calculable value – à la Silesius, what is the monetary value of witnessing a beautiful rose blooming? The sublime is replaced by *Ratio* and *the culture industry* by the previously cited, overwhelming need for calculability. The result is a self-imposed limitation of outlook. Kracauer's example of the hotel lobby highlights this innate blandness. A lobby tends to make minimal reference to the geographical particularity of the hotel itself, its purpose is purely functional, to facilitate the circulation of hotel guests and visitors and their temporary association with that particular physical environment – the particular is dominated by the general. The lobby is thus a 'space that does not refer beyond itself' (Kracauer 1995: 177) a point which Kracauer then immediately follows up by pointing to the aesthetic experience that results from inhabiting this self-enclosed space 'constitutes itself as its own limit' (Kracauer 1995: 177). Although there is an irrefutable level of activity it is essentially pointless in the sense that it does not point beyond itself.

The passive observation of this ultimately pointless activity by the denizen of the hotel lobby recalls the passage from 'Analysis of city map' with which we began this chapter. There, perambulating consumers savoured 'the spectacle of the constant disintegration of the complexes to which they belong'. But while this pleasure in the dissolution of complexes harbours at least the possibility of an eventual revolutionary realization that social structures could be organized otherwise, in the hotel lobby such a realization is neutralized and undermined by the essential banality of the aesthetic experience – the physical space of the hotel lobby thus acts as a trope for Part 2's analysis of the cultural space created by the

*Banality TV* of mass-mediated society. In both cases, existence is overdetermined in an artificially enclosed and circumscribed space of reductive self-referentiality: 'it does not refer beyond itself'. We can see it in: the tautological self-referentiality of the media's *pseudo-events* (defined as events that only have meaning/significance within the media – see Chapter 5); the predictability of *Banality TV* formats; and their hybridized interbreeding. Kracauer's analysis highlights a basic distinction to be made between critical theories and the competing theories of active audience theorists and cultural populists who tend to reject the critical theorist's right to question the fundamental quality of social activity. The observer within the hotel lobby is as free to watch the surrounding activity as the audience is to interpret the content of the mass media. Critical theory is critical, however, because it does not shy away from making the judgement that this activity is essentially worthless. The guests in the hotel lobby enter into an alienated and atomized contemplation of one another reminiscent of contemporary celebrities and Reality TV where first-hand knowledge of people is replaced by systematized, manufactured representations: 'Remnants of individuals slip into the nirvana of relaxation, faces disappear behind newspapers, and the artificial continuous light illuminates nothing but mannequins. It is the coming and going of unfamiliar people who have become empty forms' (Kracauer 1995: 183). Kracauer's hotel lobbies thus illustrate how the *then* of early mass culture speaks directly to *critical* aspects of mass media culture *now*.

We have seen how the hotel lobby acts as a trope for wider commodity culture's lack of a symbolic grounding with its environment. Marx describes how capitalism abstracts out from the use-values of objects and replaces them with the abstract, decontextualized notion of exchange value, and in the hotel lobby/ culture industry we similarly find ourselves in an 'undetermined void' in which there are only two modes of operation available. One can stand 'superfluously off to the side' or immerse oneself to the extent of 'intoxication' (Kracauer 1995: 179). The togetherness implied by social bonds of substance is replaced in this new situation by an 'invalidation of togetherness' (1995: 179). Here we can clearly see the resonant parallels between Kracauer's analysis and subsequent developments within contemporary media: Reality TV's *Big Brother* celebrity formats are analogous to the hotel lobby both in terms of a suspension in a generic non-space, and in terms of the self-referential nature of the celebrity system – 'unfamiliar people who have become empty forms'(1995: 183). It is interestingly that Kracauer discusses this invalidation in terms of the *unreal* because this is a notion that prefigures Eco and Baudrillard's much later examination of the postmodern *hyperreal*. Kracauer's description of how formerly socialized people are reduced to undifferentiated atoms predates some of Baudrillard's last writings in which he defines this invalidation of togetherness as a process of *telemorphosis*. Kracauer's insightful account of the spatially limited hotel lobby, becomes for Baudrillard a society-wide phenomenon. Reality TV formats that tend to be situated in 'any enclosed space where an experimental niche or zone of privilege is re-created – the equivalent of an initiatory space where the laws of open society are abolished' (Baudrillard 2005: 191). The enclosed space of the hotel lobby is now replaced by the *invalidly together* space of the Big Brother compound.

## Kracauer, travel and Reality TV

In the essay *'Travel and dance'* (first published in 1925), Kracauer turns his attention to the emergence of the modern travel industry. He uses it to illustrate the concealment of non-mediated reality by technologically driven capitalism. As with his concept of the hotel lobby, travel becomes an example of the way in which mass culture only apparently appears to empower when in fact it merely provides experiences to consume in an ultimately empty fashion. Kracauer is much more critical here than Benjamin. He describes how the travel enabled by mass culture is not to be understood in terms of broadening horizons, the experience of other cultures. Instead, it is simply an extension of the same pseudo-novelty that characterizes the commodity form. He establishes this by erecting a distinction between the symbolic experience of the *Here* and the *Beyond* of a pre-technological society, and the purely spatial understanding of such a distinction that predominates under capitalism. Kracauer argues that while earlier cultures recognized and cultivated an awareness and a space for an experience of a *Beyond* (a powerful aesthetic and emotional realm to be found in such spheres as religion and art), in technological society this *Beyond* is tamed, controlled and enframed: 'technology becomes an end in itself ... space and time must be conquered by the power of the intellect ... Radio, telephotography, and so forth – each and every one ... serves one single aim: the constitution of a depraved omnipresence within calculable dimensions' (Kracauer 1995: 70). Once again, the abstraction of the general dominates the physicality of the particular.

Under capitalism the potential of the *Beyond* is replaced by what is merely elsewhere, an elsewhere whose dominant feature is its accessibility: in contrast to the *Ineinander* (defined as the condition of a reciprocal inter-penetration of the *Here* and the *Beyond*) of earlier cultures, modernity posits a *Nacheinander* an 'after-each-other'. As a result both the *Here* and the *Beyond* are lost. The *Here* has become unendurable without the prospect of escape. It is dispersed in the potential of travel, while the possibility of transcendent *Beyond* is reduced to a spatial elsewhere. In effect all that remains is the novelty of motion – travel offers a 'substitute' for a *Beyond* that can no longer be accessed. In place of Benjamin's empowered, wandering masses, the mediated public is:

> confined to the spatio-temporal coordinate system and are unable to extend themselves beyond the forms of perception to the perception of forms, they are granted access to the Beyond only through a change in their position in space-time … Travel … has no particular destinations: its meaning is exhausted in the mere fact of changing locations.
>
> (Kracauer 1995: 71)

Kracauer notes that this mechanized travel is marked by an affective novelty: 'We are like children when we travel, playfully excited about the new velocity, the relaxed roaming about, the overviews of geographic regions that previously could not be seen with such scope … Technology has taken us by surprise, and the regions that it has opened up are still glaringly empty (1995: 73). He identifies something of that terrain that Benjamin will later christen the *optical unconscious*, here it is invoked as an unprecedented hybridization of the material world and our own techno-media extensions. However, the regions that travel and technology introduce to us are 'glaringly empty'. While Kracauer recognizes the novelty that they afford, implicit in his account is a fundamental difference between an apparently authentic earlier mode of *Being* (in which *Here* and *Beyond* exist in dynamic tension) and the new tensionless experience of capitalism's *Ratio* in which we consume what has already been predigested by the system that creates our systemic commodities.

Kracauer's analysis of the emergence of the travel industry prefigures a number of features that illuminate *Banality TV* and its pursuit of novelty. Shows such as Jerry Springer construct the exotic from 'trailer-trash', while 'Fenced-in nature preserves' and 'isolated fairy-tale realms' (Kracauer 1995: 66) provide good descriptions of the architecturally circumscribed manufacture of the *Big Brother* franchise. The term *franchise* is significant because its quality of geographical mobility not only points to the process of global homogenization alluded to in Kracauer's discussion of travel, but also implies the commodified need of a franchise to provide endless variations upon the same basic theme. Kracauer draws attention to how the activities of travel and dance 'have the dubious tendency to become formalized' (1995: 67). In keeping with both this insight and Weber's concept of the rationalization of charisma, Reality TV, especially in its celebrity-based formats, partakes of Kracauer's assertion that:

They are no longer events that happen to unfold in space and time, but instead brand the transformation of space and time itself as an event. Were this not the case, their contents would not increasingly allow themselves to be determined by *fashion*. For fashion effaces the intrinsic value of the things that come under its dominion by subjecting the appearance of these phenomena to periodic changes that are not based on any relation to the thing themselves.

(1995: 67; original emphasis)

For our critical purposes, the crucial phrase here is *periodic changes that are not based on any relation to the thing themselves* – this returns us to the ideological critique of the commodity and its overarching structure – the culture industry. Unlike the falsely concrete myth that still has an intimate relationship to the forms which embody that myth, the space in which the culture industry makes its profit is this essential lack of meaningful substance within the form of cultural expression (in this case, *Banality TV*). This essential lack is the same as that which exists in the notion of travel for its own sake.

Movement through homogeneous space as an end in itself closely mirrors the *self-justifying* movements (whether they be mere eye movements amid media content or physical trips between shops) of both the media viewer and commodity consumer: 'The adventure of movement as such is thrilling, and slipping out of accustomed spaces and times into as yet unexplored realms arouses the passions: the ideal here is to roam freely through the dimensions. This spatio-temporal double life could hardly be craved with such intensity, were it not the *distortion* of real life' (Kracauer 1995: 68; original emphases). The degree to which this distortion is acknowledged and the relative importance placed upon it distinguishes the culture industry critic from the cultural populist.

## Conclusion: distraction revisited and the culture industry introduced

The divergence of Benjamin and Kracauer's positions is brought into focus by considering their respective treatment of the concept of 'distraction' and its relation to cinema. Levin suggests that in the 'Cult of distraction' essay:

Kracauer locates the emancipatory potential of a distracted mode of reception in its capacity to retool perceptual and motor skills for the sensorial economy of modernity, whose most salient characteristics are its speed and abrupt transitions – the very hallmark of cinema as the school of 'shock' which Benjamin would celebrate.

(Levin, in Kracauer 1995: 26)

What makes Kracauer a more pessimistically critical thinker than Benjamin is his willingness to think through the negative consequences of such training for the 'sensorial economy of modernity'. Instead of Benjamin's rather vague notion of distraction, Kracauer was more willing to explore the negative implications of such a mode of mediated experience. For example, he saw the cinematic spectacle of the Berlin picture house as multi-sensory 'distraction factory':

> The stimulations of the senses succeed one another with such rapidity that there is no room left between them for even the slightest contemplation. Like *life buoys*, the refractions of the spotlight and the musical accompaniment keep the spectator above water. The penchant for distraction demands and finds an answer in the display of pure externality ... This emphasis upon the external has the advantage of being *sincere*.
>
> (Kracauer 1995: 326; original emphases)

Like Benjamin he calls for a heightening of those elements of the spectacle that challenge or overturn high art and its conservative dependence upon aura and outmoded cultural values. To the extent to which Kracauer shares Benjamin's sense of the empowering possibilities of the media, it rests in his previously cited concept that *Ratio* is a stalled, inhibited form of reason that needs to be pushed further forwards rather than remaining stuck in abstraction for its own sake. However, Kracauer's status as a more overtly critical thinker than Benjamin and whose mode of analysis leads us directly to Adorno's negativity, stems from his recognition that capitalism is devoted to fostering *Ratio* at the expense of reason. Unlike Benjamin, and much closer in sentiment to Adorno, Kracauer was conscious of the extent to which the empowering possibilities of distraction could easily be betrayed for ideological purposes:

> Distraction – which is meaningful only as improvisation, as a reflection of the uncontrolled anarchy of our world – is festooned with drapery and forced back into a unity that no longer exists. Rather than acknowledging the actual state of disintegration that such shows ought to represent, the movie theaters glue the pieces back together after the fact and present them as organic creations.
>
> (Kracauer 1995: 327–8)

Like Benjamin, Kracauer thought that at least in principle the media could provide the masses with insights with which to confront 'the uncontrolled anarchy of our world', but unlike Benjamin he did not regard the new media of his time as a ready-made solution to the problems of capitalism.

Benjamin placed his hope in distraction because it bypassed the cognitive process of the individual, operating directly upon the body, in contrast, Kracauer placed his faith in reason. His account of the early mediascape of his time differed from those of his peers because it offers 'the possibility of the recuperation of reason by way of the vilification of *Ratio* ... His faith in the power of reason is striking' (Koss 1997: 31). This faith in reason and its centrality in the emergence of capitalism and its media technologies brings us now to a consideration of Adorno, who, like Kracauer, placed reason's dialectical destruction of myth as the precondition for both capitalism and its possible alternatives. However, Adorno was more sceptical about the innate value of reason. It is not simply that reason's distortion in the form of *Ratio* produces the worst cultural aspects of modernity but, rather, that there is a fundamental ambivalence in rationality itself. As a result, we shall now see how Adorno was even less hopeful than Kracauer that reason in the form of a liberated consciousness would be able to break the spell of the culture industry.

# 3

# Theodor Adorno and the culture industry

## Introduction

The work of Theodor Adorno (1903–69) represents one of the first sustained meditations on the effects of mass media on culture and society. As a result it has had an enduring influence on cultural theory. Adorno's account of mass media, or what he called the *culture industry*, was developed in the context of the work of the *Frankfurt School* and their project of *critical theory*. The Frankfurt School was a group of German intellectuals who participated in the Frankfurt Institute of Cultural Research, a privately funded research group affiliated to Frankfurt University. Among its ranks were many of the most powerful minds in European intellectual life, and many of them, both within and outside the Institute, had a major impact on twentieth-century thought. The Institute began from a broadly Marxist position, however, they recognized that the direction in which Western societies were developing could not be accounted for by orthodox Marxism. This was a response to the apparent divergence between Marxist theory and the developmental trajectory of advanced capitalist societies, in particular, the integral role of culture in this context. Various phenomena, such as the emergence of avant-garde modernism, and the burgeoning influence of a range of technological media, raised questions that highlighted the inadequacy of treating culture as a superstructural expression entirely determined by the economic base. Cultural production and consumption were playing an increasing central role in capitalist societies and, as a result, a new set of theoretical tools were required to analyse these developments, as 'individual consciousness and unconsciousness were encroached upon by agencies which organize free time – for example the radio, television, film and professional sport industries – the Frankfurt theorists stressed the urgency of developing a sociology of "mass culture" ' (Held 1980: 77).

In the 1930s the Frankfurt School's continued existence in Nazi Germany became untenable, and it was forced into exile, eventually re-establishing itself in the USA. This experience proved crucial in the evolution of Adorno's media theory. In Hitler's Germany he had witnessed the powerful role that mass media could play in shaping the opinions and behaviour of populations, and arriving in America he confronted a society in which the mass media's influence was ubiquitous but apparently benign. The veneer of democracy and simple diversion that characterized American media did not convince Adorno. He believed that a common logic underlay both the propaganda of the Reich and the mass entertainment of the USA: both were manifestations of the capitalism's infiltration of everyday life, and thus any adequate theory of capitalism must factor in the role played by mass media, or what he and his colleague Horkheimer had come to call the *culture industry*.

Walter Benjamin's account of the new media had been produced under the auspices of the Institute, and Adorno had played the role of critical interlocutor in the development of Benjamin's thesis (see Jameson 1980). As previously discussed in Chapter 1, Benjamin had argued that the various technologies of mechanical reproduction held the promise of new forms of cultural expression – the possibility of a mass culture made by and for the masses. In many ways Adorno and Horkheimer's media theory is a refutation of Benjamin's *Essay*. It argues that rather than releasing the masses from the hypnotic spell of *aura*, the media of reproduction ensnared them in a sophisticated, technologically facilitated version of Marx's *false consciousness*. While Benjamin singled out reproduction as the process that emancipated culture, Adorno and Horkheimer saw reproduction as the ingression of the capitalism into the very fabric of culture and life itself. Culture had become a term in a monstrous, panoptic system, a new integral industry in the pervasive (but largely unacknowledged as such) ideology of industrial capitalism which we shall explore later in terms of *Banality TV*.

## The Dialectic of Enlightenment

Adorno's vision of the culture industry receives its fullest expression in the *Dialectic of Enlightenment* (Adorno and Horkheimer 1997 [first published in 1944])[1]. Here he and Horkheimer placed mass culture in the context of what they termed 'late' capitalism. They offered an analysis of cultural production that established its role and function within the capitalism of their time and gave it a historical context by providing an account of the emergence of capitalism itself and culture's increasingly influential role within it. The *Enlightenment* to which Adorno and Horkheimer refer is that of the seventeenth and eighteenth centuries: the intellectual movement inaugurated by figures such as Descartes, Galileo and Bacon, which championed the systematic application of reason to intellectual, material and social problems, and which found its fullest expression in the physics of Newton, the politics of revolutionary France and the American constitution, and the philosophy of Immanuel Kant. Given that its science resulted in the Industrial Revolution and its politics in liberal democracy, it is no exaggeration to say that the Enlightenment constitutes the foundation of contemporary Western society. The Enlightenment's advocates believed that it was without a doubt a major advance in human development – indeed the very notion of a linear historical progress from barbarism to culture is part of its legacy.

Adorno and Horkheimer's assessment of the Enlightenment and its consequences was somewhat different. It is encapsulated by Benjamin's famous dictum that there is 'no document of civilisation that is not at the same time a document of barbarity' (1973: 258). Similarly for Adorno there was 'no universal history leads from savagery to humanitarianism, but there is one leading from the slingshot to the megaton bomb' (Adorno 1992: 320). Reason is not some inviolate faculty embedded in the human mind, to be excavated from the slag of superstition, refined and applied to all human affairs. Instead it is always intertwined with a history of *domination*. Barbarity and reason are inextricably, or better dialectically, intertwined. Adorno and Horkheimer thus speak of 'instrumental reason' and the phrase 'dialectic of enlightenment' serves to offer an account of its various stages. But what do Adorno and Horkheimer mean by 'instrumental reason'? They argued that reason or, more generally, the intellectual faculty of the human mind was first and foremost utilitarian, its purpose to define, and so control, elements of the organic life-world in which humankind finds itself. This was achieved through *identification*, naming and thus objectifying the elements of experience and imbuing them with stable properties. The imposition of such stability where previously nature reigned involves substituting the particular aspects of the world as it presents itself in each fresh individual encounter, with a more controllable and manipulable general conception. For example, a particular sunset with all its individual properties and impressions is subsumed under the notion of 'sunset'. In this regard, thought, language and, consequently, reason have their origin in a certain kind of violence, power and domination carried out against the particular. All concepts involve violence because they seized an entity and reduced its specificity, its myriad difference, to an identity. To identify is to dominate and Adorno and Horkheimer believed this entailed the sacrifice and repression of the *non-identical* – those differences or particularities that are not accommodated in the generic concept. Instrumental reason renders objects and their concepts interchangeable.

Adorno and Horkheimer's account of the history of reason is crucial to our account of critical theories of mass media because it provides a context with which to understand how the particular attributes of reason, as they have developed under the dual influence of both capitalism and the various media technologies that consolidate its illimitable dominion, dominate ever more areas of life. The *Dialectic* proposes three phases of this domination:

- Domination over the self; self-identity is not something given but rather emerges out of instrumental reason
- The domination of labour; understood as the control of subjects, their conversion into labouring subjects
- The domination of nature (including human nature) via science and technology.

Throughout this book it is argued that, in the context of a capitalist society, mass-media technologies restrict the independence of the individual in all three of these forms. The individual thus becomes subsumed, just as the particular is under the concept of a general identity, within a life-defining system of commodities whether they be: basic commodities (objects); images (brands); people (celebrities as human brands); environments (shopping malls and themed urban centres); or processes (for example the purchasing of an education with the student reconstituted as customer).

Adorno and Horkheimer believe that man's original relation to nature is one of 'angst'. Nature is perceived as hostile and unpredictable, and in order for the human race to survive (thought's primordial function being utilitarian) it must be disciplined. In the first instance this is achieved through *myth* understood as the first dialectic turn in the evolving relation between subject and object (a relation in which both terms evolve): 'Myth intended report, the narration of the Beginning: but also presentation, confirmation, explanation; a tendency that grew stronger with the recording and collection of myths' (Adorno and Horkheimer 1997: 8). Myth abstracts, it presents the world as something other than its immediate presentation, thus it is the first step in the substitution of a system of manipulable symbols for the particularity of the real: 'language embodies the contradiction that something is itself and at the same time something other than itself, *identical and non-identical*' (1997: 15; original emphasis).

However, individual mythologies are parochial. Under pre-technological regimes of mythic signification the dialectic of identity and non-identity is under-determined and restricted by locality and ethnicity. In Kracauer's previously discussed terms, while *falsely concrete* and excessively socially determining, myths in pre-technological societies do not have the *falsely abstract* qualities that allow their unchecked spread beyond a particular locale – unlike such contemporary manifestations of the falsely abstract culture industry as the global reach of the fast-food/coffee-shop franchise. It is only with the rise of the *falsely abstract* dominance of the general over the particular that humanity begins to fully see the enormous power, and cost, of identity thinking – a fate we shall see Marshall McLuhan discuss in terms of *autoamputation*: with every media-enabled physical gain comes a concomitant psychic loss. The emergence of universal concepts represents a new stage in the relation between the thought and the world, if mythology aspired to provide a totalizing account it was compromised by the fact that it still represented that which was essentially unknowable; it was an index of all that was unknown. The universal concept in its first stages offered a more detailed account of this unknown (that is, the world of nature and the primordial fear it inspired). Nevertheless, it still dealt in abstractions, in vague totalizations. With the advent of the Enlightenment this situation is irrevocably altered. Reason is no longer the manipulation of universal concepts, but the concept of the rationality of all. Enlightenment believes that everything is ultimately accessible to reason: 'enlightenment is as totalitarian as any system ... In the anticipatory identification of the wholly conceived and mathematized world with truth, enlightenment intends to secure itself against the return of the mythic. It confounds thought and mathematics. In this way the latter is ... made into an absolute instance' (Adorno and Horkheimer 1997: 25).

What distinguishes the (necessarily) false totality of Enlightenment reason and its precursors, is the unprecedented command of the material world it presents; it does not merely cast a veil over a fearful unknown, but renders it pliable. However, the conceptual, and hence material, mastery of the external world that accompanies instrumental reason comes at a cost:

> Human beings purchase the increase in their power with estrangement from that over which it is exerted. Enlightenment stands in the same relationship to things as the dictator to human beings. He knows them to the extent that he can manipulate them. The man of science knows things to the extent that he can manipulate them. Their 'in-itself' becomes 'for him'.
>
> (Adorno and Horkheimer 2002: 6)

The unchecked spread of instrumental reason dissolves the potential of Enlightenment itself and raises in its place a pure calculability that we see later manifested in the formulaic nature of *Banality TV* and Kracauer's previously cited notion that: '*Ratio* is complete only when it removes its mask and hurls itself into the void of random abstractions that no longer mimic higher determinations, and when it renounces seductive consonances and desires itself even as a concept' (Kracauer 1995: 180). In Adorno and Horkheimer's similar terms: 'Thinking objectifies itself to become an automatic, self-activating process; an impersonation of the machine it has produced, so that ultimately the machine can replace it' (Adorno and Horkheimer 1997: 25). In this respect, Enlightenment thought is not the triumph of the individual reason (as it is often thought) because the individual itself undergoes a dialectical development – the instrumental reason that grants dominion over the realm of objects, does so only to the extent that the subject is also transformed: 'the individual is reduced to the nodal point of conventional responses' (Adorno and Horkheimer 1997: 28). The transcendental subject supposedly realized in the Enlightenment is thus reduced to a constellation of pre-encoded responses: 'reason itself has become the mere instrument of the all-inclusive economic apparatus' (Adorno and Horkheimer 1997: 30). Reason, which would recognize its own limitations and transform itself in response, is artificially arrested and rendered as debased rationality. Here Adorno and Horkenheimer can be seen as developing the distinction Kracauer makes between *Ratio* as a distorted form of reason and genuine reasoning (*Vernunft*) of a liberated consciousness.

At this point it is worth emphasizing that what may appear to the reader as a discussion of abstruse philosophical issues actually forms the theoretical basis of critical theory and its subsequent application to the cultural impact of media technologies. The instrumental reason that characterizes the Enlightenment is commensurate with the consolidation of capitalism. Both commodification and utilitarian, instrumental reason involve a decontextualization of the particular and its reduction to interchangeable units. This results in an exhaustion of what is potentiality inherent in the non-identical. The limits of what is possible become defined as limits of the established order (a weakness underpinning much of cultural populism). Thus, at the cultural level, the totalizing nature of the new myth of capitalist instrumental reason – the unknowable and all other social values are commodified. The media act as technological vessels reinforcing such commodity values (for example, it is difficult to see how the Nike swoosh could exist as a brand in the absence of media technologies of reproduction), and only that which pre-exists within the media is granted attention. This confirms Adorno's claim that 'Mass culture is a system of signals that signals itself' (Adorno, 1991: 71) – a perspective that has been variously re-described in notions such as: Boorstin's *pseudo-event*, Debord's *society of the spectacle*, Lowenthal's idols of consumption (celebrities), and Baudrillard's conception of the tautological circulation of *hyperreal* signs.

The significance of the above for the key themes of this book lies in the critical insights Adorno's work offers into the disempowering features of the media-based *culture industry*. Repetition of this phrase risks numbing the reader to its oxymoronic status. Culture has historically referred to those areas of social activity unconcerned with the needs of subsistence and commerce. This is a form of culture we shall discuss shortly in terms of 'high culture' which, despite the often repeated accusations that such a phrase contains a strong element of elitism, is used in Adorno's work not so much as a value judgement about the better quality of its content (although this may be at times implied) compared with 'low culture', but rather to distinguish high culture's autonomous status from mass culture's manipulated and manufactured nature (its negative quality of being *heteronomous* – that is, influenced by factors beyond its internal requirements, such as the profit motive which according to Adorno is more important than any previous historical distinctions to be made between high and low cultural forms. The philosophical history of instrumental reason that Adorno and Horkheimer provide is essential to understanding the otherwise seemingly natural operations of the culture industry. The *Dialectic of Enlightenment* provides an account in cultural terms of the profound *mediations* of a society of the media. We later demonstrate in our examination of McLuhan's work how instrumental reason becomes an automatic mechanism of order through the operation of media whose true effects are under-appreciated because we receive the message without fully recognizing the profoundly formative impact of the medium by which the message is delivered.

The recent history of instrumental reason has been manifested in the role media technologies have played in the 'late' phase of capitalism. These technologies have emerged as both the material consequences and further cause of the extirpation of the non-identical. Part 2's examination of *Banality TV* demonstrates how, behind seemingly politically and philosophically neutral categories, instrumental thought is alive and flourishing. An ironical development within this history of instrumental reason is that just as instrumental reason had its origins as a practical response to the unknowable nature of myth that dictated the fates of men, so this reason in turn becomes a myth of its own. Celebrity and Reality TV become aspects of new myths by which people are either manipulated unconsciously or with their full uncritical compliance. Our technological systems come to represent a 'second nature' or what Marcuse refers to as 'bad immediacy' whereby our cultural surroundings appear to be natural and therefore immune to critique. Adorno and Horkheimer suggest that this second nature (like the first of more technologically primitive societies) appears implacable, but despite this appearance it is entirely of our own making. It is an ideological construction which has the ability to make alternatives appear either unrealistic or undesirable. The culture industry is thus a crucial component of the world born from the dialectic of enlightenment; it consists of an abstract but powerful system that appears to implacably direct the affairs of men on the basis of those things that can be calculated while stubbornly neglecting to include within these calculations an assessment of the negative cultural impact of that same system. It reiterates through entertainment and information the message that this powerfully enframing situation is the ultimate embodiment of freedom and cannot be changed without a corresponding loss of what is actually only the appearance of freedom.

## The culture industry: Enlightenment as mass deception

From the above discussion we can see how Adorno and Horkheimer regard the culture industry as the heir of the dialectic of Enlightenment, as a system that partakes and extends the false totality of instrumental reason. Enlightenment is totalitarian because it subsumes all particularity under the rubric of identity. In this manner it exhibits those very aspects of mythic thought that it was formulated against; it becomes a panoptic system that deprives the individual of autonomy, and thought and culture of their freedom of expression. While these are dramatic and powerful claims, we shall see in later chapters how, if anything, the historical period in which the Frankfurt School wrote meant that their assessment did not go far enough in their exploration of the culture industry's reach. In Part 2, identity thinking now manifests itself more invasively and pervasively than critical theorists foresaw. We thus explore the spread of the panoptic system in terms of 'democratized' celebrity, Reality TV, and the formerly 'serious' news reporting of world events that now tends to be increasingly informed by the standards of the entertainment industry.

Adorno and Horkheimer argue that 'a technological rationale is the rationale of domination itself. It is the coercive nature of society alienated from itself' (Adorno and Horkheimer 1997: 120). Put another way, society has become blinded to its cultural ends through excessive attention to the technological means it has at its disposal. Thus, the output of the culture industry must adapt to the constraints of its means of distribution. In this regard the culture industry is fundamentally subordinate to the demands of industry and government, culture must assume its place within a pre-established technological order of things. The consequence for the output of the culture industry is clear – a movement towards ever

greater standardization and homogeneity; 'films, radio and magazines make up a system which is uniform as a whole and in every
part'. This uniformity is replicated in the relation of the culture
industry as a sector to the industrial system in its entirety, resulting
in a 'striking unity of microcosm and macrocosm [that] presents
man with a model of their culture: *the false identity of the general and
the particular*' (1997: 120–1; emphasis added).

Adorno and Horkheimer describe culture in industrial terms not
only because of its technological infrastructure, but also because of
its totality. This results in a fundamental tautology with regard to its
contents: advertising, celebrity, news, entertainment, all merge seamlessly and unobtrusively:

> ... the culture industry no longer even needs to directly pursue
> everywhere the profit interests from which it originated. These
> interests have become objectified in its ideology and have even
> made themselves independent of the compulsion to sell the
> cultural commodities that must be swallowed anyway. The
> culture industry turns into public relations ... each object of
> the culture industry becomes its own advertisement.
>
> (Adorno 1991: 86)

This tendency has become increasingly pronounced in the intervening decades, and today, phenomena such as product placement,
corporate sponsorship of cultural events, and advertising campaigns
in which the promotion of a 'lifestyle' or 'brand' is given greater
priority than that of any particular product's concrete qualities, bear
witness to the triumph of the spectacle over its composite forces.
Adorno's recognition of this growing environmental dimension of
the culture industry led him to argue that its analysis demanded a
certain circumspection on the part of the critical observer. If its
pervasiveness and centrality to the life of the masses precluded the
kind of retreat to elitist cultural values that Adorno's critics have
often levelled against him, this should not be taken as an invitation
to become complicit with that cultural industry and its identity
thinking. Cultural studies, for example, has tended to abandon the
patrician contempt that characterized the first intellectual reaction
to the emergence of mass culture (embodied in figures such as
Leavis and Arnold), only to replace it with a largely unreflective and
uncritical celebration of the industry's output.

For Adorno, the products of popular culture are distinguished by
their lack of autonomy. Unlike truly artistic creations, they cannot be
approached as self-contained entities that nevertheless encompass
creative tensions that point outside their own particular orbit. Art is
based upon a productive friction between an artistic format's general
rules and the particularity of the individual artwork. From this
perspective micro-analyses aimed at uncovering critique or ironic

distance, in either content or the consumer's reception, are destined to failure because the outputs of the culture industry innately lack the dialectical complexity of autonomous art and can only be understood in relation to the media systems within which they circulate. These systems, in turn, need to be understood in terms of their relations to the other organs of capitalist society. In other words, since the culture industry's 'work' is structural, only a structural critique of the culture industry will suffice. In a certain post-ideological sense, ideology is no longer to be located in any particular message or content; the entire system is an objectified ideological system – reflected in the increasing licence granted to the content of individual forms which are no longer required to promote particular perspectives or uphold prescribed doctrines. The culture industry promotes the values of tolerance, balance and democratic access to representation, because in this way it ensures any alternative remains strictly unthinkable – its ideological coup resides in the fact that it claims that as a structure it is outside ideology, when this very structure itself is nothing less than the triumph of its ideology.

## The ideology of entertainment

In analysing the structural function of the culture industry, Adorno focuses on the value ascribed to entertainment. The involvement of entertainment as 'value' and part of an 'industry' reveals the complicity of culture with capitalism. In providing amusement, distraction, relief, and so on, the culture industry ameliorates the violence that capitalism performs. This occurs on numerous levels: within the products it produces; the immediate responses they provoke in their audience; and at wider structural level where the culture industry plays an important regulatory function – the harmonizing of various elements within the capitalist system. Of particular importance is the lack of a role for tension or conflict in the output of the culture industry. As previously alluded to, for Adorno the most authentic expression of autonomous or high art involved an immanent and irresolvable tension that existed between its form and content (for example, the confinement of the classical music form and the ingenuity to be found in individual compositions), which made its progress and outcome irresolvable in advance. As a result, such art was often difficult and disturbing for its audience, since it involved a confrontation with contradiction – in the form of challenging works that refused to cater to received notions of closure, harmony and form. Whereas, within the culture industry' 'every individual product is levelled down in itself ... There are no longer any real conflicts to be seen. They are replaced by the surrogate of shocks and sensations ... smoothly insinuating them-selves into the episodic action' (Adorno 1991: 60). This logic is identified in all the industry's various forms, for instance in cinema where 'the eye of the camera ... has perceived the conflict before the viewer and projected it upon the unresisting smoothly unfolding reel' and so ensured that 'conflicts are not conflicts at all', that nothing will disrupt the resolution of all conflict within a predeter-mined timeframe. In this fashion, the culture industry banishes any possibility of real or unpredictable development, thus in popular music 'all the moments that succeed one another in time are more or less directly interchangeable with one another ... there is no real development' (1991: 61).

This situation reflects the wider conditions of production, which are those of standardization and optimization in favour of increasing profit. Thus the culture industry is a celebration of commodification, it 'simply identifies with the cues of predetermination and joyfully fulfils it'. Here sport, whose centrality to the culture industry is self-evident, proves paradigmatic. With its exaltation of performance against the clock as an end in itself, it reveals the internal logic of mass culture. The athlete 'in the freedom he exercises over his body ... confirms what he is by inflicting upon this slave the same injustice he has already endured at the violent hands of society' (Adorno 1991: 77). Thus, the individual sports person embodies the coercive optimization that capitalism inflicts on society en masse, this same process is revealed in the gestures of the actor and the musician, whose virtuosity is seen as the same soulless cultivation of performance for its own sake: 'everyone in front of the microphone or camera are forced to inflict violence upon themselves. Indeed the most rewarded are those who do not require this violence to be exercised upon them in the first place' (Adorno 1991: 77) – an appropriate evaluation of the cultural impresarios in *Banality TV*'s talent shows (for example, *American Idol*) who sit in judgement upon the contestants.

## False identity and the high/low art distinction

The notion of the false identity between the general and the particular marks a crucial point in the conceptualization of the culture industry, particularly the related distinction it makes between 'high' and 'low'/'popular' art and culture. This low/high debate is a perennial one and it is here that basic misunderstandings of Adorno's attitudes to art and its political implications are most commonly found[2]. While it is true to say that he was capable of making rather sneeringly subjective judgements upon the content of art (his critique of jazz being the most notorious example)[3], and that his dismissal of the popular culture has been refuted in numerous individual instances, this rather misses the real target of his scorn which was the *inherently* manipulative content of low art. His account of the culture industry acknowledges that high art may also be manipulated for commercial purposes but it is not created for this purpose *at the very outset of the creative process.* The contemporary mediascape contains many examples of this misuse of high art including the use of operas as advertising sound tracks for products ranging from Guinness to aftershave. It is a complex area of debate whether high art even remains possible in a society that has become so commodified but Adorno's high/low distinction is based upon the fact that at least high art has the potential to produce non-commodified[4] outcomes while low art contains commodity values within its very development structure, or creative DNA if you will.

Adorno's criticism of the culture industry is based upon the undermining of human autonomy that occurs as the historically unprecedented result of the combined effects of new media technologies in which culture is reproduced and commodified in ways not previously possible and the fact that this technical reproduction of culture is *systematically* based upon a vulgar consideration of profit. Adorno's cultural account thus builds directly upon the critical implications of Benjamin's account of mechanical reproduction and the shift this represents from a quantitative increase to qualitative change – a point further pursued in the next chapter's exploration of McLuhan's work. It should be emphasized that commercial considerations in art are not new; composers admired by Adorno such as Beethoven and Mozart were not averse to making money from their art, and glories of 'high' Western culture such as the Sistine Chapel were only possible through the patronage of rich merchants. What was new according to Adorno, was the manner in which the formal possibilities of the work of art were pre-inscribed with commercial concerns. The most immediate manifestation of this was the substitutability of the part and the whole and the reduction in artistic tension that this created.

## The part and the whole

According to Adorno and Horkheimer, 'low art is the 'social bad conscience of serious art' (Adorno and Horkheimer 1997: 132). Adorno also describes how 'high' and 'low' works of art: 'Both bare the stigmata of capitalism, both contain elements of change ... Both are torn halves of an integral freedom, to which however they do not add up' (Theodor Adorno, Letter to Walter Benjamin, 18th March 1936, in Jameson 1980: 123). The first part of the statement refers to the notion that in a capitalist society the possibility of high art only exists on the basis of the exploitation and exclusion of the masses upon whose material productivity high art relies. Low art's accessibility to the masses (the crux of Benjamin's positive interpretation) is then presented as a compensatory alternative solution – a social bad conscience. This is a false solution, however, because low art's accessibility is in turn based upon a devalued, ersatz form of art rather than truly compensating for the masses' lack of access to the original, authentic high art: the masses have *access*, but it is far from clear that they have access to the precise thing that was previously denied to them. Adorno is clear in his account of the devalued nature of mass-produced low art, but even Benjamin, as previously seen, is also clear that instead of debating the new status of art in the age of mechanical reproduction, critics should be coming to terms with the fact that the very notion of art itself is altered by the new mass media. In the second part of the above statement, integral freedom is the phrase used to describe the condition enjoyed by someone who had access to a high art un-impugned by exploitation or exclusion. Such an ideal condition is not possible in either the current form of high art or low art – the torn halves do not add up to a complete freedom – they are both now devalued.

In so far as high art once had value, it maintained this value despite high art's exclusionary and elite nature. The common critique of Adorno as an elitist thus rather misses the point because, for him, the fact that high art is based upon exploitation is part of its social truth. The ability of Beethoven, Mozart, or Michelangelo to produce beautiful artworks served to bring into sharp relief the less than beautiful or ideal social reality encountered immediately after experiencing those works (another form of high art's tension and conflict). Additionally, although high art strives within the particularity of its forms to represent an ideal, perfect whole (the artwork as an expressive totality) it will never succeed in successfully creating such a whole; there will always be something lacking in any such artistic creation – it can only ever produce an imperfect attempt. The combined effect of both these factors is that high art is inextricably linked to *non-identity*. To use a specific example, within a painting or a piece of music, Adorno points out that individual brush strokes or notes are used to create a tension with the work as a whole. The viewer or listener is made to think of the problematic relationship between the brush stroke or note and the bigger picture (both literally and metaphorically). In this manner, the high artwork does not and cannot ultimately reconcile the particular and the general, the whole and the part, or its depictions of the individual subject and the object world s/he finds themself in. This paradoxically is the truth and value of high art – its preordained glorious failure. Hence, the key distinguishing feature between high art and low art is this tension that gives the high artwork its power rather than any easy resolution of the low artwork as a commodity in which the component parts of the work are merely a microcosm of the bigger piece and the marketplace beyond it. A specific example of this would be the way in which the chorus of a pop song tends to contain the whole song in an abbreviated form and acts as an advert within the whole song that contains the chorus, but also within the wider marketing system of adverts and previews that will make use of that chorus as a sample. What lies behind this tendency of the whole to be eminently substitutable for the part and vice versa is the status of low artworks as tensionless commodities *from their very origins*.

## Pre-inscribed commercialism

In stark contrast to high art's pre-inscribed failure to reconcile the whole and the part (its inevitably glorious failure to resolve artistic tension), low art constantly conflates the two by means of the culturally defining value of the commodity. This condition can be seen as a cultural expression of the emergence of identity thinking we have explored above. Thus, just as the potential of the non-identical is over-coded by equivalence of thought and its object, and the particularity of the object further subsumed under the concept of the commodity form, so the artwork and its non-identity (those aspects of it that challenge and cannot be reconciled with existing aesthetic forms) is reduced to the predetermined schema of mass culture. What this process means in current cultural rather than abstract philosophical terms can be illustrated by the talent-based television programme *American Idol/Pop Idol*. Although not strictly Reality TV, the programme's ascendancy has occurred with the context of the former format's colonization of the screen, the reality revealed by the various *Idol* programmes is that of the music industry and its internal mechanics. It unreservedly wallows in the artifice, construction and manipulation on which this sector of the culture industry is predicated, while at the same time democratizing these techniques, so fusing the 'reality' of Reality TV with the realities of the culture industry. In incorporating the audience within this loop, *Idol* shows can be seen as explicit realization of the logic of the culture industry within a single format. The audience, the per-former, an apparently minimally mediated 'reality' and the industry are all effortlessly integrated. Here the potential of the non-identical is not subject to a brutal negation, but to a subtle co-option. In this fashion, *Idol* programmes bear witness to the increasingly minimal space that exists for authentic, spontaneous popular culture. From hip-hop to the various indigenous musical traditions market brought under the 'World Music' heading, the culture industry is exhaustive both in its pursuit of novelty, and in its elimination/commodification of any lingering trace of potential resistance.

It has been observed that Adorno and Horkheimer's vision was formulated as an indirect rebuttal of Benjamin's Essay. Benjamin talked of the extirpation of 'aura' (and an elitist order that sustained itself, in part, by reference to its authority) as a result of technical media, and believed this to represent the conditions for the advent of an authentic popular culture, made for the masses by the masses. In contrast, Adorno argued that, rather than a release from aura, the culture industry and its technologies resulted in culture's total fetishization, resulting in the triumph of a false reality. The culture industry is no liberation, it is not a mass culture in the sense of an authentic expression of the desires and dreams of the masses, but rather a determining system that directs the nature of these desires. It is even able to attempt to redefine for commercial purposes reality itself – this is the root of Reality TV and the seemingly natural way it commodifies more and more aspects of social life without ever appearing to be doing so as a deliberate ideological process:

> Reality becomes its own ideology through the spell cast by its faithful duplication. This is how the technological veil and the myth of the positive is woven. If the real becomes an image insofar as in its particularity it becomes as equivalent as to the whole as one Ford car is to all the others of the same range, then the image, on the other hand, turns into immediate reality.
>
> (Adorno 1991: 55)

This 'technological veil' whose final realization is the virtual reality of the mass-media spectacle is the result of the ongoing concretization of identity thinking in the form of technology. The 'excess power which technology as a whole, along with the capital that stands behind it, exercises over every individual thing' (Adorno 1991: 55). The principle that serves to align the sphere of culture with the large changes brought about by synergistic operation of technology and capital is *standardization*.

For Adorno and Horkheimer, standardization is the culture industry's primary characteristic. It is a process of unification which eliminates the particularity of a multitude of individual cultures and aesthetic traditions, in order that they may pass into the circuits of distribution and consumption. Since culture in all its forms can be seen as mediating between the microcosom of the individual subject (either as a creative artist or as a member of an audience) and society as whole (in the form of the materials and traditions or as the audience to which any given work of art is directed), it is of vital importance in consolidating the grip of industrial capitalism. Culture's status as the interface between the individual and society as it is taken up by the culture industry results in the description of the latter as 'psychoanalysis in reverse'. While psychoanalysis engaged in the identification and integration of unconscious mechanisms with the aim of healing the individual, the culture industry, through the capacity of cultural forms to influence the unconscious, identified the same mechanisms but sought to obscure their processes and draw upon their power in order to produce more compliant consumers. In this regard, the provision of culture was only part of the industry's output, it also manufactured the public that consumed them, and in doing this served to replicate and consolidate the system as a whole. It was for this reason that Adorno did not share Benjamin's hope in the possibility of an autonomous mass culture. Adorno believed that the mass was a product of the culture industry, and that the culture it consumed was simply a consequence of the kind of individual it created. Thus the industry was disingenuous in claiming that it did nothing more than give its audience what it desired: it had created that audience, down to the level of the individual's affective responses and aesthetic sensibility. This was true of both consumer and producer: those who worked in the culture industry were incapable of genuine creativity, because their own sensibilities had been programmed to the dictates of the industry long before they entered its service.

## Adorno applied: radio and television

### Radio

Like much of his media theory, Adorno's observations on radio issue from a particular historical context, vividly evoked in the following passage:

> The radio becomes the universal mouthpiece of the Fuhrer; his voice rises from street loudspeakers to resemble the howling of sirens announcing panic – from which modern propaganda can scarcely be distinguished anyway. The National Socialists knew that the wireless gave shape to their cause just as the printing press did to the Reformation. The metaphysical charisma of the Fuhrer invented by the sociology of religion has finally turned out to be no more than the omnipresence of his speeches on the radio. The gigantic fact that the speech penetrates every-where replaces its content.
>
> (Adorno and Horkheimer 1997: 159)

Having left Nazi Germany, where radio had become an important instrument in the dissemination of propaganda, Adorno was

confronted in America by a mediascape whose centre was occupied
by radio. This was radio's 'golden age'. It was woven into the fabric
of everyday life, a source of instruction, entertainment and information, metonymically captured in the image of nuclear family gathered around the wireless. During his residence in America, Adorno
became involved in the Princeton Radio Project, headed by Paul
Lazarsfeld, which attempted to quantify through empirical research
the role of radio in society. Adorno's treatment of radio was,
however, little influenced by empirical research. Instead he saw in it
a confirmation of his already established theory of the culture
industry (Witkin 2002: 177). The *Dialectic of Enlightenment* presented
radio as the realization of the general logic of the culture industry:
as a 'progressive latecomer of mass culture' radio drew 'all the
consequences at present denied the film by its pseudomarket',
consequently 'it is a private enterprise which does really reflect the
sovereign whole and is therefore some distance ahead of the
individual combines. In America it collects no fees from the public,
and so has acquired the illusory form of disinterested, unbiased
authority which suits fascism admirably' (Adorno and Horkheimer
1997: 159).

Adorno and Horkheimer argued that radio's development as a
medium reflected the culture industry's systemic nature. Moreover, it
was not that radio having been realized as a medium then came to
serve the dictates of an already established industry. Instead, the
evolution of radio as a technical medium was steered by the industry
that would utilize it; in particular, the clear separation of transmission and reception:

> The step from the telephone to the radio has clearly distin-
> guished the roles. The former still allowed the subscriber to
> play the role of subject, and was liberal. The latter is demo-
> cratic: it turns all participants into listeners and authoritatively
> subjects them to broadcast programs which are all exactly the
> same. No machinery of rejoinder has been devised, and private
> broadcasters are denied any freedom. They are confined to the
> apocryphal field of the 'amateur,' and also have to accept
> organisation from above.
>
> (Adorno 1991: 121)

In this fashion radio become a medium ideally structured to create
and maintain the passive consumer who would sit and receive both
explicit (political broadcasts and official statements) and implicit
instruction from the wireless. Indeed, radio's fusion of intimacy (its
sensuous contact with interiority of the subject) and authority (its
voice issues from technology itself like some *deus ex machina*)
ensured it an unprecedented capacity for control. As Adorno and
Horkheimer put it: 'the inherent tendency of radio is to make the

speaker's word, the false commandment, absolute' (1997: 122). This perspective led Adorno to reject as naive any quasi-Reithian notions that radio could instruct or educate its listeners. This is revealed most clearly in his work for the Princeton Radio Project on attempts to introduce the masses to classical music via didactic radio programmes. Adorno (1994) averred that rather than 'elevating' its audience, these misguided, if not downright cynical enterprises, served only to degrade classical music. Rather than inculcating its audiences in the art of aesthetic appreciation, radio essentially 'processed' classical music; it celebrated the triumph of the consumer, by consuming (in every sense) the classics.

This involved a transposition of the consumptive practices of the audience (practices in themselves inculcated by the culture industry) to the 'appreciation' of classical music. As previously discussed, Adorno felt that what most defined genuine aesthetic experience was a structural tension between part and whole, a tension whose resolution could only be experienced through a cogitation on the unfolding of the whole. This demanded a willingness on the part of the audience to immerse themselves in the work, to *concentrate*, to put aside immediate sensory gratification, and endure dissonance and aesthetic tension so that the whole of what they were an integral part of might be apprehended. In contrast the culture industry traffics in immediate gratification, it abandons the structural interplay between part and whole in favour of superficial affects, 'licks', melodies, repetitive choruses, and so on. In order to render classical music acceptable to a mass audience, radio must, Adorno argued, reduce it to this schema, promoting a superficial charm allied to a structural poverty. The classics must be decomposed into a succession of individual motifs. Individual melodies and so on are singled out and valorized as the choicest moment, and composers whose oeuvre comes closest to this debased aesthetic become the natural favourites of culture industry and its audiences. As always in the culture industry, these formal modifications of cultural artefacts are commensurate with wider processes and operations. Thus in promoting classical music it flattered its audience, proffering cultural capital and exploiting the self-image of the audience (a self-image that other wings of industry sought constantly to undermine). In this respect it offers an early example of the sort of consumption of signs instead of referents Jean Baudrillard described as the hallmark of postmodernity (see Chapter 8).

## Television

Adorno's views about television are, like his views on radio, heavily dependent on their historical context. In the *Dialectic of Enlighten-*

*ment,* he and Horkheimer wrote in anticipation of television (as opposed to reflecting on a established medium) and described it in terms of a monstrous realization of Wagner's dream of the *Gesamtkunstwerk* – the ultimate fusion of all the arts in single work:

> Television aims at a synthesis of radio and film, and is held up only because the interested parties have not yet reached agreement, but its consequences will be ... that by tomorrow the thinly veiled identity of all industrial products can come triumphantly out into the open.
>
> (Adorno and Horkheimer 1997: 124)

While his comments on radio reflect its golden age and grant it a centrality it has not held for more than half a century, Adorno's later observations on television (Adorno 1998) date from the early days of American broadcast television, and as a result are either speculative or confirm the general tenor of his vision of the culture industry. Given this, we cannot realistically expect Adorno's analysis to conform to today's multi-channel, narrowcast televisual ecology; nevertheless he did identify a number of trends that have proven to be enduring characteristics of the medium. He glimpsed in the advent of television the dimension of the 'spectacle' or 'hyperreality' that later media theorists were to develop. In keeping with his and Horkheimer's prognosis, Adorno argues that television does not disrupt or alter in any significant way the culture industry but, rather, it occupies the place this industry has prepared for it. Indeed, Adorno seems to question whether it is even possible to differentiate television's characteristics or qualities from the media that pre-date it: 'one should not exaggerate the specific character of television productions ... their similarity to films attests to the unity of the culture industry: it hardly makes any difference where it [the culture industry] is tackled' (Adorno 1998: 60). Whatever factors may be attributed to television alone in fact have their origin in the latter's position within the culture industry.

From this perspective, television's significance resides in its revelation of the fundamental trajectory of the culture industry, namely, 'to transform and capture the consciousness of the public from all sides' and so 'approach the goal of possessing the entire sensible world ... in a copy satisfying every sensory organ' while 'inconspicuously smuggling into this duplicate world whatever is thought to be advantageous for the real one' (Adorno 1998: 49). Television's particularity is elusive because it represents a new threshold in the operations of the culture industry as a whole – the fusion of media and environment, or what Debord would come to describe as the *society of the spectacle.* If we are to identify an individual trait or function for television in Adorno's account, it seems that its relationship with the individual and collective unconscious is the best candidate. As noted above, Adorno saw the culture industry as a form of 'psychoanalysis in reverse' and the theorists of the Frankfurt School attempted to adapt Freud's insights regarding the structure of the individual psyche for a better understanding of mass-media culture. In contradistinction to psychoanalysis, the culture industry sought to construct and install complexes within the audience's unconscious: 'the psychoanalytic concept of a multilayered personality has been taken up by the culture industry ... in order to ensnare the consumer as completely as possible and in order to engage him psychodynamically in the service of premeditated effects' (Adorno 1991: 143).

Adorno believed television to be particularly powerful in this regard, since it raised the creation and control of the collective unconscious to a new level. This was the result of its status a visual medium, which bypassed 'the mediation of the concept' and acted directly upon its audience's subconscious. Adorno countered the objection that since television is an amalgam of sound and image it cannot be said to entirely bypass the verbal, by arguing that speech as rendered on television was effectively subordinated to the image; it was nothing more than 'a pure appendage of images ... a commentary on the directives that issue from the image', its function comparable to that of the speech balloon in comics (Adorno 1998: 53). The affective power of the visual hinders attempts to apprehend the television's specific influence because viewers when questioned will always offer rationalized, verbal responses, for instance, declaring it mere 'entertainment'. In this manner, the true consequences of television are literally unspeakable. Television's scopic regime is infantilizing, it induces a literal regression in the viewer, and in the collective, which is returned to the darkest and most impulsive strata of the group mind. Television lulls the viewer with its play of images into a condition of passive receptivity. It is in every sense the 'boob tube' or 'glass teat' at which the infant-viewer suckles in unthinking dependency: 'Addiction is regression. The increasing dissemination of visual products plays a decisive role in regression' (Adorno 1998: 53). Here Adorno suggests a psychoanalytic source for the often observed parallel between television and various substances of abuse, such as that made by Winn:

> Not unlike drugs or alcohol, the television experience allows the participant to blot out the real world and enter into a pleasurable and passive mental state. ... [But] it is the adverse effect of television viewing on the lives of so many people that defines it as a serious addiction. ... it renders other experiences vague and curiously unreal while taking on a greater reality for

itself. It weakens relationships by reducing and sometimes eliminating normal opportunities for talking, for communicating.

(Winn 1977: 24–5)

Given that Adorno's claims are founded on television's ability to access the *optical unconscious*, it could be argued that its effect in this regard would be no greater than that of film. Hence the second factor that Adorno saw as facilitating television's greater capacity for control. Unlike cinema, which required its audiences to enter a space clearly demarcated from the quotidian, television colonizes the domestic sphere. It becomes an electronic hearth of flickering images around which family life increasingly revolves, while providing a pseudo society for those deprived of the real thing. From this position of centrality television entrains in turn the mind of the individual, the behaviour of the family unit and, by extension, the values of society at large. This infiltration of the private sphere by the culture industry builds upon the achievements of radio, which as we have seen installed a 'voice from on high' in every household. Thus Adorno speaks of the power television possess to 'form a community, to bring family members and friends, who have nothing else to say to each other, mindlessly together' that is at once satisfying a continuing desire for collectivity and ensuring that those aspects of the latter that threaten the hegemony of the culture industry are neutralized. In this manner, television 'obscures the real alienation between people and between people and things. It becomes the substitute for the social immediacy which is denied to people. It confuses what is thoroughly mediated, deceptively planned, with the solidarity for which they hunger' (Adorno 1998: 52), Adorno's words being extremely apposite to the Introduction's critique of cultural populism and its misguided valorization of ersatz sociability. It is now worth, in anticipation of our later analysis of celebrity culture and Reality TV, considering Adorno's remarks on the presentation of identity and subjectivity on television.

His observations on these arose from a study of scripts for television drama that Adorno carried out for the Hacker Foundation in 1952–53. At this stage of television's development, the majority of schedule time was given over to dramatic entertainment and, in the absence of the technical means to analyse programs themselves, of necessity, Adorno had to confine himself to their scripts. Not surprisingly Adorno claimed that these scripts revealed a systematic promotion of personality traits fitted to the operations of late capitalism, while at the same time stigmatizing those that implicitly challenged its values. For instance he spoke of the ambivalence of television with regard to the figures of the intellectual and the artist, combining a servile respect for high culture and its geniuses with the profound contempt it displayed when it portrayed them on the screen. Intellectuals and artists were represented as effeminate, weak or morbidly sensitive, as the antithesis of the decisive, upright, square-jawed man of action: television drama 'glorifies the virile man ... and insinuates that all artists are in fact homosexual' (Adorno 1998: 64). Similarly it policed expressions of female subjectivity, vilifying the 'good time girl' and the over-assertive 'shrewish' self-directed women, upholding a traditional image of women as subordinate. Talking of television farce or situation comedies (sitcoms), Adorno identifies a structural reconciliation to the violence of late capitalism. Broadly stated, this can be understood in terms of an objectively exploitative or immiserized situation, within which the characters both struggle to survive and escape. Humour is generated from their attempts at doing this (we might think for example of the Trotter family in the classic British sit-com *Only Fools and Horses* who each week appear to have found a means to escape their poverty but who at the end of each episode are firmly relocated in their position, with humour and family ties held up as compensation).

For Adorno the ideological message of such farces was the absolute futility of challenging the objective structure. Put simply, one might as well laugh because structural change is an impossibility. In this fashion, television drama both exposed and concealed the underlying logic of capitalism; indeed through it, late capital, like a tyrant that homeopathically eliminates the threat of poisoning by immunizing themselves through the consumption of small doses of a given poison, absorbs and neutralizes discourses and desires that threaten to challenge the status quo. This is most clearly revealed in the case of psychoanalysis, which had at the time of Adorno's studies made considerable inroads into the American cultural landscape, acting as an explanatory device for the motives of characters and providing a thematic framework in Hollywood films. Adorno argued that this adaptation of psychoanalytic themes and theories served the purpose of conjuring away the threat that it might otherwise constitute. This was achieved through the presentation of superficial psychoanalytic motifs whose aim was their subsumption within traditional notions of identity and morality: 'The psychological process that is put on view is fraudulent ... psychoanalysis ... is reduced and reified in a way that not only expresses disdain for this type of praxis but changes its meaning into its very opposite' (Adorno 1998: 65).

## Conclusion

This chapter has demonstrated how Adorno and Horkheimer's *Dialectic of Enlightenment* provides a solid theoretical foundation for a critical account of the mass media, one which locates the latter within the ongoing evolution of human rationality and development of capitalism. In addition, it has highlighted the various points of contact between this work and Kracauer and Benjamin's body of thought, and noted the key issues on which these various accounts differ. It has been pointed out that while certain elements of the culture industry thesis are now primarily only of historical significance, other aspects are remarkably prescient. For example, the thesis anticipates Baudrillard's notion of *hyperreality*, Debord's concept of the *society of the spectacle*, as well as the emergence of Reality TV and new, democratized forms of celebrity culture. It would appear, therefore, that rather than being a reactionary elitist, Adorno articulated with great foresight and in a manner cultural populism could still learn much from, the underlying logic of the culture industry, its conservative attitudes. He vividly described a colonizing commodifying logic whose grip on the individual and collective has grown ever more firm in the intervening decades.

# 4

# Marshall McLuhan's understanding of the media

## Introduction: The media-friendly theorist

Marshall McLuhan (1911–80) was arguably the single most important media theorist of the twentieth century. Indeed, through his willingness to engage directly with the masses via the media itself, McLuhan was the figure who introduced the wider public to the notion that the media required any theory at all. McLuhan's cultural and intellectual milieu was quite different to that which produced the critical thinkers addressed in the previous chapters: while they were products and self-appointed heirs of Europe's intellectual heritage, McLuhan was a son of the New World. Similarly, while their readings issued from, and assumed the perspective of, Freud, Marx and Nietzsche, McLuhan's intellectual background was in the anglophone world of literary criticism. He is not usually considered to be a critical thinker but, after outlining his key concepts, this chapter demonstrates that it is relatively easy to see his work as an implicit and sometimes explicit critique of the profoundly negative cultural impact of media technologies. In the context of our previous discussions of the decline of auratic symbolic culture (Benjamin and Kracauer) and the subsequent industrialization of culture (Adorno) McLuhan's work helps us to highlight the specific role played by media technologies in these culturally destructive processes.

During his lifetime, and in the decade following his death, McLuhan's academic standing remained low. His critics accused him of sensationalism, self-promotion and a lack of any formal rigour. Reading McLuhan it is easy to see the reasons for this hostile reception; his prose is often flashy, modish, abounding with (not always successful) puns both verbal and conceptual, and his ideas are often driven by an 'associative' rather than synthetic logic. Genesko affectionately terms this provocative style 'McLunacy' (Genesko 1999: 3), while McLuhan himself referred to it as a *mosaic* or *field approach*. It could be argued that both the strength and weakness of

McLuhan's mediology reside in his refusal to engage with the grand narratives of continental thought. This meant that he has, in Kroker's words: 'no systematic, or even eclectic, theory of the relationship between economy and technology' (Kroker 1984: 79). For our purposes, however, McLuhan's work provides a highly useful assessment of the specific properties of media technologies, which gives an illuminating context for such contemporary critiques of the mediascape as Baudrillard's notion of a totalitarian semiotic order encountered in Chapters 7 and 8.

Readers of Adorno's work may suspect that he has forgone any real encounter with the particularities of specific media in favour of a predetermined position on the general determining features of the culture industry. McLuhan, by contrast, captures the genuine novelty of media technologies. He believes that instead of merely being manifestations of the abstract dynamics of capitalism and commodification, the media are active components in the transformation of the very nature of our society. From this perspective, many of the supposed shortcomings of McLuhan's work attest to the degree to which he allowed the object of his study to transform his conceptual schema. But rather than a result of sloppy thinking, the absence of an overall theoretical framework is born of a profound recognition that media demand new ways of thinking. It is in this regard that McLuhan spoke of his books as 'mosaics', that is, constellations of interrelated concepts which the reader could access at random, rather like the television viewer channel hops, or the web user navigates the Internet. His work conveys the singularity and potentiality of media, adopting the tactics of his object of study and articulating them in an immediate and engaging manner to the extent that his theory has often been adopted and adapted as good public relations for the media's positive social role. Such attention to the specific qualities of the media tends to be lacking in the more overtly critical, but also more philosophy/political economy-based accounts of critical thinkers such as the Frankfurt School. McLuhan's work has been a direct inspiration for other major critical media theorists, in particular, Baudrillard, Kittler and Virilio. His insights have stood the test of time, remaining relevant in the face of 40 years of accelerated media evolution.

Our critical reading of McLuhan is made with full acknowledgement of his own tendency to act as a consultant to the prime movers of the culture industry and his willingness to educate them in the application of his ideas in the creation of an ever more docile consumer culture (albeit in a more deliberate and self-conscious manner than Freud whose psychoanalytical insights were transformed into marketing techniques by his nephew 'the father of public relations[1]' Edward Bernays). McLuhan's critical potential can only be fully realized when his work is reinforced with the more resolutely oppositional writings of the other writers in this volume. This avoids the pitfalls of an uncritical reading which reduces him, in the words of Debord, to 'the spectacle's first apologist ... the most convinced imbecile of the century' (Debord 1991: N33). This notion of McLuhan as a critical theorist of the media can be justified without too much need to read him against the grain of his own apparent enthusiasm. His position is far more ambivalent than his posthumous canonization as the patron saint of the techno-enthusiast *Wired* magazine might lead us to believe. In the following presentation of McLuhan's key concepts, this critical edge to his work is brought out, allowing the reader to see that in the midst of his celebration of the possibilities created by the mass media, he was also a hugely important theorist for those who have been the sternest critics of the media's cultural effects. Indeed, McLuhan's first study of the media, *The Mechanical Bride* (1951), was an unreservedly critical account of advertising. It stressed the potential for the emergent media technologies to create conditions of control and manipulation. Indeed, its terms are reminiscent of Adorno, as McLuhan argued that mass-media culture erodes cultural values so that 'low, middle, and highbrow, are consumer ratings, nothing more' (McLuhan 1951, cited in Stevenson 2002: 122), and he unflinchingly acknowledges the system of false values and dehumanizing images that results in order to enhance profits. Although McLuhan repudiated the terms of his early critique as the imposition of outmoded literate values on radically new media culture, beneath the vertiginous play of references and examples of his later texts a significantly critical element remained as an undercurrent throughout his work.

## Key concepts in McLuhan

### Media determine the nature of cultures/societies

The fundamental shift from McLuhan's original perspective on mass media to that of his later, more central, work results from a rejection of question of content and value, in favour of a structural analysis. That is, from McLuhan's perspective, media create technological environments – the nature and extent of which should override any concern with the apparent effect of their specific content, or particular message. While the McLuhan of *The Mechanical Bride* evaluated the impact of media technologies from the surety of accumulated cultural values, the later McLuhan sees such values as entirely determined by media technologies. This raises an immediate question as to the suitability and appropriateness of interrogating the nature of media-induced cultural shifts with approaches and perspectives that have been undermined and made outdated by those same media. In the face of this situation, McLuhan turned his attention to the history of such shifts in perspective. He investigated the relationship between the cultural superstructure, and its techno-medial infrastructure.

## McLuhan then: acoustic/pre-literate cultures

McLuhan argued that the predominant medium or media defined *the nature of knowledge in any given epoch*, and that these mediatically determined cultures in turn dictated the form that 'man' would take within them. Thus, according to McLuhan, preliterate tribal cultures were characterized by an 'acoustic' space, within which the human mouth and ear were the main organs of communication, serving as transmitter and receiver respectively. This acoustic space is continuous – in it, individual elements and their background are never truly separate; they rise out of and return to a single aural dimension from which they are only partially differentiated. Moreover, the designation of this space of communication as aural/oral is largely for convenience, in truth, mouth and ear are mere points within a multi-sensory field of discourse in which gesture, intonation and location constituted integral components in communication. The preliterate word was 'asignifying' – a co-participant in a complex 'speech' act in which the body was as articulate as the voice. Its tactility, immediate sensuousness, and omnipresence meant that acoustic space was effectively coterminous with the collective space of tribal life. The nature of the individual was in turn prescribed by the primary medium of communication; indeed McLuhan argues that acoustic space did not support the kind of individuated subject that we now take for granted. In preliterate culture the individual and collective are intertwined to such a degree as to be effectively interchangeable. There is minimal distance between the responses of the individual and those of the collective, and McLuhan depicts the affective life of the oral society in terms that recall the fearful tremulousness of a flock of birds and a herd of gazelles: 'Terror is the normal state of any oral society, for in it everything affects everything all the time[2]' (McLuhan 1962: 32).

Similarly, the production and preservation of knowledge is enmeshed in the collective; thus McLuhan speaks of a 'tribal encyclopaedia', an oral repository of the accumulated experience and wisdom of the collective. The reproduction of this 'encyclopaedia' is co-extensive with the life of tribe. In the absence of any external means of preserving information, rites of passage, various rituals, celebrations and seasonal migrations, as well as material activities such as hunting, cooking, and so on, at once apply and preserve the knowledge of the collective. In this manner, the knowledge of preliterate cultures is truly encyclopaedic, that is to say a totally integrated system in which each element reflects the other so as to make up a cohesive whole. Resonant with Kracauer's previously cited discussion of the grounded nature of symbolic culture and of Baudrillard's later critique of the contemporary mediascapes groundless, infinitely circulating signs, McLuhan describes how knowledge in non-technological society is not transcendent but immanent – embodied in the practices of everyday life:

> Coercing reality to do one's bidding by manipulating it in the prescribed manner is, for the non-literate, a part of reality ... It is necessary to understand that non-literate people identify themselves very much more closely with the world in which they live than do the literate peoples of the world. The more 'literate' people become, the more they tend to become detached from the world in which they live.
>
> (Montagu, cited in McLuhan 1962: 76)

From this perspective the various prohibitions, superstitions and taboos that characterize oral cultures, and that often appear to the literate as folly, can be understood as strategies of data storage, as a means of preserving 'signal' from noise or degradation. Of course, this tactic of 'rite words in rote order' (Joyce, cited in McLuhan 1962: 19) inevitably results in an inflexibility, since there is no distinction between (what the literate would regard as) genuine causes and mere superstition, and there is little inducement to experimentation or improvement. Thus the oral society dwells in an eternal repetition of a static body of knowledge; if evolution occurs at all, it is at the pace of genetic drift: 'the culture controls behaviour minutely ... Little energy is directed toward finding new solutions to age-old problems' (Riesman, cited in McLuhan 1962: 29).

## McLuhan now

McLuhan's account of acoustic pre-technological culture offers important insights into social conditions within the contemporary mediascape – the latter represents a technologically mediated return to the former. For example, subsequent chapters demonstrate how the phenomenon of 'rite words in rote order' reappears in the apparently flexible, but ultimately deeply enframing, cultural forms of Reality TV. On the one hand, McLuhan's account of modern media technologies and the associations to be made with pre-literate culture strongly suggests a loss of certain rational aspects in cultural life. On the other hand, the mediascape replaces the cultural vitality of pre-literate societies, grounded as they are in physical proximity and face-to-face ties, with pseudo-social media events and celebrity-driven news reporting. Part 2 examines how this creates an *eternal now* of fresh affective images (that are, however, always the same in their essence) that dominate and undermine rational discourse. This produces what Langer (1998) calls the *Other News* and Nichols (1994) calls an *ideological reduction* of the *discourses of sobriety.*

## Literate/visual cultures

The emergence of writing constituted a fundamental rupture with acoustic culture. In introducing an external means of preserving and transmitting information, writing alters every aspect of culture. Indeed, McLuhan argues that writing introduces a new form of subjectivity, a novel form of self-identity radically different to the form it took in oral societies. The scope and scale of this transformation cannot be overestimated: for McLuhan civilization *is* writing. Phonetic writing is the first real *medium* because it translates or carries an extrinsic content, namely, oral communication. According to McLuhan every subsequent medium will have as its content a pre-existing medium, a process that begins with the alphabet. Moreover, it is not a case of simple transposition; the nature of the spoken is itself modified in literate societies. McLuhan regards many of the characteristics of the culture and technology of the West as direct consequences of the phonetic alphabet's impact upon culture – a consequence of the arbitrary and linear nature of script. The arbitrary nature of the elements that make up phonetic script contrasts with ideographic scripts. It marks a break with any form of symbolic or pictorial reference. Script's linearity serves to reduce a continuous chaotic flow of sense impressions into an orderly sequence of discrete units. In this respect, writing involves a 'lossy' (to adopt the terminology of today's media technology) compression of information; whereas the oral word was replete with nuances and entered into a complex interplay with other sensory streams, the written word is resolutely visual. It contracts the multi-sensory interplay of non-technological, symbolic culture into a single sensory data stream, substituting 'an eye for an ear'. This ultimately resulted in a fundamental disruption of the sensory world of man. It tore him out of the archaic multi-sensorial acoustic space and located him in the harsh and exacting world of the visual.

## Abstraction

McLuhan stresses that the effects of alphabetization were incremental and unfolded over many centuries. Drawing on the work of Harold Innis (whom he regarded as the main stimulus for his media theory), McLuhan argues that writing served as the defining source of political and social organization that allowed the development of technological civilization in various forms that we would not normally associate with writing. For example, he saw the numerical ordering of troops as an application of the abstract system of writing to human affairs. Perhaps most significantly, he argued that the extensive network of roads that enabled the coordination of the far-reaching Roman Empire was an extension of what he regarded as the technology of writing. Roads aided writing's accelerated transmission in the form of papyrus, allowing the Empire to function as a veritable information system in which signals were transmitted from and to a command centre (Rome) which evaluated and responded to them. More generally, this reflects McLuhan's belief that an adequate definition of media must encompass not only explicit means of communication and representation, but those material technologies (such as the wheel, roads, clothes, and the built environment) with which the former enter into complex interrelations.

According to McLuhan, it is only with the West's adoption and subsequent adaptation of the technology of the printing press that the full impact of alphabetization is realized: 'it was not until the experience of mass production of exactly uniform and repeatable type, that the fission of the senses occurred, and the visual dimension broke away from the other senses' (McLuhan 1962: 54). It is no exaggeration to state that, for McLuhan, printing is the driving force of the destiny of the West, a destiny whose direction is entirely determined by the aforementioned disruption of the senses, and the consequent privileging of vision. Printing results in a cultural transformation of both the subjective and objective worlds. It is the manifestation of a mediated process that involves a reformatting of the subjectivity in accordance with its technological needs. Let us briefly consider some of the results attributed to print by McLuhan.

McLuhan asserted that printing begins to produce the first suggestions of mass, standardized society. The book as medium generates the first media audience, in which society is now formulated in terms of its spectorial status. From this position it appears that the process of corporatization and standardization of populaces bemoaned by Adorno, occurred within a space already prepared by a vestigial, culture industry of standardized print. Indeed, according to *The Gutenberg Galaxy* (McLuhan 1962), industry is an entirely appropriate term to use in the context of print culture. For

McLuhan, industry, both as process and as function, is entirely attributable to the book. However, as in all of McLuhan's 'mature' work, it is television that serves as the ultimate medium of the brave new world of media, television is the wafer and wine that transports the masses *en masse* to a 'electric communion', its images and affects are the currency of global village, as Cronenberg's caricature of McLuhan presciently (given the rise of Reality TV) puts it in his seminal *Videodrome* (1983) 'the television screen is the retina of the mind's eye and what appears on that screen emerges as reality, therefore television is reality, and reality is less than television'. There are hints here of the de-realization of traditional reality previously found in Benjamin's Essay. In subsequent chapters it is shown how Boorstin and Baudrillard pursue the radical implications of this with their notions of the *pseudo-event* and the *hyperreal*, respectively. But television for McLuhan, embodied all of the promise and risk of the electronic age. In Part 2, what seemed as nothing more than the hyperbole of McLuhan's interpretation of television now appears as an extremely insightful anticipation of the Reality TV-dominated focus of the contemporary mediascape.

## *Understanding Media:* – central themes in McLuhan's media theory

First published in 1964, *Understanding Media* is probably McLuhan's most important and certainly his best-known text. It begins where *The Gutenberg Galaxy* left off, namely, at the point at which the lineal-visual hegemony of print technology begins to unravel in the face of a proliferation of new media. *Understanding Media* places itself at the intersection of two worlds, and attempts to use each to explain and investigate the other. The electronic media reveal the contours and characteristics of print culture, while at the same time print culture provides us with a negative image of what is emerging. Stylistically, it announces a shift in McLuhan's work. It moves away from the scholarly proliferation of detail and citation that characterized his previous work, towards a mode of discourse that attempted to replicate the speed and simultaneity of the information age (a strategy that won him at once the attention of masses, and the hostility of the academic community): 'McLuhan worked very hard in public writings to fail the standards typical for written texts. And he largely succeeded in his failure' (Meyrowitz, cited in Katz 2002: 193).

In the texts that followed *Understanding Media*, McLuhan accentuated this tendency to adapt print to the needs of media understanding by collaborating with graphic artists. He produced artefacts in which print was effectively deposed from its privileged position, and interacted 'horizontally' with graphic elements. Indeed, from *Understanding Media* onwards, McLuhan's texts become one factor in a multimedia profile (a profile that was managed by a public relations company). This was a strategy that yielded initial benefits but, as with many who seek the attention of media, it resulted in an equally rapid fall into obscurity. However, while McLuhan's later work can possibly be said to mark an advance in terms of their form, *Understanding Media* stands as the most coherent and thorough articulation of his theory, offering a general theory of modern media, and close readings of the technologies (for instance, radio, the typewriter, and so on) which make up the new techno-medial environment. McLuhan is keenly aware that his anatomy of mass media is inevitably partial, compromised, and incomplete, since so much of its environment is beyond his full understanding. Despite their oracular rhetoric, McLuhan's analyses were intended primarily as provocations to further enquiry. He saw all his statements as works in progress or as 'an index of possibilities' and was content solely to provoke comment and reflection on the nature of the media. To this extent, McLuhan can be seen to fit quite naturally with the radical group of thinkers labelled in this book as critical due to the way in which they seek to interrogate, from a perspective beyond the conventional, the basic processes of our mediated society.

*Understanding Media* begins programmatically. The first chapter 'The medium is the message' announces McLuhan's best-known slogan, and the basic principle of his media theory. As noted previously, McLuhan's thesis is that the real import of media technology is not their apparent content (the narratives, stories, genres, cultural forms and personalities they present for our consumption), but rather their material presence, as discrete technologies, and more importantly, the reticulated networks of production and consumption they create. McLuhan's undiluted media determinism results in an image of society as entirely defined by its means of communication. This collapse of message into medium is a polemical gesture designed to discredit a number of orthodox, and in McLuhan's view, reactionary positions. These include:

- The Frankfurt School's ideological interpretation of the media, in which they function as the tools of control and mass obedience
- Active audience and cultural populism theories that, from a critical perspective, risk assuming the role of public relations for triumphant capitalism – they create semiotic interpretations, which focus on the forms of signification that can be found within media, without reflecting on the manner in which the semiotic is itself media determined

- What Winner (1977) refers to as *the myth of neutrality* – a simple minded instrumentality which might argue, for example, that the media is neither good or bad, it only becomes so when directed to these ends by external factors. McLuhan is scathing about this attitude calling it: 'the voice of the current somnambulism. Suppose we were to say, "Apple pie is in itself neither good nor bad; it is the way it is used that determines its value." Or, "The small pox virus is neither good nor bad ..." ' (McLuhan [1964] 1995: 11).

For McLuhan, all these approaches are predicated upon a fundamental ignorance of the true nature of technical media and so they cannot help but fail to give an accurate account of the subject. He compares those critics of the mass media who focus on the questions of content and ideology to a guard dog duped by a juicy steak while the burglar goes about his business (McLuhan [1964] 1995: 32). Such critics who pride themselves on their ability to penetrate the surface and expose the occult agenda that drives media culture, are in fact, entirely superficial according to McLuhan. Paradoxically, it is only by ignoring the explicit content of a given medium that its real features and functions become apparent.

McLuhan's refusal to succumb to what he sees as the appeal of the message's meretricious novelty reveals that at another level the content of a given medium is in fact the 'form' of a previous medium. To use some of the examples offered by McLuhan:

1  The content of writing is speech.
2  The content of the first books is made up of earlier manuscripts.
3  The content of film incorporates the theatre and photography (and later phonography).
4  Radio has the gramophone as its content.
5  Television's content adapts both radio and film.

The implication of this series of mediations of content is that media are essentially tautological: the message of the medium is the fact of mediatization itself. This has obvious and profound consequences for the status of what normally passes for a message. In representing any term, media necessarily represent themselves, everything spoken of in the media to a greater or lesser extent, speaks of the media. Midas-like, the media turn everything they touch into media.

This process creates the rise of what Boorstin ([1961] 1992) calls the *pseudo-event* (dealt with in the next chapter and developed further in relation to Baudrillard's work in Part 2). Boorstin argues that mass media resulted in the creation of 'events', whose nature was inseparable from the media, in other words one could not talk of the media as mediating or representing an inviolate, prior 'event', but must instead recognize that they are an integral, co-productive term in all that 'passes through' them. Although McLuhan was openly critical of Boorstin's work, believing it subject to fallacy of content analysis (because the true import of media effects relates to the medium and not the message), Boorstin's concept does help to develop one consequence of McLuhan's argument – the medium dominates the message.

## 'Outering' the body: media as extensions

One significant element introduced in *Understanding Media* is the central role McLuhan ascribes to the human body. Subtitling his book *The Extensions of Man*, he argues that it serves as the reservoir from which disparate media are extricated and externalized, and as the locus of their operation (as we shall see this position implies a certain vision of what constitutes the human subject). Let us explore these propositions in turn. McLuhan argues that media technology is an externalization, an 'outering' of the various structures of the human body and thus the manner by which the human body extends its influence. While McLuhan was not the first thinker to approach technology in terms of an extension of the human body (see, for instance, Samuel Butler, Ernst Kapp, Marx and Alfred Espinas), he was the first to systematically apply this proposition to media technology and take his conclusions to a wide audience.

McLuhan's 'presupposition of corporeality' (Wellbury, in Kittler 1990: xiv) was timely. It serendipitously coincided with a growing awareness of the body and its role in culture. During the same period artists and activists began to turn their attention to the body as a terrain to be explored and fought over. This concern with corporeality is inextricably bound to another dimension of McLuhan's media theory, namely, a suspicion of the human subject. As we have already seen in his analysis of tribal and literate cultures, McLuhan argues that different communication technologies generate different forms of subjectivity. Thus aural culture induced a collective form of identity in which the boundaries between the self and the social were indistinct. In contrast, print culture created the interiority of the private subject. Implicit in this is his assumption that the subject 'man' is a reconfigurable assemblage made up of his technologies of communication, and the manner in which they distributed his sensory functions. Media alter the sensory ratios of the human organism, and when these ratio's change then 'man' changes, as Blake's lines, cited approvingly by McLuhan, have it: 'If Perceptive Organs vary, Objects of Perception seem to vary' (McLuhan [1964] 1995: 55).

The 1960s witnessed much talk of a 'generation gap', as youth embraced a lifestyle increasingly incomprehensible to their elders (over and above the usual, perennial differences of outlook between generations). McLuhan saw this as a result of the new media: the youth of the 1960s the television generation. As such they were configured differently, equipped for a bright electronic future, while their parents gazed backwards to the nostalgic comfort of the certainties of the age of print. However, McLuhan's account of the relationship between the body and its extensions is marked by a distinct ambivalence that is frequently passed over by those commentators keen to emphasize the optimism of his reading of media developments. Exploring such ambivalence further provides strong evidence that McLuhan's media theory has a strongly critical element. This is perhaps best captured in his presentation of the myth of Narcissus as an allegory of media effects. Drawing on the etymological relation between *narcissus* and *narcosis*, McLuhan argues that Narcissus rather than falling in love with his reflected beauty, was narcotized by his own 'extension'. Narcissus became the 'servo-mechanism' of a cybernetic media circuit, and in this process became terminally absorbed in his own extension. This terminal absorption in terminals recalls the twenty-first century narcissists who sit enraptured in the electric glow of their own extensions. For McLuhan the crucial factor is that these extensions induce a narcosis, a numbness, which means that those who use them are singularly unable to comprehend the true nature of their condition.

Given the centrality of the body, and his suspicion of conventional boundaries and distinctions, McLuhan's description of this as a process of *auto-amputation* is not simply figurative. He argues that sensory channels and organs are tuned out if their input becomes overwhelming; in order to preserve the psychic and physical integrity of the overall organism, individual components are disowned. Thus Narcissus becomes numb to his own (extended) organism, just as a narcotic releases one from the pressures of the immediate environment. The status of media technologies as prosthetic sense organs, results in an unbearable level of stimulation. Therefore we collectively perform various acts of 'auto-amputation'; we not only 'outer' but *other* our senses, and so regard them as external. It is this narcosis that conventional debate about the media's content consistently passes over. Thus to focus on content or to argue that media are neutral and simply reproduce the intention of their owner's is to succumb to a narcissistic narcosis. To truly apprehend media as extensions of ourselves is a painful, overwhelming experience that, McLuhan argues, we instinctively avoid.

Narcosis aids our functioning at the cost of inhibiting our recognition of the nature of the situation. It both extends and diminishes us: thus McLuhan notes that like those deprived of the use of organs or sense, who compensate by developing their remaining faculties to their highest power, the auto-amputated social body results in the proliferation of specializations, collectively and individually we respond to the loss of various channels, by a hypertrophy of those that remain. We can see here that implicit in McLuhan's theory is a critical rereading of Kracauer's notion of the potentially empowering aspect of the media (see Kracauer's use of the myth of Medusa's shield in the Conclusion) and an intimation of Baudrillard's later sustained account of that which is hypertrophied in the contemporary mediascape: the etiolated *hyperreality* of a society in which aura has all too effectively been eradicated. We shall see in subsequent chapters that McLuhan's theory allied to that of Benjamin, Debord, Boorstin and Baudrillard provides us with a critical basis from which to understand the cultural effects of the disproportionate role of images whether manifested in affect-driven news reporting or television formats and their obsessive attention to increasingly inflated and conflated voyeuristic formats (see Chapters 7 and 8 in particular).

Another aspect of McLuhan's work that tends to be given scant attention by media-optimists is the way in which he needs to compensate for the implicitly critical aspects of his presentation of the relationship between man and prosthesis with his various appeals to a quasi-Catholic belief in an ultimate communion, that is, at both a restoration of humanity to a pre-lapsarian state, before the fall into language and separation, and the ultimate rapture:

> Electricity points the way to an extension of the process of consciousness itself, on a world scale, and without any verbalization whatever. Such a state of collective awareness may have been the preverbal condition of men ... Today computers hold out the promise of a means of instant translation of any code or language into any other code or language. The computer, in short, promises by technology a Pentecostal condition of universal understanding and unity.
>
> (McLuhan [1964] 1995: 83)

We can perhaps get a better sense of the critical implications of McLuhan's theory in relation to the work of various artists such as J.G. Ballard, Cronenberg and Burroughs. McLuhan's comments on the latter are particularly informative. He finds in Burroughs's visceral satires, an allegory of the function of media as translators and consumers of previous environments. In Burroughs's work the relationship between body and media is vividly confronted; if media consume their forbears' form as content, and if media are sensory extensions or reproductions, then can it be said that media are in the process of consuming the form of the human body? Is the human organism in the process of being digested by its technical

extensions? This is the sinister vision that McLuhan finds in Burroughs's eschatological landscape of organs without bodies and
technologies:

> All men are totally involved in the insides of all men. There is
> no privacy and no private parts. In a world in which we are all
> ingesting and digesting one another there can be no obscenity
> or pornography or indecency. Such is the law of electric media
> which stretch the nerves to form a global membrane of
> enclosure.
>
> (McLuhan 1997: 89)

This quotation prefigures Part 2's discussion of the notion of the
*obscene*. It is a term Baudrillard uses to address the *implosion* of social
distance in a manner that directly counters Benjamin's excessively
optimistic notion of the camera's *explosive* power. Part 2 explores in
detail how a similar all-consuming quality is attributed to the
commodity form and it is this combination of the 'greedy eyes'
nature of cameras and the wider commodity culture that contains it
that devours all previous social forms to create a one-dimensional
commodified mediascape.

## 'Hot' v. 'Cool'

In contrast to many of the key concepts put forward in *Understanding
Media*, McLuhan's division of technical media into *hot* and *cool*
appears irrelevant and idiosyncratic. McLuhan's notion of *hot* meant
that a medium presents itself as a single sensory stream in high
definition. Examples of this might include radio and film. McLuhan
saw *hot* media as passive, since they did not require the audience to
supply detail. *Cool* media in contrast were marked by their low
definition, and presented schematic or minimal data. Television was
the privileged example of the *cool*. As a low-definition image (as
television was in the 1960s) McLuhan argued that the audience was
actively involved in developing the image, and so it was a more
participatory medium. This coolness on television's behalf underpins
McLuhan's assertion that the viewer is the real screen; the television
image is assembled in and by the viewer. Thus the participation
occurs at the level of the medium as technology rather than in terms
of any meaningful level of interactivity with the content itself – this
mirrors Part 2's treatment of the various modes of pseudo-
interaction promoted in daytime and Reality TV (and even previously 'serious' news programmes).

## Understanding individual media

Having explored the key principles of McLuhan's theory media
theory, it is now time to turn to the analysis of individual media that

make up the bulk of the text. It is in his readings of individual media that McLuhan offers suggestive details that serve to flesh out his broad generalizations and hint at its darker, critical potential.

## Ear

The role of what we might call the media of the ear (radio, gramophone, telephone) is critical in disrupting the hegemony of the text. For McLuhan they induce a re-tribalization, a return of the repressed aurality that characterized pre-literate cultures. Given this, as well as McLuhan's belief in the environmental and corporeal impact of media, they are seen as the locus of wide-ranging cultural shifts. Similarly, the revolution in literary form that took place in the opening decades of the century is seen by McLuhan as a registration of the environment and sensibility produced by the new media. James Joyce (McLuhan's Virgil) and T.S. Eliot, among others, reflect the breakdown of standard lineal, textual perception in favour of the plural, inclusive sensibility engendered by the media.

## Radio

The development of radio illustrates many of the key ideas of *Understanding Media*. McLuhan regards it as a product of hybridization, absorbing the content of pre-existing media, such as newsprint, phonography, and the theatre. Its evolution in the increasingly crowded media ecology of the twentieth century is marked by various renegotiations which serve to accentuate certain characteristics of the medium, while at the same time relieving it of other functions. At the most general level McLuhan regards it as the crucial operator in reawakening the 'tribal' sensibility that he sees as characterizing post-literate culture. Radio affects a re-tribalization, functioning as 'a subliminal echo chamber of magical power to touch remote and forgotten chords' ([1964] 1995: 264). Thus McLuhan attributes the rise of Hitler to the impact of radio and its effects upon the German unconscious, which he argues was not sufficiently inoculated by print as the Anglo-Saxon mind had been. Certainly, the Nazis recognized the unique power of radio as a propaganda tool, Goebbels describing it as 'the Eighth Great Power', and many have noted the unique 'radiogenic' power of Hitler's voice, and its ability to access some atavistic stratum of the German collective mind (see, for instance, the discussion of Adorno and Horkheimer's analysis of radio in Chapter 3). Difficult as it is to entertain McLuhan's rather crude, emphatic declarations, behind them there lies a subtler observation: namely, that radio has a

paradoxical quality. It is at once the archetypal broadcast medium –
it scatters its signal on the four winds – but at the same time it
establishes an intimate, sensual relationship to the listener speaking
directly to their shell-like ear.

In its first capacity, radio functions in the manner of a new
sensory environment: an omnipresent sonic envelope that surrounds
the collective, providing an incessant stream of consciousness. Dissolving space and disrupting the atomized individual of print
culture, radio is a crucial catalyst in fomenting the global village.
McLuhan argues that radio's role as an artificial sensory environment only becomes apparent after its displacement as the prime
broadcast medium by television. This relieved radio of its duty to
provide mass entertainment (the phase of its development discussed
by Adorno); the family no longer gathered around the wireless of an
evening. Instead, radio becomes a system of myriad transistors
making up what McLuhan described as a 'nervous information
system'. This information system's function is reflected in monitoring
of environmental conditions, thus 'weather is that medium that
involves all people equally. It is the top item on the radio, showering
us with the foundations of auditory space or *lebensraum*' ([1964]
1995: 261). This mixture of the environmental and tribal makes
radio a nervous system in the sense of constant inquisitive disquiet,
a medium of rumour, gossip and chatter: 'talk radio'. In this respect,
radio exemplifies the darker aspects of the global village: 'Radio is
the medium of frenzy, and it has been the major means of hotting
up the tribal blood of Africa, India, and China' ([1964] 1995: 270).
This is, of course, an area in which the danger of crude media
determinism are readily apparent, in which circumspect analysis is
preferable to McLuhanite generalization. Nevertheless, it is interesting to note the integral role of radio in the instigation of the
horrors of the Rwandan genocide, in which a constant background
chatter of hate and dehumanizing rhetoric primed a civilian popu-
lace to perform atrocious acts of ethnic cleansing. Even a relatively
modest outbreak of inter-ethnic tension, such as the Birmingham
riots of 2005, reflects radio's power in this regard; pirate radio
stations, broadcasting rumour as fact raised existing tensions to flash
point.

## Eye

McLuhan's treatment of visual media is set against his history of the
senses and their extension, and involves the coalescence of the
ocular bias of typographic culture with the resurgent aurality of the
preliterate. For McLuhan, television is the culmination of this

process, and the various technologies that are seen as its precursors, are read in terms of their anticipation of, and divergence from, this ideal.

## Photography and McLuhan's criticality

The technologies of the eye (for our purposes primarily film and television) have their inception in the photograph. McLuhan regards the camera as a technology of objectification, arresting the vital continuity of its subject and reducing it to a static tableau. As we have seen in Chapters 1 and 2, objectification is a consequence of commodification, and the photograph both as an object and as an objectification is the result of technology commensurate with the emergence of capitalism. McLuhan's definition of photography as a brothel without walls ([1964] 1995: 169) is in keeping with this perspective, and his imagery recalls Benjamin's study of Baudelaire as the poet of high capitalism (Benjamin 1985a), in which the figure of the prostitute is used to symbolize the interplay between commodification, urbanism and capitalism. However, McLuhan, lacking the syncretic resources of Freudo-Marxist theory, does not make this connection.

What McLuhan does do is charge the camera with introducing a hitherto undreamt of degree of exactitude into culture. This has several aspects: first, a temporal exactitude. By capturing the evanescence of the external world, the photographic image institutes a new relation to time, and this relation has a vital role in 'creating a world of accelerated transience'. In an observation that recalls Kracauer's meditation on the temporality of the photographic image, McLuhan states that:

> If we open a 1938 copy of *Life*, the pictures or postures then seen as normal now give a sharper sense of remote time than do objects of real antiquity. Small children now attach the olden days to yesterday's hats and overshoes, so keenly attuned are they to the abrupt seasonal changes of visual posture in the world of fashion.

> ([1964] 1995: 176)

This exactitude has the paradoxical effect of transubstantiating the 'real' that it preserves, so that it increasingly takes on dream-like malleability. Photography's recording of reality, soon becomes a writing of reality. Photography not only confers the power to translate all it beholds into an object, but initiates a change in the nature of the object itself. This process affects both the psychology and physiology of the individual and the external environment – indeed it serves to problematize any clear demarcation between these realms.

This represents an interim theoretical position between Benjamin's work upon the notion of aura and Baudrillard's later concept of the *hyperreal* as more real than the real itself. McLuhan's interpretation underlines the profound changes to our experience of the world represented by the advent of the camera. Photography provides a concrete example of the interplay between technology and the body, and the essential plastic nature of subjectivity within it. McLuhan argues that photography initiates a physiological education, as the body adapts itself to a new servo-mechanism. Gaze, deportment, posture: all these are refashioned to fit the new environment. The apparent naturalness of those who are 'photogenic' is the height of artifice; in this manner photography's immediate corporeal impact corresponds to a shift in the status of the individual:

> the complete transformation of human sense-awareness by [photography] involves a development of self-consciousness that alters facial expression and cosmetic make-up as immediately as it does our bodily stance, in public or in private. This fact can be gleaned from any magazine or movie of fifteen years back. It is not too much to say, therefore, that if outer posture is affected by the photograph, so with our inner postures and the dialogue. The age of Jung and Freud is, above all, the age of the photograph ...
>
> (McLuhan [1964] 1995: 197)

The reformatting of subjectivity takes place within the context of an increasingly complex relationship between the material world and its representations/simulations. This intersection between subjectivity, photography and psychoanalysis has already been noted by some of the other, more ideologically orientated theorists of earlier chapters. What sets McLuhan apart, is his particularly relentless commitment to the centrality of the medium. A commitment that may make him appear to avoid the kinds of engagement with political questions that we have observed in other explicitly critical theories of mass media, but which remain implicit in his work none the less.

For instance, there are a number of points of convergence between McLuhan's account of the impact of photography and Debord's thesis of the spectacle. For example, Debord's account of the increasing convergence of urban space with the spectacle finds an echo in McLuhan's observation that the city is designed and redeveloped in response to its photographic representation. Similarly, McLuhan's observation that 'One immense area of photographic influence that affects our lives is the world of packaging and display, and ... the organization of shops. The newspaper that could advertise every sort of product on one page quickly gave rise to department stores that provided every kind of product under one roof' ([1964] 1995: 179). In other words, the exaltation of the packaging, presentation surrounding the commodity, is a direct response to the proliferation of images, and can be seen as confirming Debord's thesis that under the spectacle the commodity is essentially by an image that determines material forms and relations, so that the media does not present images of commodities, rather the commodity is a concrescence of the spectacle.

## Film

*Understanding Media* casts film as a Janus-faced technology; it recalls the discrete, sequential technology of print, while at the same time intimating the dynamic gestalt of television. Film, like the phonetic alphabet, arrests an unbroken flux, fragmenting it into separate units, which are then recombined to produce the impression of a continuum. In this manner it looks back to the age of print, and forward to the age of television. Film is a *hot* medium, and so is treated as a passive experience in which the viewer, ensconced in the dark, hands over their nervous system to an external input. Film inherits and greatly accentuates the camera's paradoxical relation to the real, and McLuhan treats it as the medium of the imaginary, such that the illusion of movement that is its formal premise is replicated in its content. It provides, a *hot* instant gratification for its viewers who for an hour or two are immersed in a simulation of lives and times they can never know: 'The movie is not only the supreme expression of mechanism, but paradoxically it offers as product the most magical of consumer commodities, namely dreams' (McLuhan [1964] 1995: 254). But this dream is predicated upon the mechanical, and in this sense the description of Hollywood as the 'dream factory' (and the commercialization of this idea in such ventures as Spielberg's *Dreamworks* animation company) is telling, not least because it involves a collective mode of production that sets it apart from the more atomized labours of text and introduces it to the full operational capability of the culture industry.

## Television

Television is the locus of McLuhan's media theory. In television the fusion of eye and ear is complete. Television involves a re-education of the eye, which must be relieved of the habits of centuries of print culture and trained in the holistic or depth perception that television requires. Indeed, McLuhan argues that television is not a visual but a tactile experience, something not watched but 'felt'. As established above, new media necessitate a reorganization of the human sensorium, and this results in a restructuring of human subjectivity: 'the rigorous separation and specialisation of the senses ... [cannot] withstand ... the radio and TV waves that wash about the great visual structure of abstract Individual Man' ([1964] 1995: 275). The critical approach promoted in this book finds McLuhan's account of the dissolution of the Individual Man a convincing one – it is what makes his work an important contribution to critical theories of mass media despite the fact that he tended to celebrate such dissolution (although the various points in his work in which he voiced profound concerns were frequently overlooked by commentators [see Harris and Taylor 2005: 7–8]).

McLuhan's analysis of television is exclusively dictated by the technical conditions of the medium at the time of its formulation, conditions that led him to characterize it as a *cool* medium[4]. Whereas the *hot* medium of film was seen as a transitional form which drew on the discrete, sequential technology of print to create the illusion of a moving image, television is clean break with the typographic paradigm: 'The TV image is low on data ... It is not a photo in any sense but a ceaselessly forming contour of things limned by a scanning-finger. The resulting plastic contours appears to be light *through*, not light *on*, and the image formed has the quality of sculpture and icon, rather than picture' ([1964] 1995; 273: original emphasis). Here is the source of the qualities of participation and tactility ascribed to the medium. For McLuhan tactility does not designate touch so much as an immediate interplay between different sensory channels – *synathesia*. Television by presenting an audio-visual image that is marked by its modulation 'the ceaselessly forming contour of things' replicates the interplay of senses. This interplay results in a new form of image, which he terms the 'mosaic', this is a synthetic image in which elements continually coalesce to preserve a continuum – a high-technology continuation of the urban shock and distraction identified by Benjamin.

In spite of this apparent over-investment in certain aspects of the technical conditions of the television of the time, McLuhan did identify a number of significant trends. Although most commentators would today question the degree of television's impact, the trend toward decentralization, the blurring of public and private spheres, and clear demarcation of roles that McLuhan, on the basis of his analysis of television, predicated has been confirmed. Similarly, while his definition of television as a participatory medium is for the most part confused and confusing, it remains the case that television is still the most powerful media in terms of simultaneous collective experience, as clearly demonstrated in the epochal events of 9/11 – a televisual event watched live, and later in a loop of traumatic images, by millions. Indeed, it could be argued that it is this function rather than any particular set of technological conditions that defines television today.

## Conclusion

For Adorno any reconciliation or dissolution of high and low culture takes places within the context of a homogenization; if high and low meet it is because the former has been reduced to the level of the latter. Nothing could provide a greater contrast than McLuhan's account of this process:

> Perhaps it is not very contradictory that when a medium becomes a means of depth experience the old categories of 'classical' and 'popular' or 'highbrow' and 'lowbrow' no longer obtain ... When [the] l.p. and hi-fi and stereo arrived, a depth approach to musical experience also came in. Everybody lost his inhibitions about 'highbrow' and the serious people lost their qualms about popular music and culture. Anything that is approached in depth acquires as much interest as the greatest matters ... Depth means insight, not point of view; and insight is a kind of mental involvement in process that makes the content of the item seem quite secondary. Consciousness itself is an inclusive process not at all dependent on content
>
> (1964: 247)

During the course of the chapter we have repeatedly encountered a fundamental ambiguity in McLuhan's attitude toward his subject. This is an ambivalence writ large in the trajectory of his published work, which begins with the highly critical *The Mechanical Bride* and moves toward increasingly eulogistic accounts of media. Yet even in the white heat of technological euphoria a shadow remains, an awareness of the darker possibility of the forces at play in the electronic environment, and McLuhan is able to pass from exhorting his readers to prepare themselves for the techno-medial rapture, to observing that: 'Electric technology is directly related to our central nervous systems, so it is ridiculous to talk of "what the public wants" ' ([1964] 1995: 68). We have seen that McLuhan felt under no obligation to resolve these tensions, and in an illustration of Whitman's declaration 'Do I contradict myself? Very well I contradict myself, I am large, I contain multitudes!', was happy to serve as the site of multitudinous contradiction, as long as they served to provoke debate. Indeed, McLuhan saw the demand for consistency as part of the cultural legacy of print, as a rear-view Guttenberg hang-up, which prevented an apprehension of the inherently plural space of the new media.

This places McLuhan in a curious relation to the other theorists we have examined, most of whom adopt a uniformly critical position in relation to the mass media. Raymond Williams powerfully articulates the case against McLuhan in this respect when he says:

> If specific media are essentially psychic adjustments, coming not from our relation with ourselves but between a generalized human organism and its general physical environment, then of course intention ... is irrelevant ... and with intention goes content ... All media are in effect desocialised: they are simple physical events in an abstracted sensorium ... If the effect of the medium is the same, whoever controls or uses it, and whatever apparent content he may try to insert, then we can forget ordinary cultural and political argument and let the technology run itself.
>
> (Williams 1974: 127)

If on one level McLuhan's fidelity to the medium as message resulted in a failure to consider the very real social, economic and political conditions in which it was installed, it also provided him with fundamental insights into unique experiential and cultural opportunities generated, and enabled him to anticipate, amid a welter of pseudo-prophecy, a number of very real trends. Thus Williams's further judgement that the influence of McLuhan's media theory 'is unlikely to last long' appears today, given the rise in McLuhan's stock in the digital era, as misguided as McLuhan's most foolish pronouncements.

Williams's criticism prefigures some of the analysis of the profound cultural harm caused by the media, encountered in Part 2. Whereas Williams and more contemporary theorists (like Benjamin before them) frequently see room for the development of positive social forces within such powerful media trends, critical theorists tend to take Williams's fears as an accurate summary of social and political conditions within the mediascape. As an introduction to Part 2's latest versions of these critical accounts, in the next chapter we see how, in the 1960s, Guy Debord combined a McLuhanite account of specific media properties with a much more politically informed sense of the wider environmental effects to produce his critical concept of the *society of the spectacle*.

# 5

# Guy Debord's *society of the spectacle*

## Introduction

An important theme of the preceding chapters is the degree to which mass communications *align* or *co-opt* the cultures and societies in which they operate. For instance, Kracauer's concept of the *mass ornament* recognizes that media do not simply slot into prior social structures, but serve to shape or restructure their whole environment in a complex mix of social and technical interactions (a point further developed in McLuhan's work). From this book's *critical* perspective, rather than media producing a qualitative change that offers new forms of social empowerment, they represent a subtle but pervasive vehicle for the enhancement of capitalist dynamics and commodity values. In this chapter we explore the work of the French activist and thinker Guy Debord (1932–94), and argue that the account of the mass-media society presented in his most influential text *The Society of the Spectacle* (first published in 1967)[1] represents a crucial moment of transition between those thinkers that we have addressed in historical terms – representatives of the *then*, and contemporary critical assessments of the role of the media *now* – Debord's concept of the *spectacle* represents a crucial hinge point between the work of the Frankfurt School and those offered by later figures encountered in Part 2. In presenting his thesis, Debord drew heavily on the conceptual legacy of Hegelianism and Western Marxism, and in this regard he employed the same theoretical 'tool kit' as the Frankfurt School. This places him in a transitional position, at once indebted to dialectics, while at the same time furnishing the insights that allowed a later generation of media critics (in particular Baudrillard) to break with this tradition and fashion a 'post-Marxist' critique of media.

Debord's thought is essential for a critical account of the contemporary mediascape. It further develops Benjamin's key insight that mechanical reproduction creates qualitative change in social conditions (through its quantitative expansion of mediated content) by adopting a more specific focus upon the ways in which those new social conditions so created are suffused with commodity values. The Frankfurt School's analysis addresses this qualitative change in terms of increased alienation and exploitation from a relatively traditional Marxist perspective. Debord's analysis provides a fresh critical insight that focuses more upon the role the image plays in this alienation. We have previously seen how Kracauer explored some of the cultural implications of Marx's account of the commodity form. A defining feature of capitalism, is the way in which the specific properties of an object (use-value) become subordinated to a new abstract, generic property (exchange-value). Using concepts such as *Ratio* and *mass ornament*, Kracauer is a key critical theorist for the way in which he traces how this process of abstraction reaches further and further into cultural life so that the previously discrete and autonomous realm of culture increasingly becomes merely the aesthetic reflex of underlying economic influences. Critical accounts of the media from Debord onwards have focused upon this process of abstraction and its various manifestations of which Benjamin and Kracauer were only able to see the beginnings.

In the age of mass media, exchange-value has in its turn morphed into the society-wide spread of *sign-value*. Heavily processed images have now become a defining social category. The mass media are no longer instruments of re-presentation, as mirrors of pre-existing socio-political conditions, but, as McLuhan argues, they can be described as total environments. The media annexes and transforms its social and cultural milieu, refashioning it in its own image. As such media come to dictate the structure and expression of everyday life, they permeate and determine all personal and collective relations, they construct and determine the wishes, desires and thoughts of the individual, who becomes merely a relay station, a medium among media. This situation in its totality, Debord christened *the spectacle*, and he believed that its logic lay beneath the transformation of the West into a consumerist culture in the post-war period.

## Debord's theory of the spectacle: the background

Before dealing in detail with his key concepts, it is worth outlining the very particular circumstances under which Debord formulated his ideas. He is unique among our assembled company in having never attended university (Hussey 2001). He operated quite outside the world of scholarly journals, conferences, and research grants. Thus, while his life corresponded with the great flowering of radical thought that took place in post-war France, he was far removed from the world of its more celebrated intellectual stars whom he regarded as bourgeois ideologues incapable of truly radical thinking. His sphere was that of the avant-garde and underground politics with their fractious alliances of creative and unpredictable individuals. For Debord, theory was inseparable from an avowed commitment to action, theory was born of praxis, and its primary function to effectuate further praxis – to hasten full-blown revolution. The main vehicle of these ambitions and operations was the *Situationist International* – an unstable collection of theorists, artists and activists, over which Debord (in stark contrast to his egalitarian politics) presided imperiously. Although the history, operations and legacy of the Situationists or 'situs' (as Debord and his followers were popularly known) is outside the scope of this chapter, certain elements are worth outlining in order to better contextualize Debord's notion of *the spectacle* and help establish more clearly its continuity, and departure, from earlier media critique.

The Situationists argued that the consumer society effectively subordinated all aspects of human endeavour to capitalism. It follows from this that any political struggle to change this would need to extend beyond challenging the economic relations of production (hitherto the central arena of left-wing politics). Consequently, they developed an armoury of tactics adapted to the conditions of modern mass-media society, in particular they identified *culture* as a vital 'theatre of operations'. In other words, given the fact that culture had become an industry (to use Adorno's term), then the task at hand was to develop corresponding forms of 'industrial action', the cultural equivalents of 'wildcat strikes' or 'work to rule'. As Debord's 1958 *Theses on Cultural Revolution* put it, the: 'Situationists can be seen as a union of workers in an advanced sector of culture ... as an attempt at an organisation of professional revolutionaries in culture' (Debord, cited in McDonough 2004: 62). Thus, like the thinkers of the Frankfurt School, Debord recognized the centrality of culture (and by extension the technologies by which it was produced and disseminated) to any proper understanding of contemporary mass society. Unlike the Frankfurt School, however, Debord was committed to what might be termed *aesthetic terrorism* – a direct intervention in cultural production.

Situationist activity coincided with a fundamental transformation of the culture of the developed nations. The arc of the Situationists's rise and fall encompassed the optimistic consumer boom of the 1950s and then the turbulent cultural and political upheavals of the 1960s, while their demise corresponded with the disillusionments of the 1970s. The zenith of this trajectory was the 'event' of May 1968, in which France teetered on the brink of full-scale revolution. It is difficult to establish, given competing accounts and self-publicity, the true extent of the Situationist role in events as they unfolded. What is incontrovertible is their contribution to the style or 'spin' of those heady weeks. The irreverent and playful slogans, which blossomed on the walls of Paris (for example, 'Be realistic, demand the impossible', 'Beneath the pavement the beach') were either inspired, if not put up, by Debord and his cadre. In this regard, it could be said that the Situationists' input set May 1968 apart from predecessors. In conjoining the personal and the political the Situationists fused revolution and play, and in a gesture whose ambiguity haunts their legacy to this day, provided an enduring image, *a spectacle* no less, of revolution. Indeed, the proliferation across the international media of images of the May insurrection, ensured the propagation of Situationist theory: mimeographed copies of hastily translated Situationists texts circulated in universities, the 'underground' press in Britain and America gave their readers crash courses in 'situ' theory and groups such as the New York based *Up Against the Wall Motherfucker* [*sic*], Holland's *Provos* and London's *King Mob* (on the fringes of which were to be found Malcolm Maclaren and Jamie Reid – who a decade later would stoke a situ style moral panic in the form of *The Sex Pistols*), recognized the power of Debord's thought, and embraced its programme of cultural disruption. But with this influence and notoriety came *recuperation* – that is, the neutralization, and re-commodification by capitalism of those tactics designed to break its fetishizing spell of signs.

## *The Society of the Spectacle*: early influences and key terms

Debord's *The Society of the Spectacle* is his most famous critique of the media. However, it is worth noting that he arrived at this position through the refinement of a number of earlier perspectives. An important tributary to Debord's thinking and to the structure and aims of the Situationists were the avant-garde art movements of the early twentieth century. These movements (in particular Dada and the Surrealists) subscribed to the belief that the freedom formerly consigned to the confines of the work of art could be liberated. Unbound, the aesthetic could intervene directly in social life, as a force of radical transformation. In keeping with Benjamin's desire (voiced at the end of his Essay) for a politicization of aesthetics, the Situationists offered a fusion of art and politics. They hoped to produce an art that would break the spell of bourgeois culture and so emancipate the revolutionary energies that Benjamin and Kracauer believed to lay beneath mass-mediated culture. The early avant-gardes adopted the structure of political organizations, complete with manifestos, leaders, pogroms in the name of ideological purity and the inevitable splintering attendant upon such structures. Debord both inherited and transformed these ambitions, like these precursors the Situationists aimed to rupture what they saw as an artificial division between art and life. Like Dada they celebrated negation, the utter rejection of the false and contemptible values of the culture surrounding them ('negation, historically associated with dadaism, must end up in every subsequent constructive position as long as those positions manage to resist being swept up by the force of social conditions' [Debord in McDonough 2004: 32]) and, like the Surrealists, they did this in the name of a revolutionary politics.

The Situationists proposed a move 'beyond art'. No longer would their revolutionary aspirations be channelled through the artwork or its negation, rather the life of the spectacle itself was to be their material. Allied to this was their commitment to the power of play or the *ludic*. Liberated life was to be a game, an aesthetic pleasure palace, underwritten by the advances in industrial technology born of capitalism. In this sense the Situationists did not seek the restoration of alienated life that had been consumed by the commodity but, rather, to liberate the positivity inherent in the commodity. To this extent they were practising Kracauer's disdain for outmoded cultural values and his belief that the path out of *Ratio's* alienation was to be found by pushing through it rather than withdrawing from it. In contrast to the nihilistic conception of negation found in the Dadaists concept of anti-art, the Situationists saw negation in Hegelian terms, that is, as a *aufhebgen* or *sublation* – in which something is negated to the extent that one moves beyond it, but in a process of creative transformation in which elements of the old are contained in a radically new version, rather than the simple destruction of what went before. In this manner Debord saw all of the Situationist International's various activities in terms of a coherent strategy perfectly attuned to its historical situation; the Situationist movement must necessarily manifest 'itself simultaneously as an artistic avant-garde, an experimental investigation of the free construction of daily life, and finally as a contribution to the theoretical articulation of a new revolutionary contestation' (Debord, in McDonough 2004: 159).

One of the first expressions of this commitment to the dialectical development of revolutionary theory and aesthetic and experiential praxis was *psychogeography*. Psychogeography worked over the legacy of the avant-garde's attempt to apprehend and express the shock and cacophony of the metropolis (as touched upon in Chapters 1 and 2's discussion of the 'shock' and 'distraction' fostered by the advent of the mediascape) within the context of the urban renewal that took place in post-war Europe. The Situationist International defined *psychogeography* as the 'study of the exact laws and precise effects of the geographical environment'. In language reminiscent of Benjamin and Kracauer's previously cited descriptions of the disorientating effects of the metropolis, they argued that it arose from the recognition that cities 'have a psychogeographical relief with running currents, stable points, and whirlpools that make entering and exiting certain zones very uncomfortable' that act 'directly on the affective deportment of individuals' (McDonough 2004: 301).

## The dérive

Debord believed that urban development was producing a homogenized cityscape whose essential interchangeability paralleled that of the commodity form. The organic flows of the city were being subordinated to the dictates of central planning, functioning as the handmaiden of capital. In keeping with principles of the Situationist International, psychogeography as theory implied its own particular form of praxis, namely the *dérive*. This described a sort of spontaneous drift through the cityscape that rejected the logical order of the city, in order to discover its secret singularities of space and atmosphere. The *dérive* was thus a means of reclaiming the streets, and accessing the hidden city that lay beneath its regulated exterior. Recalling Benjamin's belief in the emancipatory potential of the sensory education involved in adapting to the technological reality of the metropolis, the *dérive* involved an ambulatory derangement of the senses, in order to create new forms of space. The *dérive* is thus a foray into another way of being – the non-alienated life that exists beyond the commodity.

## The situation

The *situation* builds upon the recognition that culture in late capitalism is no longer confined to the boundaries of the artwork. Life itself has become mediated, and it must be disrupted if people are to awake from the spell of commodity culture. The concept of *the situation* constitutes a generalized and refined form of the *dérive*, it is not only urban space that is to be reclaimed but the passage of life itself. This is achieved by the construction of *situations*, moments in which the alienated script of commodified life can be rewritten. The situation is the generation of 'an integrated ensemble of behaviour in time', 'a temporary field of activity' (Jorn, cited in Knab 1981: 43) in which unalienated desire can find forms of expression. The aim of such situations is to provide an intimation of a life beyond the dictates of the spectacle.

## The détournement

The *détournement* can be seen as an extension of the *dérive*, in which the elements that make up the mediascape are themselves overturned and rerouted. The Situationists thus took adverts, comic strips, section of film and inserted subversive commentaries. *Détournement* is thus the creative re-appropriation of cultural fragments that are then reassembled to expose the hidden dynamics of consumer capitalism.

## The Society of the Spectacle: the argument

*The Society of the Spectacle*, Debord's major text was published in French in 1967, and translated into English shortly after. It offers a singularly timely, systematic and comprehensive account of the forces at play within the new consumer society. At the most rudimentary level the spectacle can be understood in terms of the infiltration of the mass media (in particular visual media such as television, film, and photography which offer vivid but essentially false images of life) into many aspects of contemporary life.

### *Origins: commodity capital and consumerism*

For Debord it would be a grave error to see the media and the spectacle as synonymous. While *The Society of the Spectacle* can be defined as one in which the media has an active role in creating what passes for reality, such a society cannot be explained solely in terms of media. An adequate account of the spectacle must describe its genesis, that is, how a spectacular society emerges from an earlier industrial capitalist society. Debord locates this in the processes of commodification and reification as originally described by Marx and developed more explicitly by Lukács[2]. The spectacle represents an unprecedented development within society due to the qualitative change it brings to social experience and thus to this point Debord is in agreement with Benjamin. Its nature is determined by the basic operations of the capitalist system. This is set out most clearly in the text's second chapter 'Commodity as spectacle', prefaced by the following citation from Lukács:

> The commodity can only be understood in its undistorted essence when it becomes the universal category of society as a whole. Only in this context does the reification produced by commodity relations assume decisive importance both for the objective evolution of society and for the stance adopted by men towards it. Only then does the commodity become crucial for the subjugation of men's consciousness to the forms in which this reification finds expression ... As labor is progressively rationalized and mechanized man's lack of will is

reinforced by the way in which his activity becomes less and less
active and more and more contemplative.

(Lukács in Debord 1977: N35)

By citing Lukács in this manner, Debord effectively proposes the
spectacle as the final form of the commodity, and retroactively
defines capitalism as the process of its progressive realization. The
dissolution of categories, the sublimation of 'all that's solid to air'
described by Marx and Engels is now revealed as part of the
spectacle's evolution. As the commodity approaches the condition of
the 'universal category of society as a whole', labour (as a means of
generating surplus) becomes increasingly 'contemplative'. Debord
perceives this term in a much more negative way than Benjamin's
use of it in order to critique the manner in which art absorbs the
masses rather than vice versa. Debord uses it to describe a much
more superficial visual interaction. Passive consumption rather than
active labour becomes the means of generating surplus, labour has
become 'immaterial', production has been superseded by consumption.

The commodity form 'reaches its absolute fulfilment in the
spectacle, where the tangible world is replaced by a selection of
images which exist above it, and which simultaneously impose
themselves as the tangible par excellence' (Debord 1977: N35), thus
the media does not bring, but is rather brought, into being by the
spectacle. Conceptualized in this fashion the spectacle can be seen as
standing in the same relation to the commodity as the commodity
did to earlier forms of exchange. Just as the commodity absorbed
and abstracted the economic relations that pre-dated it, so the
spectacle absorbs and abstracts the commodity form. Money as a
medium of exchange permits a false equivalence to be established
between two incommensurate objects (that is, whichever physical
items are being expressed in monetary terms). Capitalism extends
this equivalence to the point where it does not simply mediate, but
begins to determine the nature of the objects themselves. Marx
described this process of abstraction in terms of *reification* and
*commodity fetishism,* and it can be readily seen from the way in which
objects come to achieve an exchange value out of all proportion to
any apparent usefulness due to their status as desirable brands. For
example, the Nike swoosh creates a disproportionate increase in
value if it is present or absent on the same pair of athletics shoes.
Debord's use of the term *spectacle* to describe a unique cultural
phenomenon arises at the point where money becomes a whole
environment that structures our lives: 'The spectacle is the developed modern complement of money where the totality of the
commodity world appears as a whole, as a general equivalence for
what the entire society can be' (1977: N49). Debord's essential point

here is that, in a mass-media society, the commodity form and the media become so well aligned that they mutually reinforce and inter-penetrate each other. A crucial aspect of Debord's development of the theorists we have previously encountered in these pages, is his account of how the environment created by this intertwining assumes a society-wide presence – McLuhan's notion that *the medium is the message*. Whatever the nominal content of the mass media, Debord argues that its ultimate effect is to be found and felt in the environment it creates irrespective of any attempts to use individual media for specific purposes.

If nineteenth-century capitalism concentrated primarily on the worker as a source of mechanical labour, and treated other needs and desires (for instance those of leisure and pleasure) as irrelevant, then the capitalism of the spectacle involves bringing these external aspects of life inside the circuit of capital[3]. Subsequently, under the spectacle the proletariat finds itself 'suddenly redeemed from the total contempt which is clearly shown ... by all the varieties of organization' and 'in the guise of the consumer' is subject to displays of 'zealous politeness' (1977: N43). In this manner capitalism recuperates the elements of life from which the worker was formerly alienated, but in doing so it in fact alienates all the more. Moreover, to the extent that alienated life forms the basis of the spectacle, life is doubly alienated: *under the spectacle we are alienated from alienation by alienation!* The *society of the spectacle* thus represents a general process of abstraction that proceeds from a pre-capitalist condition of unmediated 'being', to the original distinguishing feature of capitalism – its investment in possessing or 'having' – to a further stage of evolution, namely, the spectacular valorization of image or 'appearing' from which 'all actual "having" must draw its immediate prestige and its ultimate function' (1977: N17). The spectacle becomes life's double – the material real becomes increasingly subordinate to its mediated appearance as a society-wide expression of the original move from use-value to exchange-value.

Debord concisely defines the spectacle as 'the concrete inversion of life ... the autonomous movement of the non-living' (1977: N2). It is a spectre – a form of 'non-life', the accumulation of dead labour converted into images that haunt the living. Although the image is privileged and most immediate expression of the spectacle it is not simply 'a product of the techniques for the dissemination of images' but a 'social relation among people mediated by images'. It is an image of the world that has become concrete. Just as exchange (in the form of the commodity) remade the object of human labour in its own image, so the spectacle as a radical disembedding of exchange from physicality remakes the world literally in its own image. This results in a culturally pervasive and domineering tautology that is powerfully resistant to perspectives other than its own self-enclosed one. The spectacle in the form of the media, fashion, advertising and the entire spectrum of mass-produced objects continually affirms itself: its 'form and content are ... the total justification of the existing system's conditions and goals' (1977: N6). Debord's thesis is explicitly iconoclastic and characterized by a certain *scopophobia* – a contempt or hatred for images[4]. Recalling McLuhan's delineation of the literate, ocular-centric European sensibility, Debord regards the spectacle as the heir of the 'Western philosophical project' and its commitment to 'comprehend activity in terms of the categories of seeing', which has been realized in the form of media technologies and the 'precise technical reality which grew out of this thought' (1977: N19). The spectacle becomes a paradoxical concretization of an otherwise immaterial ocular-centric bias based on images to create a technological milieu in which abstract images produce very real effects.

## Boorstin and the *pseudo-event*

Additional insight into Debord's spectacle can be approached through the work of an American contemporary – Daniel Boorstin. While far removed from the avant-garde aesthetic and revolutionary Marxist politics of the Situationists, Boorstin's *The Image: A Guide to Pseudo-Events in America* (first published in 1961) nevertheless articulated the crucial elements of the spectacular society, and in this respect demonstrates that it was not simply a Parisian phantasm but a phenomenon apparent even to the soberest of commentators (Boorstin was a historian by training, and *The Image* his only work on the media). Boorstin argued that contemporary (that is, those of 1961) media operating in combination had resulted in the emergence of what he calls the *pseudo-event*, which had the following closely related and cumulative characteristics:

1 *It is not spontaneous: it has been planned or spun in advance.* For example, a press conference or staged interview. Reminiscent of Benjamin's account of the way in which traditional aura becomes undermined by mechanical reproductions, and prefiguring Baudrillard's later writings about the undermining of reality by simulations, Boorstin argues: 'We begin to be puzzled about what is really the "original" of an event. The authentic news record of what "happens" or is said comes increasingly to seem to be what is given out in advance ... The story prepared "for future release" acquires an authenticity that competes with that of the actual occurrences on the scheduled date' (Boorstin [1961] 1992: 19).

2 *It is produced, from the beginning, in order to be reported or reproduced.* The press release illustrates this particular quality of an event whose whole meaning resides only within the media itself and

according to a number of critical theorists both then and now, the combined effects of mediation and commodification serve to produce a realm of culture in which meaning and representations become autonomous and self-generating – increasingly divorced from any prior reality.

3 *Its relation to any underlying concept of reality is unclear.* For example, media reports are frequently based on *human interest* stories related more to the motivations and the psychological contexts surrounding the actors involved in various *pseudo-events,* rather than any actual substantive significance to the events themselves. Thus, an exclusive television interview on the breakdown of Princess Diana's marriage and her subsequent mental state constitutes a self-evidently important 'news' item – without any attempt to assess the importance of such issues in a wider, more genuinely political sense.

4 *It is an essentially tautological phenomenon.* Related closely to the previous point – the fact that an event is presented as being important creates its own importance. Ultimately all media representations tend to valorize the representative power of the media largely irrespective of the actual content (once again McLuhan's *the medium is the message*).

Thus Boorstin argues that reality has been replaced by a largely separate world that is capable of reproducing itself. He offers a number of direct explanations for the proliferation of *pseudo events*:

- They are more dramatic.
- Once disseminated they create the conditions for other 'events'.
- Subsequent events in their turn are amenable to the networks and technologies through which they are relayed and so tend to supplant alternative non-*pseudo-events*.
- Within an environment that privileges the *pseudo-event* knowledge of *pseudo-events* assumes its own importance.
- Because they are artificially generated and created to be disseminated they are inherently repeatable, and so can be manipulated and processed to occur to fit in with schedules and audience demand.
- Given their relationship to the systems that re-present them, *pseudo-events* both generate and require money to create in the first place.

The above combination of causes, effects and explanations leads to these further issues to be considered:

- *Pseudo-events are more dramatic*: their staged element brings 'manufactured spontaneity' to news reporting. This can range from reporters rather needlessly standing outside an appropriate building (for example, the court building for a high-profile court case), to photo-opportunists such as President Bush speaking to the media upon an aircraft carrier.

- *Pseudo-events are easier to disseminate because they were designed to be propagated and repeated*: stemming from a combination of their dramatic nature plus their circulation within a self-referential media matrix within which 'newsworthiness' is defined by the media itself, easy dissemination of *pseudo-event*s becomes the inevitable, self-justifying process of a system that is both the gatekeeper for their prior identification and for subsequent circulation. The formulaic nature and innate reproducibility of news events adds to their potential for dissemination to contribute to a general environment of spectacle where *pseudo-events* become the filler for round-the-clock news bulletins. The viewer becomes quickly acclimatized to this new grammar of the *society of the spectacle* – the *pseudo-event*.
- *Pseudo-events cost money*: although rather an obvious statement, the financial investment made in *pseudo-events* provides further encouragement for their wide dispersal and repetition in order to justify their expense by creating a return upon the investment – hence yet more momentum for the dissemination of *pseudo-events* is created.
- *Pseudo-events are designed to be easily intelligible*: although desirable in some senses, it is important to note that this is a particular form of intelligibility peculiar to the media. Deeper levels of meaning and sophistication are sacrificed for immediate accessibility with media-friendly forms of communication such as the soundbite. The depth to which the media's *pseudo-events* penetrate the wider social life is vividly illustrated in the way in which US Presidential television debates now closely follow the form of a quiz show. The previous political practice of 'debating' is redefined into soundbites that better suit the television format – carefully timed two-minute responses to questions of national and global importance.
- *Pseudo-events are socially convenient*: their intelligibility is thus enhanced by the way in which they are packaged for our consumption at the most appropriate and regular times. Thus, for example, irrespective of world events on any given day there is always enough news to fill the requisite half-hour long news bulletins at a time to suit the viewers. In the first Gulf conflict, for example, military actions were at least partially coordinated with television news schedules rather than vice versa.

- *Awareness of pseudo-events becomes knowledge*: the self-referential media community that decides the newsworthiness of items is reinforced by a cultural environment in which knowledge of *pseudo-events* increasingly becomes more important than more traditional forms of knowledge.
- *The geometric progression of pseudo-events*: as a result of all the previous factors, *pseudo-events* propagate further *pseudo-events* to provide the basis of the contemporary media-sponsored blurring of reality and the simulated world of media. In Boorstin's words: 'By this new Gresham's Law[5] of American public life, counterfeit happenings tend to drive spontaneous happenings out of circulation' (Boorstin [1961] 1992: 40). The exception to this trend is the periodic occurrence of truly spontaneous events such as Hurricane Katrina. However, even here, there is a tendency for reporting to quickly revert to the grammar of *pseudo-events* once the initial trauma of the natural disaster has been extensively covered.

## The alienation of the image: separation perfected

Debord argues that Boorstin's *pseudo-event* does not equate to his concept of the spectacle because he thinks he can exempt private life, or the notion of 'the honest commodity', in other words to uphold a preserved space which is not infiltrated by the values of the spectacle:

> Boorstin finds that the results he depicts are caused by the unfortunate ... encounter of an oversized technical apparatus for image diffusion with an excessive attraction to the pseudo-sensational. Boorstin fails to understand that the proliferation of '*pseudo-events*' which he denounces flows from the simple fact that ... history itself haunts modern society like a spectre, pseudo-histories are constructed at every level of consumption of life in order to preserve the threatened equilibrium of present frozen time.
>
> (1977: N200; emphasis added)

The spectacle is part of the process of alienation and separation produced by the combined and related effects of capitalism's increasing commodification of traditional social life and the decline of aura brought about by media technologies. Capitalist production fragmented the life-world of the worker. In other words it alienated him from the object of his labour and separated him from the traditional creative experience he would previously enjoy with fellow workers and his role within the wider community. This alienation was a by-product of the institution of industrial capitalism, more than a deliberate strategy. However, consumer capitalism as embodied in the spectacle engages directly with the alienation of the industrial process. The spectacle involves the recuperation of the masses' alienation – the very fact that the masses are distanced from traditional values by the industrialized process of manufacture, provides the space for the spectacle to be sold to them as an additional aspect of manufacture, the manufacture of a pseudo-reality to replace their traditional reality – hence Debord's description of the spectacle as 'separation perfected'.

The spectacle offers a false totality, an imminent but ultimately elusive image of completion and integration, whose apparent cohesion merely disguises actual alienation. The allure of the spectacle is in direct proportion to the estrangement felt by its individual members. Each product offered by the consumer society reflects the lustre of the spectacle in its totality 'every individual commodity is justified in the name of grandeur of the production of the totality of objects' (1977: N65), and promises the consumer the chance to cross the divide between their alienated, fallen state and spectacle's perfection. This lustre, however, being merely reflected, vanishes as soon as the commodity is removed from its setting within the spectacle, and becomes a mere object – the possession of an alienated individual as distant as ever from the spectacle's pseudo-totality:

> Therefore the already problematic satisfaction which is supposed to come from the consumption of the whole, is falsified immediately since the actual consumer can directly touch only a succession of fragments of this commodity happiness, fragments in which the quality attributed to the whole is obviously missing every time.
>
> (1977: N65)

This analysis is reminiscent of Adorno's conception of the relationship between the general and the particular within the culture industry. Instead of the tension between the two that is indicative of true art, in the culture industry and *society of the spectacle*, a false identity is created so that in consuming commodities the buyer continually buys into an illusion of fulfilment (Adorno's notions that 'the diner must be satisfied with the menu' and we continue to practise the magic of commodities upon ourselves). The spectacle is the avowed enemy of all forms of community and (non-mediated) collective action. All conceptions of collectivity are carefully policed, and are either incorporated or, if resistant, stigmatized. The spectacle jealously guards its unifying force, it must be the only representation of the life-world it denies. Hence the importance the media places on generating various forms of ersatz community – the *Banality TV* explored in the following chapters. Banal and formulaic

intrigues are manufactured to imitate village life along with organized expressions of collective sentiment, such as national days of
mourning and televised 'charithons'.

## Time and space in the spectacle

We have established that for Debord the spectacle cannot be
reduced to the image and its technologies, which are the result of a
pre-existing dynamic within capitalism. The media emerges within an
environment already radically altered by capitalism, not least in the
form of a wide-ranging reconfiguration of the categories of space
and time in conformity with its demands. This is in keeping with our
previous exploration of Benjamin and Kracauer's work given that, as
previously cited, Benjamin starts his Essay with an epigraph from
Paul Valéry claiming that time and space have been irretrievably
changed due to the advent of the camera, while Kracauer argues
that it profoundly alters traditional forms of human cognition and
memory. Building upon these insights by tracing more closely the
complex links between media technology and culture, Debord
argues that industrial capitalism involves an increasing spatialization
of time 'a commodity-time, namely exchangeable units and the
suppression of the qualitative dimension' (1977: N149). According to
Debord, spectacular capitalism represents a significantly more culturally invasive development from previous mode of industrial capitalism. The capitalism of the *society of the spectacle* colonizes those
aspects of life industrial capitalism still left alone. For example,
pre-capitalist time could be described as cyclical, it involved various
recurring cycles, marked by holidays, feasts, and so on.

Reminiscent of Kracauer's 'Travel and dance' essay, in *The Society of
the Spectacle* we observe a 'pseudo-cyclical time' assembled from the
remnants of a pre-capitalist cyclical time. It subjects any cyclical
elements to manipulation as an opportunity for profit. Thus vacations, festivities, the alternation of working week and weekend, these
occasions serve as sites of consumption. Vacations are festivals of
image-consumption, in the sense that a certain image of leisure is
purchased in a form of conspicuous consumption, as well as the
consumption of images in the more restricted sense of taking
holiday snaps or 'taking in the sights'. Spectacular time involves a
spatialization of cyclical time in accordance with the logic of
production. It is sold back to the producer qua consumer in the
form of time-saving goods, which in turn free up time for other
forms of consumption. In this fashion capitalism: 'orientates itself
toward towards the sale of "completely equipped" blocks of time,
each one constituting a single unified commodity which integrates a
number of diverse commodities' (1977: N152). The modern vacation

highlights the space/time transformation under the spectacle. Space like time becomes a consumable commodity, the particularity of place is converted into a consumable (as in having 'done Thailand'). For Debord this reflects a more general banalization of space, a reconstruction that eliminates all singularity, capitalism thus remakes the totality of space into its own setting. Although this process involves the extirpation of particularity it nonetheless involves the creation of various forms of second-order distinctions between spaces, forms of zoning and differentiation that accord with opportunities for profit. Thus Debord provided an early description of what has subsequently been examined in terms of urban theming (see Sorkin 1992; Hannigan 1998; Gottdiener 2001). In space as in time, capitalism at once homogenizes and differentiates, in order to return at a profit what it has appropriated.

## The spectacle revisited: Debord's *Comments*

In 1988, on the twentieth anniversary of the appearance of *The Society of the Spectacle,* Debord published a small pamphlet, translated into English as *Comments on the Society of the Spectacle* (1991) in whose pages he reassessed his theory of the spectacle in the light of the social, cultural and political trends of the intervening decades. His conclusions were far from optimistic. And while deriving some grim satisfaction at his accurate diagnosis, as he wrote in 1992 in the introduction to the third edition of his major work: 'A critical theory of the kind presented here needed no changing ... the general conditions of the long historical period that it was the first to describe accurately were still intact. The continued unfolding of our epoch has merely confirmed and further illustrated the theory of the spectacle' (Debord 1994: 1).[6] Debord could only despair at the naivety of the solutions he formerly entertained. Gone is the confidence in the possibility of cultural revolution. Indeed the spectacle of 1988 mocks such aspirations, for under the 'integrated spectacle' art has fused with life, the aesthetic has infiltrated every dimension of social (as evidenced by the emergence of 'designer' as a free floating prefix in the 1980s). Likewise the language of Marx and Hegel, and the unshakable certainty of an analysis framed in its terms is conspicuous for its absence in contemporary political and ideological discourse. *Comments* is therefore uniformly pessimistic, and offering no alternative to dominant conditions, is confined 'to recording what is' and refuses to speculate 'on what is desirable, or merely preferable' (1991: s. N1). This pessimistic inventory is founded in a recognition of the recuperative power of the spectacle. The spectacle like a spectre cannot be killed but rises with redoubled vigour from each fresh challenge to its hegemony.

The spectacle, like the culture industry that preceded it, has a stubborn ability to turn everything to profit no matter how radical the critique. This is exemplified by the fate of Debord's own thesis. *The Society of the Spectacle* is a condition that all acknowledge, that society is spectacular becomes unworthy even of mention. Debord argues that: 'The empty debate on the spectacle ... is thus organized by the spectacle *itself*: everything is said about the extensive means at its disposal, to ensure that nothing is said about their extensive deployment' (1991: s. N3; original emphasis). The cultural role of the spectacle is thus both acknowledged and at the same time left unaddressed. The thesis's explanatory force is diffused through the efforts of numerous minor commentators who offer revisions and refinements that effectively renounce the all-important totality of its critique (the uncritical cultural populists). In concentrating on individual factors and *pseudo-events*, ultimately empty debates encourage the illusion that the spectacle can be redeemed through the reforming of a given component (such as advertising, political and corporate propaganda, sex, violence, and so on). For Debord the substitution or elision of 'the spectacle' and 'media' performs an allied function. It conceals the agency of the system behind an apparently neutral technical network. The spectacle thus hides in plain sight (a paradox that forms a consistent theme in Part 2), a situation that leaves its anonymous consumers with the 'vague' but widespread 'feeling that there has been a rapid invasion which has forced people to lead their lives in an entirely different way; but this is experienced rather like some inexplicable change in climate' (1991: s. N2). Debord's reassessment in his *Comments on the Society of the Spectacle* awards technology a minor role in the evolution of the spectacle, arguing that while technology has undoubtedly advanced in the intervening years, it cannot be seen as major force behind the spectacle, since the latter was already well established. Thus the spectacle thesis remains unimpressed by the developments in media technology, and the radical changes that have taken place in the decades since Debord's *Comments*, would, if Debord were alive today, elicit the same response.

## The integrated spectacle

In 1967 Debord distinguished between two forms of spectacular society – the diffused spectacle of Western Europe and the 'concentrated' spectacle of the Eastern bloc. This concentrated spectacle came to an end with the collapse of the Soviet Union in 1989. According to Debord this was the occasion of a new form of spectacle, *the integrated spectacle*, a 'rational combination' of the most successful features of its precursors. The integrated spectacle is both more diffuse and more concentrated than its predecessors. While the former 'hovered above the surface of society' allowing areas of life to escape the spectacle (so providing a space for détournement) no aspect of culture is outside the purview of the integrated spectacle. As its name implies, it permeates every strata of society. This pervasiveness is matched by its concentration, its 'controlling centre has now become occult, never to be occupied by a known leader, or clear ideology'. Thus the integrated spectacle 'integrates itself into reality to the same extent that it speaks of it, and that it reconstructs it as it speaks', as such it is the ultimate realization of the *society of the spectacle*: 'the unbridled accomplishment of commodity rationality has quickly ... shown that the becoming-world of the falsification was also the falsification of the world' (1991: s. N4). Part 2 explores the topical manifestations of the integrated spectacle in relation to Banality TV and its political consequences.

Debord argues that the integrated spectacle is a combination of four characteristics, namely:

- Fusion of state and economy
- Generalized secrecy
- Incessant technological renewal
- A perpetual present.

The *fusion of state and economy* is the defining feature of the integrated spectacle. If in its earlier incarnation these two sectors had enjoyed an uneasy relationship, the new spectacle is characterized by a mutually beneficial alliance whose end result is a totally administered environment. Accordingly 'it is absurd to oppose them, or to distinguish between their rationalities and irrationalities'(1991: s. N5). Indeed, the integrated spectacle is precisely this integration of economy, state and media. The condition of *generalized secrecy* is the direct result and ultimate aim of this integration; in other words, the successful concealment of the true centre of power. Since technology is not a driving force in the institution and evolution of the spectacle, the technological innovations that sustain the integrated spectacle are for Debord simply cosmetic phenomena: 'Gizmos proliferate at unprecedented speeds; commodities out-date themselves almost every week; nobody can step down the same supermarket aisle twice' (Merrifield 2005: 125). This incessant technological innovation is for Debord largely aimed at consolidating the grip of the spectacle, and reinforcing the status of various specialists and technicians. The final characteristic, the institution of a perpetual present 'where fashion itself, from clothes to music, has come to a halt, which wants to forget the past and no longer seems to believe in a future' (1991: N5), is a strategy of self-protection, a deliberate reduction of the world to the scope of the spectacle's past, the photo-shopping out of history and culture, its editing in conformity with a 'ceaseless circular passage of information': 'When social significance is attributed only to what is immediate, and to what will be immediate immediately afterwards, always replacing another, identical, immediacy, it can be seen that the uses of the media guarantee a kind of eternity of noisy insignificance' (1991: N6).

The institution of a perpetual present is one example of the manner in which the spectacle eliminates the forces that threaten its reign. Another strategy discussed by Debord is the destruction of rational thought by the image. In losing their immediate access to the external world in favour of the mediation of the image or screen, the individual is deprived of their autonomy of thought, since the processed pseudo-experience of the spectacle entirely determines thought. Consequently, whoever 'governs at will this simplified summary of perceptible world', ensures a continued control over the viewer. The spectacle's programmers minimize the opportunity or temptation for independent thought. This editorial control of the image and, equally importantly, of the juxtaposition of images, presents the spectacle with new tools for subjugation of thought. The image, as Debord notes, is a schematic summary (recall here McLuhan's comments of the televisual mosaic) of the 'real'. As such it is compressed, and stripped of 'extraneous' information. This editing when combined with global reach of the spectacle creates a compressed, contracted double of the 'real', in which what is shown is isolated 'from its context, its past, its intentions and consequences', that is, divorced from its causal and therefore logical relations. Moreover, in its ability to combine these decontextualized images, the integrated spectacle effectively substitutes its combinatory power for synthetic operations of independent logical thought. False associations and judgements are generated and disseminated en masse, via the technologies of the image. Thus Debord observes:

> Since no one can contradict it, the spectacle has the right to contradict itself, to correct its own past. The arrogant attitude of its servants, when they make known some new, and perhaps still more dishonest version of certain facts, is to harshly correct the ignorance and bad interpretations they attribute to the public, while the day before they themselves were busy disseminating the error, with their customary assurance.

> (1991: s. N10)

Anyone familiar with the perplexing, protean shifts in the justifications of such Anglo-American policies as the Gulf conflicts as related by the mass media will appreciate the contemporary relevance of these comments. Debord argues that in berating spectators for their supposed misapprehensions, the spectacle falsely generates a dichotomy between representation and reception, and so obscures the fact that its own deeply ideological natural mode of operating has deliberately generated these misunderstandings in the first instance.

## Terrorism

*The Society of the Spectacle* argued that the theatrics of adversarial politics concealed the underlying hegemony of a unitary system, but under the integrated spectacle simulated conflict is replaced with a manufactured consensus, a 'third way' for which the dominion and logic of the commodity and spectacle are beyond question. All 'legitimate' participants accept as the price of entry a commitment to the fundamental values of the integrated spectacle (evoking Adorno's notion that talented individuals seeking to be successful within the culture industry belong to it in spirit before they even begin their quest), which come wrapped in the sugar-coating of the radical political ideals of the earlier centuries (democracy, free speech). This creates a situation in which to fundamentally question the integrated spectacle is effectively to question the inalienable right to question, and therefore to be an enemy of freedom. This double bind is part of what Debord describes as the 'fragile perfection' of the integrated spectacle, whose perfection in terms of its scope and self-sufficiency means that all contradiction assumes the guise of an irrational 'other':

> Such a perfect democracy constructs its own inconceivable foe, terrorism ... The story of terrorism is written by the state and it is therefore highly instructive. The spectators must certainly never know everything about terrorism, but they must always know enough to convince them that, compared with terrorism, everything else must be acceptable, or in any case more rational and democratic.
>
> (1991: s. N9)

Being unable to accept the principles on which the integrated spectacle apparently rests, means that this contradiction cannot be accommodated, but only extirpated. Moreover, in the face of an alterity that appears to refuse all forms of democratic representation, 'anything goes', up to and including the suspension of the very rights that terrorism will not honour. The intrinsically shadowy nature of terrorism is perfectly suited to the spectacle's own agenda, and its 'rumors ... after three or four repetitions acquire the weight of secular historical proofs. According to the legendary authority of the day, strange characters eliminated in silence can reappear as fictive survivors, whose return can always be evoked ... and *proved* by the mere say-so of specialists' (1991: s. N18; original emphasis).

## Conclusion

The relevance of Debord's analysis to today's mediscape is obvious from the immediately preceding comments and the ease with which they can be applied to the ongoing War on Terror and various aspects of the media's coverage of world events, and this is explored in more detail in Chapter 8. The various forms of contemporary celebrity also demonstrate the continued pertinence of Debord's work. Celebrities now incarnate the very ideas of integration, autonomy, self-confidence and fulfilment whose force and appeal resides precisely in the glaring absence of these qualities in the lives of most consumers. Celebrities as 'the spectacular representation of a living human being' promote the illusion of 'equal access to the totality of consumption' and serve as 'the object of identification with the shallow seeming life that has to compensate for the fragmented productive specializations which are actually lived ... They embody the inaccessible result of social labour by dramatizing its by-products magically projected above it as its goal' (1977: s. N60). Through the *cult* of celebrity the spectacle ensures that the desire for the false totality of the spectacle remains both constant and unsatisfied. Debord asserts a fundamental polarity between the celebrity and the individual, in which the former is the enemy of the latter, sustained by the power it has expropriated. Moreover, entry into the charmed circle of celebrity involves the systematic suppression of spontaneous individuality 'passing into the spectacle as a model for identification, the agent renounces all autonomous qualities in order to identify himself with the general law of obedience to the course of things' (1977: s. N61). This 'general law of obedience' has evolved from the cult of beauty Benjamin identified *then* as a residual ritualistic element of the Hollywood star system, to the contemporary *cult* of celebrity that now appears in the democratized form of Banality TV, and it is this to which we turn *now*.

# Part 2

Now

# Introduction to Part 2

An important aspect of Part 1's critical analysis of the media is its unwillingness to take the media's content at face value. Rather, past writers illustrated the subtle (but all the more, not less, powerful for that) 'structure of feeling' (Raymond Williams) created by the media in the wider social environment.

Benjamin optimistically explored the *decline of aura* and the rise of *distraction*. He found hope in the qualitative changes that occur in our experience of *mass* culture due to the rapid quantitative increases in its content produced by mechanized technological reproduction. In Part 2 we develop further the more negative implications of the socio-technical processes he tried to view positively. We suggest that contemporary manifestations of the culture industry require a complete and critical re-evaluation of Benjamin's Essay to explore in:

Chapter 6 – the decline in aura in the context of new democratized forms of celebrity.

Chapter 7 – his concept of distraction as revisited in the light of daytime and Reality TV – *Banality TV*.

Chapter 8 – the political consequences of the decline of aura and the rise of distraction.

Kracauer's terms *mass ornament* and *Ratio* provide the basis of a consistently pessimistic assessment of the rise in mass-media culture and its alienating cultural properties. The topical examples in Part 2 illustrate the essential accuracy of his early analysis of media culture.

Adorno's *culture industry* explains the operational functioning of the commodified and mechanically reproduced culture explored by both Benjamin and Kracauer. The culture industry of *now* incorporates 'active' audience involvement into the inherent structures of its culture industry products. This provides a powerful rejoinder to the active audience/cultural populist emphasis upon interpretive activity as *a priori* evidence of empowerment. Reality TV, for example, provides 'continuous interactive originals' – which are in fact constant repetitions of the same format merely with new faces. This is a topical illustration of Adorno's early analysis of the fake originality of the culture industry's products. Adorno's work is particularly applicable to the themes of Part 2 for the way it provides an early explanation of the way in which mass-media audiences are not deceived into false consciousness but, rather, willingly participate and connive at their own oppression within a culture of excessive explicitness. In Chapters 7 and 8 this theme is discussed in relation to theorists of the *now*, such as Slavoj Žižek and Jean Baudrillard.

McLuhan's provocative notion of *the medium is the message*, read in a critical fashion, adds a prescient interpretation of the technological underpinnings to the concepts of all three previous thinkers of the *then*. In particular, it provides a theoretical basis for understanding the contemporary mediascape's powerfully innate grammars explored in the themes of celebrity, Reality TV and a global politics of the spectacle in Chapters 6, 7, and 8 respectively.

Debord's notion of the *society of the spectacle* provides an integrated account of the previous thinkers. It explains how the culture-defining nature of the spectacle derives from the close cultural alignment of the technical power of the mediated image and the wider commodity culture of which it is an intrinsic part. Part 2 uses recent illustrations to explore how this alignment works in practice to produce our excessive contemporary dependence upon the mediated image.

# 6

## The *cult*ure of celebrity

## Introduction

> The celebrity in the distinctive modern sense could not have existed in any earlier age, or in America before the Graphic Revolution. *The celebrity is a person who is known for his well-knownness* ... He is the human pseudo-event.
>
> (Boorstin [1961] 1992 : 57; original emphasis)

> Celebrities function in consumer culture as a connecting fiber between the materiality of production and culturally contextualized meaning of consumption and its relation to collective identity. The celebrity then, is a commodity that possesses in its humanness and familiarity an affective link in consumer culture to the meaning that is bestowed on consumer objects by groups.
>
> (Marshall 1997: 245)

As Boorstin points out above, the modern celebrity is well known for being well known (and, as we shall soon see in relation to Reality TV, such a status is often gained irrespective of any significant talent). Replacing traditional aura and charisma, fame now circulates in a self-justifying fashion. This chapter demonstrates the complex cultural alignment between this form of fame and commodity culture in general. It builds upon Part 1's detailed treatment of the links that exist between media technologies and the culture industry – what Marshall refers to above as 'a connecting fiber'. An under-acknowledged aspect of celebrity within cultural populist accounts is this ideological role by which it provides a human face for commodity values. The celebrity's role as a friendly personification of the commodity process is highly significant because of the non-threatening manner with which it allows critical analysis of the commodity system's malign consequences to be voiced – one suspects that if the honorary Knights of the Realm, Bono and Bob Geldof did not exist, capitalism would need to create them. While the essential elements of the commodity system remain undisturbed, ebrity faces effectively distract us from the much less glamorous and more mundane structural economic causes that continue to dominate social relations within the heavily mediated West and the wider global political order. As embodiments of the enigmatic and irrational aspects of commodity culture, even their various well-intentioned charity campaigns ultimately serve to reinforce the system as they appear to challenge it.

Just as the medium becomes the message for McLuhan, so the specific qualities or use-values of both commodities and celebrities have been supplanted by their status within the realm of circulation. In both cases, the mode of circulation (the general) is more important than the content being circulated (the particular). Our routine interaction with familiar yet unknown (in any meaningful personal sense) celebrities mirrors our similarly ambivalent yet routinized relationship with the branded commodity. Both are premised upon abstract desire. Any use-value they might have is subordinate to their primary appeal as iconic representations and the value of this appeal stems from an essentially circular and self-regarding process. The logo on a sports shirt or shoe has no real usefulness beyond the status it derives from being instantly recognizable. There is no inherent reason why the Nike swoosh logo has to be a swoosh, or why this should make its running shoes more desirable, and so too beyond the particularly talented or charismatic, the cultural value placed upon celebrities is predominantly arbitrary. Part 1 demonstrated the roots of this now highly developed social valuation of circulation for its own sake and how its cultural tipping point arose with the advent of photography. In the mechanically reproduced images of *then* lie the origins of the celebrity culture we inhabit *now*.

Adorno argued that the culture industry relies upon an unhealthy denial of the marginal nature of the supposed differences between what are essentially the same commodities. The illusion of difference is created by the advertising industry's manufacture of superficial distinctions and purported attributes. This aspect of the culture industry's output is equally true in relation to celebrities and brands. Successfully advertised goods mean that inanimate objects become celebrity products. For a human celebrity well-knownness creates its own justification, while for commodities 'best-sellerdom' fulfils the same function: 'As a celebrity of the book world, a best seller has all the dignity and appeal of other *pseudo-events*' (Boorstin [1961] 1992: 164; emphasis added). A key aspect of celebrity is its ideological function as the human face of this otherwise alienating and tautological process. The *pseudo-event* is labelled *pseudo* because its meaning derives only from the media system for which it was created. Within advanced capitalist culture, the increased irrelevance of an object's use-value compared with its status as a sign to be circulated, creates a situation in which meaning is reduced to the recognition of how different objects and people share a relationship within a self-referential commodity system. Marx described the enigmatic 'theological subtleties and metaphysical niceties' (Marx [1887] 1983: 76) of the commodity form and Benjamin saw potential in the way photography helped to explode conventional and the traditional categories of experience. However, given the limitations of their historical perspective, neither could foresee the ever more pervasive and invasive ways in which commodity values would enter previously insulated realms of culture. Against their better hopes, the close alignment between media technologies and their commodified content has become increasingly resistant to any radical reinterpretation and re-appropriation by the masses. Despite their betrayed hopes, Benjamin's notion of *distraction*, Kracauer's concept of *Ratio*, Adorno's *culture industry*, McLuhan's *medium is the* (narcotic) *message* and *Debord's society of the spectacle* all retain their importance as terms with which to revive a critical interrogation of the current mediascape and the specific ideological role played by celebrity[1].

## Fame in the age of mechanical reproduction

Just as in Highland Park, Michigan, Henry Ford's Model Ts began rolling off newly-developed assembly lines in their thousands, starting around 1913, so the concept of mass production began to be applied to movie stars. The entertainment business became the first industry to treat the creation of fame as if it were an industrial process.

(Gritten 2002: 19)

Celebrity is an industry like many others. Celebrities are manufactured as attention-getting bodies, a process complicated but not negated by the fact that celebrities are human beings. Knownness itself is commodified within them.

(Gamson 1994: 105)

I am my own industry. I am my own commodity – Elizabeth Taylor

(cited in Gamson 1994: 85)

We can see from Gritten's above reference to Henry Ford's Model T (the first mass-produced motorcar) that the most significant distinguishing feature between modern celebrity and other modes of social renown from previous epochs is its newly industrialized nature. As Gamson then points out, the consequence of this industrialization is that aspects of social life that were formerly exclusively cultural, now become commodified. In Kracauer's previously discussed terms, rather than being 'permeated by cognition' our recognition and memory of key figures becomes increasingly open to manipulation by the culture industry. In opposition to the old-fashioned notion of heroes who were known for great deeds or qualities (whether moral or immoral), as human embodiments of the commodity system, celebrities differentiate themselves primarily through marginal differences in their personalities to the extent that the term 'personality' is now used as a synonym for celebrity. In his seminal essay 'The triumph of mass idols' (in Lowenthal 1961) Leo Lowenthal uses detailed empirical data from the USA between 1901 and 1941 to trace and contrast the rise of the entertainment industry's particular form of celebrity with the previous tradition of public figures drawn predominantly from the world of politics, industry or finance. The central point he makes is that at an empirically identifiable point in history, a large-scale cultural shift took place. *Consumption* became the overarching frame of reference for understanding public figures. The idols of consumption Lowenthal described represented an early example of the much more sophisticated role played by today's celebrities as embodiments of commodity values. The fact that the culture industry can be so open about this process is indicated by the very title of *American Idol* in which the critical import of Lowenthal's original phrase is effectively undermined by its blatant appropriation. More subtly, today's Reality TV, docudramas and so on are often based in sites of commerce (for example, *The Apprentice*, *The Hotel*, *The Restaurant*, and so on) while celebrity reportage in various forms frequently focuses upon the consumption patterns of their lead characters either explicitly (*MTV Cribs*) or implicitly (*The Osbournes*).

While active audience enthusiasts emphasize how viewers exercise their interpretive skills, Lowenthal's tone is unequivocal as he describes the ideologically driven consequences of the social shift he has outlined:

> While we found that around 1900 and even around 1920 the vocational distribution of magazine heroes was a rather accurate reflection of the nation's living trends, we observe today the hero-selection corresponds to *needs quite different from those of genuine information.* They seem to lead to a dream world of the masses who no longer are capable or willing to conceive of biographies primarily as a means of orientation and education. They receive information not about the agents and methods of social production but about the agents and methods of social and individual consumption. *During the leisure in which they read, they read almost exclusively about people who are directly, or indirectly, providing for the reader's leisure time.*
>
> (Lowenthal 1961: 116; emphasis added)

Here Lowenthal clearly prefigures two crucial aspects of the contemporary mediascape that the remaining chapters address in detail:

1   *A decreasing amount of media content can validly claim to be information in any substantive sense.* This point is particularly marked for Lowenthal by the fact that a significant part of his research was conducted during a period of two world wars – yet the media's output was still dominated by trivial content.
2   *This loss of informational content is exacerbated by the tautologically enframed nature of the data that is provided.* The sort of distance needed to assume a critical perspective upon what one is interpreting is curtailed by its systematic focus upon consumption to the exclusion of other cultural values.

Lowenthal is once again explicit in his emphasis upon the hermetically sealed, self-serving nature of the frame of reference so produced:

> Our content analysis not only revealed impressive regularities in the occurrence, omission, and treatment of certain topics, but also showed that these regularities may be interpreted in terms of the very same category of consumption which was the key to the selection of the biographical subjects. Consumption is a thread running through every aspect of those stories. The characteristics ... can all be integrated around the concept of the consumer.
>
> (Lowenthal 1961: 118)

Cultural populism frequently either fails to notice the tightly circumscribed nature of this severely limited frame of reference, or alternatively, recognizes it but fails to see it as a problem. The Introduction highlighted Barker's uncritical use of such commercial terms as *investment* to describe audience engagement. Elsewhere he also provides an admirably frank account of the extent to which, unlike critical theory, he values consumption for its own sake. Explaining his personal selection methods of holiday reading, Barker celebrates shallowness over depth:

> The novels all have one characteristic – they are fat enough (I buy by the inch thickness) and narratively driven enough, that I 'consume' them at great and undemanding speed ... the manner of my consumption is such that I can't even remember their titles. I am in real danger of re-buying the same books – though it would hardly matter since I probably could re-read most of the book and not recall even that I had read it before, let alone how it went. To 'consume' in this sense is to retain as little as possible.
>
> (Barker in Dickinson et al. 1998: 186)

'To consume … is to retain as little as possible' is hard to beat as a succinct summary of the parallel nature of the critical and populist accounts of contemporary consumer culture. For critical theorists, this form of consumption is the basis of mass docility rather than empowerment.

Lowenthal's analysis of the overall ideological effect of this combination of the banally shallow and the tautological fits closely with Adorno's account of the culture industry – for both writers, culture was traditionally at least partially insulated from commerce while now it plays an instrumental role in preparing populations for lives in industrialized society (as terms such as audience *investment* would seem to bear out): 'the routine and repetition characteristic of leisure-time activities serve as a kind of justification and glorification of the working day … the horizon is not extended to the realm of the unknown, but is instead painted with the figures of the known' (Lowenthal 1961: 135). Thus Benjamin's acknowledgement that media technologies psychologically train people for the shocks of urban life is reinforced at the further subtle level of the cultural values promoted by the pervasion of celebrity. However, while Benjamin hoped that, suitably trained, the masses would be politically empowered, for Lowenthal and other critical thinkers any such potential for empowerment is fatally undermined by the fact that the masses are diverted and *distracted* in a one-dimensional world of commodities: 'The large confusing issues in the political and economic realm and the antagonisms and controversies in the social realm – all these are submerged in the experience of being at one with the lofty and great in the sphere of consumption' (1961: 136).

Unlike Benjamin, for critical theorists, distraction produces a much more negative political outcome. Celebrities ideologically underpin the capitalist system because the relationship between the audience and the celebrity is intrinsically surface based. It is premised upon *abstract* desire – the venerated celebrity figure is greatly admired but intrinsically intangible. The audience thus relates to the celebrity as a human being but one that embodies abstract value – pre-designed for circulation. The notion of an embodied abstract quality may appear an oxymoron, but in much the same way, the relationship that contemporary consumers have with physical commodities is mediated by such abstract yet valuable signs as brand logos (once again the Nike swoosh being an archetypal example). Relating to the increasingly immaterial qualities of the desire/affection that celebrity helps to produce and maintain, Rojek points out that there are two basic differences between the traditional notion of 'renown' and the much more recent notion of 'celebrity'.

1 *Social Distance*: renown is traditionally associated with a person whose uniqueness is derived from their standing within a social network that has direct experience of their celebrated qualities. Celebrity in contrast involves a much greater social distance between the celebrity and the admirer, a distance that has evolved from the proscenium arch of the theatre to the separation provided by the cinema or television screen (see Chapter 8's discussion of the *ob*-scene [against-the-scene]).

2 *Transience*: celebrity is more closely associated than renown with the pace of change in social life. While some celebrities develop into 'idols' or 'icons', most have a short shelf-life related more to the fickleness of fashion than any personal talent.

Based upon *space* and *time*, these differences between *then* and *now* forms of fame illustrate Benjamin's account of the decline of aura and its loss of a unique point in both the physical and temporal realms. Celebrity's dual attributes of distance and transience are closely aligned to media technologies that are also inherently based upon these premises. The powerful force of abstraction that dominates both creates a deeply imbricated mix between the media's manufacture of celebrity and the preordained readiness with which it is received by a mass public trained for consumption of the short-lived and instantly forgettable (à la Barker's holiday reading).

Benjamin's political optimism rested in the masses being able to develop a form of radical political consciousness from their interactions with the mass media, but the likelihood of this occurring through his poorly defined notion of distraction would seem to be further away than ever given the much more highly sophisticated forms of distraction now employed by the culture industry. It is the seamless nature of the integration of personalities produced by the culture industry and the uncritical acceptance of the wider commodity culture that make Debord's *Society of the spectacle* such an important 'hinge' piece between relatively early analyses of media culture *then* and the latest theories of the *now*. The *spectacle* becomes such a powerful culture-forming entity because of its ability to assume the status of a general background against which social meaning is then constructed. Because there is a relative lack of critical recognition that our dominant cultural values are so deeply commodified *in advance* and why this should matter, culture consequently suffers from a loss of symbolic, non-commercial values. It becomes industrial in ever more immaterial yet effective/affective ways and celebrity plays an important supporting ideological role in this process.

## The components of celebrity

Rojek (2001) employs five main categories of celebrity to trace the evolution of celebrity:

1   Ascribed
2   Achieved
3   Attributed
4   Celetoid
5   Celeactor.

### Ascribed celebrity

This is the most traditional form. It relates to family lines and dynasties whether they are based upon historical royal families or newer forms such as US political dynasties – the Kennedys, the Bushes, and so on.

### Achieved celebrity

This form is based upon some sort of rare talent or skill and applies to fame that has been achieved in the face of competition with others in such realms as sports, the arts, business, and so on.

### Attributed celebrity

Attributed celebrity is closely related to Boorstin's *pseudo-event*. It is the purest and most tautological form of celebrity as it consists of being famous for being famous. It results from the disproportionate representation of an individual based upon the efforts and machinations of various media impresarios and intermediaries more than any particular talent. Due to its image-based largely content-free nature, the particular significance of attributed celebrity is the manner in which it seamlessly aligns itself with the similarly pure sign-value nature of modern commodities.

### The celetoid

> I propose celetoid as the term for any form of compressed, concentrated, attributed celebrity. I distinguish celetoids from celebrity because, generally, the latter enjoy a more durable career with the public ... Evanescence is the irrevocable condition of celetoid status.

> (Rojek 2001: 20, 22)

Such is the pace and breadth of celebrity's powerful incursion into popular culture that Rojek uses the term *celetoid* to describe an extreme form of attributed celebrity. Compared to conventional celebrities, celetoids assume even more temporary and manufactured forms. Their rise to fame is based upon contingent factors surrounding the entertainment industry rather than any innate talent and when those contingent factors lose their short-term salience, the original lack of talent hastens an inevitable decline into obscurity. The *celetoid* is a particularly useful concept to explain the generally short-lived and eminently disposable nature of the celebrities produced by the various genres of Reality TV.

## The celeactor

> The celeactor is a fictional character who is either momentarily ubiquitous or becomes an institutionalized feature of popular culture.
>
> (Rojek 2001: 23)

A sub-category of the *celetoid* is the *celeactor*. Its fictional status does not prevent it having a large media impact as illustrated by the success of such virtual stars as Lara Croft and the simulated band *Gorillaz*. Rojek uses the 'deaths' of two celeactors from British television, Inspector Morse and Victor Meldrew to illustrate the phenomenon as a media institution. The deaths became national media events despite their fictional status. The institutional nature of Victor Meldrew was underlined by the 45-minute obituary programme that preceded his television death – an honour Rojek points out that is normally reserved for members of the Royal Family. The blurring of the mediascape and the 'real world' implied by this prominent status given to mere celeactors is further highlighted by the death, subsequent to the publication of Rojek's book of the real-life actor, John Thaw, who played Inspector Morse. This event also received national media attention, although ironically, not as much as for the television character.

## Celebrity and the co-optation of the masses

> They are allowed to express themselves quite individually and idiosyncratically while the rest of the members of the population are constructed as demographic aggregates.
>
> (Marshall 1997: ix)

Max Weber's account of the historical development of modern society describes the way in which charisma is expunged from society through the increased application of rationalized, bureaucratic structures – there is a 'routinization of charisma' (Weber 1968: 246–54). Weber describes a growing social condition of disenchantment and loss of traditional cultural symbolism. In this context, celebrity can be viewed (like Benjamin saw the Hollywood star system) as a disenchanted reclaiming of art's ritualistic element – the fulfilment of the atavistic human need for narrative but in a heavily commodified and enervated form. It re-appropriates and re-enlists charisma in order to maintain the appearance of a society in which individuality is prized but also pre-inscribed with standardized, rationalized qualities (Kracauer's *Ratio*). This is in keeping with Adorno's claim that those entering show business already belong wholeheartedly to it: 'Talented performers belong to the industry long before it displays them; otherwise they would not be so eager to fit in' (Adorno and Horkheimer 1997: 122). Anyone with individual talent is already primed to adapt that talent to the requirements of a system that tolerates such individuality – but only in so far as a profitable place in the industry can be found for it: 'Anyone who resists can only survive by fitting in. Once his particular brand of deviation from the norm has been noted by the industry, he belongs to it as does the land-reformer to capitalism. Realistic dissidence is the trademark of anyone who has a new idea in business[2]' (Adorno and Horkheimer 1997: 122). Celebrity is thus appealing to the mass audience because it acts as a compensatory force for its own anonymity but it is, nevertheless, a negative and reactionary social phenomenon: it is constructed as a palliative for the anonymity of the mass rather than representing any intrinsic, worthwhile qualities of its own. The celebrity reasserts the importance of the individual – but merely at a rhetorical level. Individuality only exists in a sublimated, commodified form in what otherwise stubbornly remains a homogeneous mass society.

Although their subsequent interpretations may be radically different, advocates and detractors of the culture industry thesis agree about some of its basic processes. Both those who emphasize the empowerment of audiences and consumers, and those who argue they are disempowered, tend to agree that their participation is often active and self-conscious. For advocates of audience empowerment this is obvious; the culture industry thesis fails for them because the act of consumption does not stop alternative interpretations and meanings from being pursued alongside those desired by the dominant interests of the culture industry. In contrast, one of the most significant features of Adorno's analysis is the way in which consumers within the culture industry do indeed actively engage in the process of consumption but do so as an act of bad faith. They connive at their own oppression, by practising the 'magic' of commodities upon themselves: 'The triumph of advertising in the culture industry is that consumers feel compelled to buy and use its products even though they see through them' (Adorno and Hork-heimer 1997: 167). In shows like *American Idol,* a good illustration of this process is provided by the public's emotional (and financial in relation to the premium phone charges involved) *investment* in the progress of contestants presented as talented individuals. The pre-packaged nature of the cultural product into which such talent has to fit, however, is reflected by the fact that a number one hit is normally guaranteed before the eventual winner is first announced and then typically signed up to a lucrative contract with one of the music industry impresarios who double as judges. Rather than causing any criticism, if anything, these manoeuvres add to the enjoyment and significance of the event for the audience who are in on the trick, indeed, their *active* involvement is necessary for the trick to be so successful and profitable.

The irrational energies of the crowd/public to which charisma traditionally appealed is transformed by the culture industry into the much more easily controlled (and exploited) commodified phenom-enon of celebrity for the pre-primed mass-media audience. Weber talks in terms of charisma's qualities becoming: 'transferable, person-ally acquirable and attachable to the incumbent of an office or an institutional structure regardless of the persons involved' (cited in Marshall 1997: 21), a process which has little essential difference with contemporary celebrity given the increased importance given to attributed rather than achieved fame. Especially with such democra-tized forms such as Reality TV, but to a lesser but still significant extent with conventional celebrity, fame can now move readily from one person to another in a systemic process largely independent of the particular individuals involved. This is evident from a spate of 'conveyor belt' television formats that either 'discover'/produce new talent as already pointed out in relation to *American Idol,* or in instances such as *Reborn in the USA* where past celebrities have their careers recycled. The advent of democratized celebrity can be seen as an example of the Frankfurt School's concept of *repressive desublimation*[3]. This constitutes a return of the repressed whereby the original rejection of sublime, ecstatic charisma reappears in the desublimated and more easily socially controlled form of celebrity. Marshall points out, for example, how the pop singer: 'represents the physicality of the affective power of the people' (Marshall 1997: 197). In Weberian terms the potentially unruly crowd is simultane-ously energized by the pop star's charisma yet nevertheless still channelled into consuming his/her CDs, T-shirts and so on[4]. Per-haps the clearest example of the practical co-optation of audiences by pervasive commodification is provided by the 1999, 30-year anniversary revival of the Woodstock pop festival (*The Guardian*

1999). The original 1960s Woodstock pop festival was widely seen as a defining representation of hippy counter-cultural values. A largely spontaneous and free-form rock concert took place with volunteer food providers and a general share-and-share-alike atmosphere. The 1990s version fully exemplified the full meaning of the music *industry*. The event was corporately organized with expensive ticket prices and a large array of band-related merchandise. It culminated with a full-scale riot, looting, arson and the deployment of riot police. The purported catalyst of the riot was the perceived over-charging for fast food and bottled water. Audience empowerment in this instance evolved from the original anti-capitalist peace-advocating stance of the hippy ethic to a violent form of protest whose radical action was not to object to the commodity system – just its prices.

Rojek terms celebrities as 'the embodiments of surplus' (Rojek 2001: 31) and argues that they tap into: 'the surplus material and symbolic value that is inherent in the economic and moral frameworks governing everyday life' (Rojek 2001: 31). They represent human channels for the processing of the excessive material and symbolic capital produced within contemporary capitalism. In a form of semiotic potlatch[5] their frequently over-the-top transgressions against the moral codes of behaviour that constrain the rest of the non-celebrity masses act as a lightening conductor for the discontent of the masses that might otherwise arise. Citing the work of Morin as support, Rojek argues that celebrity can be understood in a way that overturns the Frankfurt School's culture industry thesis and its emphasis upon the deliberate manipulation of celebrities as commodities by capitalists. Instead, the public is said to be attracted to celebrities because they represent: 'the antithesis of a generalized psychological lack in ourselves' (Rojek 2001: 35). If this assertion is true, critical theory would suggest that this does not so much overturn the culture industry thesis, as reinforce its emphasis upon the escapist element of the masses' consumption of the mere images of otherwise unobtainable personal freedom and power not present in their everyday lives. Identification with the celebrity becomes a substitute for correcting the 'psychological lack' for which it is used as a temporary solution. Even for those directly enjoying fame: 'The agency of the celebrity is more often reduced to a privatized, psychologized representation of activity and transformation – it rarely moves into a clear social movement' (Marshall 1997: 244). The celebrity-fixated nature of such celebrity-based initiatives as *Live Aid* and *Live 8*, accounts well for the 'privatized, pyschologized representation of activity and transformation' that prevents the effective reform of ongoing geopolitical structural sources of inequality – an impasse reflected in the complaints of the celebrity campaigners themselves at the G8 summit of June 2007 (see Blair 2007).

## The culture of distraction

> Celebrities are part of the culture of distraction today. Society requires distraction so as to deflect consciousness from both the fact of structured inequality and the meaninglessness of existence following the death of God.
>
> (Rojek 2001: 90)

Rojek traces the way in which the narratives of celebrity frequently involve a decline and fall, followed by renewed success to closely mirror the major religious theme of redemption. The rise of celebrity as a religion substitute, the celeactor and all its kitsch implications, and the identification by the masses of celebrities as embodiments of surplus are all made possible by the loss of traditional aura initially identified and welcomed by Benjamin as a socially empowering phenomenon. Like Benjamin, Rojek interprets this loss of aura positively. The rise of celebrity is symptomatic of the decline of more traditional, ascribed forms of power to the extent that he claims: 'Celebrity culture and the celetoid are the direct descendants of the revolt against tyranny. The celeactor is a symptom of the decline of ascribed forms of power and a greater equality in the balance of power between social classes' (Rojek 2001: 29). However, the notion that celebrity draws its appeal from non-traditional sources does not provide persuasive grounds for optimism. It does not address the argument that celebrity culture merely presents an idealized version of the empowerment of the masses. In reality, this superficial appearance disguises the deeper and deeper imbrication of this new form of power with another tradition, albeit a newer one – commodity culture.

Despite arising from the masses and thereby having the potential to act as a countervailing force to previous forms of elite power, this argument does not move us much further than Benjamin's previously explored hopes for the masses. The technologically enabled, historically new quality of the mass also enables celebrity to be produced and set squarely within the operational requirements of a capitalist society and its particular form of elites – *plus ça change, plus c'est la même chose*. For a profit, capitalist society will meet the false needs of the masses it itself has generated but, as Marcuse (1968) points out, needs derived from beyond the commodity realm are marginalized by society's one-dimensional nature. More than this, the 'new' traditional elite's ideological manipulation of the public is at once stronger yet less explicit than previous forms of social power and domination. The media's exercise of power is more subtle, but no less effective.

Rojek's response to the argument that celebrity may simply provide a new take on Marx's conception of false consciousness is illuminating. He asserts that debates over the positive or negative social aspects of celebrity are fruitless and that the social impact of each individual celebrity needs to be assessed on the basis of its own individualized empirical study[6]. This claim is puzzling to the extent that its emphasis upon the non-generalizability of celebrity's impact somewhat contradicts Rojek's own admirably systematic approach to its various processes and effects. Furthermore, the illustrative example he uses to further his case raises more questions than answers. Thus, he argues in relation to Princess Diana's anti-land mines campaign and its success at raising public awareness that: 'Whether this outcome was the accomplishment of an essentially meretricious and self-serving personality is beside the point. The campaign helped to relieve suffering, and this relief could not have been accomplished so readily by other available means' (Rojek 2001: 91). From a more critical perspective, it is certainly not 'beside the point' nor politically insignificant if the only available means to ensure the greater equality of power between the social classes is dependent upon the manufactured and heavily mediated appeal of 'an essentially meretricious and self-serving personality'. Highlighting the significance of this lamentable lack of 'other available means' is a major and persistently relevant contribution of critical theory to today's mediascape.

Like Benjamin's attempt to find socialist potential within the then new medium of photography, optimistic interpretations of the way in which celebrity undermines traditional authority fail to undermine the central case of the culture industry thesis. They ultimately rest upon a notion of re-enchantment based upon either the transference of religious beliefs to the new field of celebrity or the ironical consumption and re-appropriation of celetoids/celeactors for the enjoyment of the masses. In the first instance, the mere transference of religious feelings from one realm to another represents exactly that, a transference rather than their radical undermining of the traditional practices that cultural populists are keen to claim as a positive function of celebrity. In the second case, such a transference may actually suggest that, rather than being subverted, traditional authority has in fact become transformed into a more deeply entrenched, yet less immediately obvious process of cultural commodification. Oppressive, traditional forms of authority and the focal points of their power were at least easily identified and subjected to various forms of open and covert resistance. In contrast, the simultaneously pervasive and invasive nature of commodity culture makes it subject to more, not less, manipulation by vested interests: the greater dispersal of traditional authority does not necessarily equate to a decrease in its power. Increased cultural commodification in such forms as celebrity would not seem to promise the 'greater equality in the balance of power between social classes' that Rojek seeks. The tyranny of tradition that Benjamin and later cultural populists have claimed is undermined by mass culture, has been replaced by a much more subtle and voluntaristic, but nevertheless, still freedom-denying regime of commodification all the more effective for its apparently radical properties.

## Voluntary servitude[7] and the knowing wink: practising commodity magic upon ourselves

> Why such widespread interest and consumption in the face of what ought to be extremely damaging, even shameful, revelations of technique? How does the celebrity system survive, even thrive, under these conditions?
>
> (Gamson 1994: 144)

> Nike and its advertising agency, Wieden and Kennedy, have built their reputation on advertising that is both distinctive and avoids claims of packaged individualism. Their ads have garnered public admiration because they seem to speak in a voice of honesty and authenticity. Paradoxically, their aura of authenticity has been a product of their willingness to address alienated spectators about feeling alienated from media-contrived images.
>
> (Goldman and Papson 1998: 3; emphasis added)

It has been argued that a strong element of the culture industry thesis is the way in which the surreal power of commodities relates less to overt ideological manipulation and much more to the way in which we practise their magic upon ourselves. Commodity culture is thus premised upon the profuse circulation of generic, frequently cross-referencing, image-based brands and the manufacture of desire, all to cultivate the type of individual consumer who will demand such products. What makes this process so insidiously effective is not that deception or *false consciousness* occurs but, rather more disturbingly, the way in which the individual consumer is voluntarily co-opted into the ideological process. In a closely related manner, Gamson (1994) describes how celebrity fans are sophisticated interpreters of the manufactured nature of postmodern celebrity and in fact become fans, of not only particular celebrities, but more importantly, the skilful management and reinvention of their images that takes place within the broader process of celebrity production. The fans thus positively identify with an abstract overarching atmosphere of manipulated inauthenticity of which particular celebrities are but individual manifestations. There is thus a twofold process that cultivates deep-rooted consumption practices in relation to celebrity culture:

1 *The consumer of celebrity culture identifies closely with the abstract generic notion of celebrity* – this makes him/her particularly predisposed or *culturally aligned* to more general commodity consumption.
2 *The consumer's identification process with the manipulative overarching celebrity superstructure is an active and ongoing one.* Pleasure is derived from being media literate enough to recognize the commercial nature of the manipulation and, rather than under-mining the whole celebrity structure, exposure of the process reinforces the effect.

Using the Nike company for their focus, Goldman and Papson (1996, and 1998) describe in detail the various processes by which the cultivation of commodity values in the individual takes place through this mode of active identification:

> The advertisers ... sensed that they must buffer Nike from the logic of the spectacle, the logic of commercialism, and the logic of advertising, even though they are enmeshed up to their ears in these logics ... Nike ads draw attention to metacommunica-tion in order to distance Nike from the processes of commer-cializing sport and thereby legitimize its own contradictory commercial practices which contribute to the corruption of sport.
>
> (Goldman and Papson 1998: 44)

The metacommunication Goldman and Papson refer to above relates to the way in which the Nike company incorporates a multilayered (for example, commercials within commercials), self-conscious aware-ness of the ultimately bad faith nature of their advertising. For example, within its own adverts, the company makes fun of its contribution to the commercialization of sport despite its simultane-ously contradictory message that Nike represents the true spirit of sport. Goldman and Papson term this element *the knowing wink* – possible resentment is disarmed by full acknowledgement of the manipulation taking place. The contemporary culture industry exhibits an inherently ambivalent social atmosphere to produce a paradoxical situation of *ambiguous transparency*. Products are adver-tised using deliberately obfuscatory or exaggerated language, yet often this process is deliberately left open for detection by the consumer so that it mirrors McLuhan's axiom, the medium is the message, to the extent that admiration of form supersedes attention to the ideological effect of its content: 'The citizen-consumer enjoys the satisfactions of being at the same time the bewitched, the bewitcher, and the detached student of witchcraft' (Boorstin [1961] 1992: 227). The complicity required from the audience is calibrated in the advertising process as enough to diminish any resistance to the commercial project, but not so complicit as to obtain a full critical view of the social process as a whole – which might lead to a fundamental questioning of the commodity project itself. Most troubling of all from Goldman and Papson's analysis is their highlighting of how critical resistance itself tends to be co-opted back into the process even if such a fundamental questioning does take place. They describe how Nike's 'aura of authenticity' is paradoxically created by their ability to manipulate as yet another element of the production of profit, the very feeling of alienation felt towards their own profession.

## Ideological manipulation: playing with aura

> Celebrity is a never-ending series of images to be read, so that even those whose truth appears to be that they are in control of their own manufacture cannot be known to be so and must also be read as essentially fictional. Reading the celebrity text from this angle is like encountering mirrors facing one another: there is no end-point, no final ground.
>
> (Gamson 1994: 158)

> As we have watched and marvelled in ways that used to be reserved for shocking fictions, the frames that separated the real and the contrived are continually being shattered, making us less able to distinguish the public from the private, friend from stranger, and legal due process from merely the televised version of crime, trial and punishment – in short, everything that frames our lives and gives it meaning and predictability.
>
> (Abt and Mustazza 1997: 49)

Gamson's above interpretation of the disorientating effects of celebrity and Abt and Mustazza's assessment of *Banality TV*'s (celebrity's democratized form) effect upon US culture contrasts sharply with Benjamin's savouring of photography's explosion of the everyday. Both suggest that the disorientating effects of the media inspired explosion do not result in a radical reappraisal of the status quo as Benjamin hoped. Rather, in the midst of these disorientating effects, reliable, formulaic and ultimately conservative tropes are enlisted to help reorientate what would be an otherwise confused viewing public. The ideological move thus consists of a simultaneous reliance upon the more mature media-induced fragmentation of meaning that began with photography along with the provision of commodified formulaic formats that provide reorientation. In this way ritual returns in a way unforeseen by Benjamin. Citing Carey's (1989) distinction between ritual and transmission modes of communication, Grindstaff points out that participants in chat shows are less concerned with the content of their contributions than the act of participation itself (once again, the medium is the message) – this makes them much more cooperative with the structuring needs of the producers. In contrast to those who seek to emphasize audience empowerment, this ritualistic element of *Banality TV* makes the individual a participant from whom dramatic performances of an often deeply personal nature are extracted, yet it treats them as easily interchangeable and replaceable elements in an essentially repetitive process. It is difficult to see how this commodification of people's vulnerability represents empowerment more than exploitation. Any short-term agency of the shows' guests or audiences rarely, if ever, successfully challenges the core production values of the genre. For example, even the most violent attempts to damage studio sets merely provides dramatic footage for programme previews, while any attempt to produce considered arguments can be cut short by the ubiquitous commercial break. It is important to emphasize that these excessively willing and active participants represent an extreme form of the generally much more passive viewing audience at home, whose various interpretive acts merely disguise their similar submission to the overarching structural framework within which the producers operate.

Above, Gamson cogently describes the fictional or unreal element of celebrity that makes it difficult to critically pin down. The *hyperreality* of the phenomenon is taken as proof of either its harmlessness or its neutrality. This domination of the event by the *pseudo-event* encapsulates in microcosm an important feature of wider celebrity culture. Issues such as what constitutes truth or meaningful, substantive content are subordinate to the enjoyment to be derived from consuming celebrity images. These can consist of unusual instances (pictures of Michael Jackson dangling his baby from a balcony, reports of Mel Gibson drunkenly ranting anti-semitic comments) or more structured interview situations (Martin Bashir's famous individual interviews with Michael Jackson and Princess Diana). Gamson succinctly describes how: 'celebrity watchers continually *ride* the belief/disbelief and fiction/reality axes but with no particular destination' (Gamson 1994: 178; emphasis in original). General celebrity watchers may indeed be more critical than the stereotypical image of the obsessed fan would imply because they frequently do not ultimately care about particular celebrities and may actually enjoy witnessing their downfall. But unlike the fan who is merely obsessed with one particular celebrity and who can therefore (hypothetically at least) discover their hero has feet of clay and so end their celebrity worship, generic celebrity watchers are much less easily dislodged from their devotion to celebrity's overall culture industry framework.

In *the knowing wink*, the grip of celebrity culture is tightened by the very revelations of artifice that one might otherwise assume would weaken its hold on the popular consciousness. Baudrillard (1983a) explains this in terms of the specific instance of the Watergate scandal as serving to hide the fact that US politics in general is pervasively corrupt. What superficially appears to be an incident that may undermine the credibility of the political system, in fact becomes a *pseudo-event* that reinforces the system by providing the false impression that such moral lapses are the exception rather than the rule: 'It is always a question of proving the real by the imaginary; proving truth by scandal ... Everything is metamorphosed into its inverse in order to be perpetuated in its purged form' (Poster 1990, cited in Gamson 1994: 171). At best, celebrity watchers seem resigned to the apparent difficulty of achieving a stable critical perspective within the cultural industry's manipulative hall of mirrors, while at worst, their enjoyment of the mirror show precludes normatively evaluating it. Rather than fuelling criticism of its artificially manufactured nature, any deconstruction of the celebrity production process, tends merely to promote further enjoyable consumption of celebrity by providing yet more material for gossip. It is this circular and self-augmenting nature of celebrity culture that makes it such a close ideological fit with the wider commodity society that contains it – premised as it is upon the expansive circulation of signs as an end in itself.

## Celebrity: the seductive occurrence

Our experience tends more and more to become tautology – needless repetition of the same in different words and images ... Celebrity is made simple familiarity, induced and re-enforced by public means. The celebrity is therefore the perfect embodiment of tautology: the most familiar is the most familiar.

(Boorstin [1961] 1992: 60–1)

The ascension of the cinema idols, the masses' divinities, was and remains a central story of modern times – it still counterbalances all political or social events. There is no point in dismissing it as merely the dreams of the mystified masses. It is a seductive occurrence that counterbalances every productive occurrence.

(Baudrillard 1990a: 95)

In the context of mass-media audiences, Marshall distinguishes between the *admiring identification* cinema encourages and television's *sympathetic identification* (Marshall 1997: 154–6). Admiring identification is a useful way of conceptualizing Hollywood's ability to domesticate and pacify art's originally ritualistic/magical/contemplative quality (as identified in Benjamin's Essay and Baudrillard's notion of a 'seductive occurrence'). Sympathetic identification appositely describes televisions's more homely contribution to the role of celebrity. Television's superficially more domesticated quality, however, should not distract one's attention from the crucial ideological work it nevertheless unobtrusively manages to carry out. Its primary status as an overwhelmingly domestically situated medium, in conjunction with its close links to the advertising industry, means that it plays a major political function linking the expansion of capitalism and increasingly privatized and domesticated forms of consumption. The tautological element of celebrity that it symbiotically shares with the equally tautological commodity form is much more evident in television than cinema. Aura is still present enough in cinema to allow great performances to create *stars*, while in television discussion tends to centre more upon *personalities*. In our previous discussion of Kracauer's work (particularly his comments about the essential contiguity of photographic images), we saw how photography laid the groundwork for the media's tendency to privilege contingent detail over more substantial content and the subsequent naturalization within a widely mediated culture of a pervasion of discrete, fragmented images with only loose conceptual connections. Television speeds this process up by technologically facilitating the seamless joining together of photographic output in a continuous flow while at the same time slowing down and deepening the amount of attention that can be given to contingent detail in such trivia-based personality-dominated formats as chat shows and lifestyle programmes.

The role of the television personality combines with the structure of programmes to reinforce televisions role as an ideological support for commodities. In a domesticated, tamed version of Weber's charismatic authority, personality traits become unique selling points. They play their part within several additional layers of commodification. For example:

1 The programme's celebrity presenter literally becomes an individual brand.
2 Presenters work within a show that as an entity is itself branded and franchised.
3 The strength of the programme brand is used to sell other brands during the commercial breaks.

4   During the programme, celebrity guests frequently 'plug' their latest performance/book and so on.
5   Even the various experts used in various chat shows tend to be partially identified as the author of a best-selling self-help book.

Programme structures themselves frequently involve fragmented narratives that have less in common with the more unified artistic format of a movie[8] and more with the disjointed, imagistic, and relatively shallow narrative presentation of commodities found in advertising. This occurs in a manner similar to Kracauer's comments about illustrated magazines and their contribution to a 'strike against understanding'. *The Oprah Winfrey Show*, for example, 'constructs the conception of currency; the issues being discussed are of vital concern for that particular moment' (Marshall 1997: 132). Currency in this instance, however, does not just only refer to the topicality of the show's content. Like Barker's use of the term 'investment', *currency* becomes an apposite term for the connotations it has with the commercial values underpinning of-the-moment, fashionable content. Premised upon the same short-term values as the fashion industry, topical items and news stories readily present themselves for repackaging and further reselling in 'new' formats even though there is little change in their true content.

## Conclusion

Contemporary celebrity plays a crucial part in the naturalization of the strange and metaphysically ambiguous commodity form described by Marx as 'abounding in metaphysical subtleties and theological niceties'. The Hollywood star system played an important role in the industrial manipulation of charisma, but as Benjamin recognized, it still contained vestigial forms of art's ritualistic properties – the cult of beauty that grew up around its most famous faces. Newer forms of celebrity embodied in *Banality TV*, to which we now turn, provide a much more sophisticated way of further taming the aura Benjamin saw being pumped out by media technologies, 'like water from a sinking ship'. New forms of celebrity translate the concept of distraction Benjamin sought to invest with radical potential into a process that serves to hide the media's sponsorship of an ultimately irrational (but highly rationalized) reversal of human/object relations (an image-based irrationality explored in depth in Chapter 8). For example, the fame-for-fame's sake element of today's celebrity produces the format inflation of Reality TV's endless variations upon the same basic theme. The particular qualities and achievements of the competitors (human relations) become less important than the competitive element of the formats themselves (object relations). Perhaps even more important than this element of competition between and within formats, however, is the transparency with which the production process of celebrity-hood is exposed as part of the viewing experience. While at one level the celebrity figure may help to distract attention away from the ideological nature of the commodity form, the forensic way in which the production of celebrity itself is uncovered for all to see can perhaps be seen as a type of double bluff: if there is anything so significant to hide, then why are we so happy to show you everything?

The ideological aspect of the production of celebrity thus becomes an organic part of the audience's viewing process and ironically difficult to spot because of its very obviousness (as previously pointed out, McLuhan once said 'whoever discovered water wasn't a fish'). A self-perpetuating circle thus closes itself off from critically minded questioning through the excessive transparency and explicitness of a society dominated by an *obscene* form of images explored in Chapter 8. By providing openly forensic accounts of the production of individual celebrities, the culture industry escapes equally close scrutiny of the wider social aspects that go into creating the appearance of the celebrity system as an apparently natural and even inevitable social order. This inevitability is presented either on the grounds of talent so great that it can only be imitated by other extraordinarily gifted individuals (*Bend it like Beckham*), or pure chance beyond anyone's control[9]. In either scenario, a potentially critical understanding of celebrity production is displaced by a distracted fascination with the contingent and contiguous details of celebrities themselves.

Both celebrity culture and the closely related personality-based politics, share the exposure of people's private lives as a distraction from more substantive structural issues – political, social and economic questions – emotional affect replaces political effect. As Benjamin pointed out, the public is a critic, but an absent-minded one. The following chapters explore the rise of democratized forms of celebrity within *Banality TV* and show how rational discourse is displaced by the privileging of traumatic events and individual opinion to the extent that Dovey claims: 'in Foucauldian terms we are witnessing the evolution of a new "regime of truth" based upon the foregrounding of individual subjective experience at the expense of more general truth claims' (Dovey 2000: 25). The following chapters suggest that a well-developed political awareness of the ideological role played by the seemingly trivial is supplanted by pleasure in the false intimacy and everyday banality of the trivial itself (Langer's *Other News*). It is now time to examine the notion of *Banality TV* to explore what the culture industry does best – encouraging the diner to be satisfied with the menu.

# 7

# *Banality TV*: the democratization of celebrity

## Introduction

> How is it that *the pre-digested detail of banal everyday life* has become the ratings phenomenon of late nineties UK prime-time?
>
> (Dovey 2000: 1; emphasis added)

> At a time when television and the media are increasingly unable to give an account of the world's (unbearable) events, they have discovered daily life and *existential banality* as the most deadly event, the most violent news, the very scene of the perfect crime. And indeed it is. People are fascinated, fascinated and terrified by the indifference of the Nothing-to-say, Nothing-to-do, by the indifference of their very existence.
>
> (Baudrillard 2005: 182; emphasis added)

Baudrillard argues that essentially empty, tautological and vacuous media content can still be fascinating in an absorbing rather than revealing sense. It produces much interpretive activity (the focus of cultural populism), but from a critical perspective this activity reflects, rather than challenges, cognition's enervation at the hands of *Ratio*. *Banality TV* resonates with Dovey and Baudrillard's cogent phrases 'the *pre-digested* detail of banal everyday life' and 'existential banality' – descriptions of the excessively personalized and trivial approach, tone and content of entertainment programmes that have now also become standard features of news programmes to the extent that *factual entertainment* is now used as the title of television company departments (for example, the UK's Channel 4). The sentiment behind the term *Banality TV* is already evident in Kracauer's comments about the cultural films that prefigured Reality TV. More critical than McLuhan's enthusiastic embracing of the media's *mosaic* quality, Kracauer is scathingly unambiguous about the banality of its cultural consequences in everyday practice:

The monotony of this hodgepodge is the just revenge for its inconsequentiality, which is heightened by the thoughtless way the individual sequences are combined into a mosaic ... almost all of them avoid the most urgent human concerns, *dragging the exotic into daily life rather than searching for the exotic within the quotidian* ... From horse breeding to carpet weaving, no out-of-the-way subject is safe from the clutches of the popular pedagogy of cultural films.

(Kracauer 1995: 311; emphasis added)

The political implications of celebrity's pervasion is that all political action becomes subject to the same indifference to truth content that, depending upon your viewpoint, produces at worst a passive, subordinated population or, at best, a passive population whose very inertia becomes its only hope of assuming radical status as Baudrillard (1983b and 1990b) argues somewhat tongue-in-cheek. Formats like Reality TV and docudramas play an ideological role in the obfuscation of this essential passivity. Whereas the conventional documentary was reflective and investigative, this new form is revelatory and observational. The superficially participatory nature of these shows merely either distracts attention from the inertness of the viewing public or offers the false promise that meaningful participation is freely available to all. More generally, the apparently most transgressive shows such as *Jerry Springer* actually demonstrate *the paradox of conservatism* for the manner in which they routinely caricature and commodify the whole notion of transgression itself. Their ritualistic and systematic formats are complete with sermonizing elements (for example, Jerry Springer's homily at the end of each show). Of key concern for critical theory is the fact that this ideological function has important social implications beyond the immediate sphere of entertainment.

Drawing from the critical heritage outlined in Part 1, *Banality TV* is the phrase used to refer to a large swathe of media content derived from highly formulaic but predominantly unscripted programmes. They share a sustained ethos of *revelation* and *explicitness* (explored in more detail in the next chapter) but are both ultimately hamstrung from a critical point of view by their structural constraints. *Banality TV* thus describes the cultural manifestation of McLuhan's *medium is the message* and Baudrillard's yet more radical contention that modern communications technologies actually fabricate non-communication. The dominant value they sponsor is the act of transmission rather than any meaning behind that transmission. *Banality TV* incorporates three main categories – lifestyle programmes, chat shows, and Reality TV. Two key criticisms arise from *Banality TV* as the latest manifestation of the *society of the spectacle*.

1   *The fascination it generates is a dumb fascination much more akin to McLuhan's notion of narcosis than Benjamin's hopes of empowerment.* In authentically seductive and symbolically rich forms of exchange, social meaning is derived from the interplay of unpredictable interactions. Unlike the pre-encoded nature of the culture industry's products, empowered play is indeterminate and truly fascinating. In *Banality TV*, open-ended and unpredictable outcomes are expunged from culture (just as Benjamin described aura being 'pumped out like water from a sinking ship') by the combined effects of the dumb narcotic fascination of the screen and the formulaic nature of the content: 'Any system that is totally complicit in its own absorption such that signs no longer make sense, will exercise a remarkable power of fascination' (Baudrillard 1990a: 77)[1].

2   *The banality of non-symbolic media content seeps into areas of social life traditionally devoted to more substantial symbolic cultural practices.* Critical resistance is increasingly replaced by uncritical engagement with Reality TV as a defining and normalizing frame of reference. Examples of this include: Reality TV-influenced academic studies of parliamentary and television voting behaviour[2], and a selection model for the granting of Western university scholarships to students from the developing world – *Scholar Hunt: Destination UK*[3].

For critical purposes, Kracauer's crucial phrase is his claim that 'urgent human concerns' are avoided by 'dragging the exotic into daily life rather than searching for the exotic within the quotidian'. In today's mediascape his comment pertains to:

*Chat Shows* – the appearance of celebrities drags the exotic into daily life. Their star status is displayed in a highly structured and staged demonstration of how they are both like us with their everyday, down-to-earth nature, but also part of a lifestyle that the rest of us can only dream about. Non-celebrities provide the flip-side of this made-for-admiration exoticism. 'Trailer-trash' with their bizarre personal problems and family situations are presented for judgement by 'normal standards' (hence the ritualistically aggressive questioning by members of the audience and the typically strong moral judgments made by the presenter).

*Reality TV* – the exotic is found within the quotidian *but in a pre-packaged manner*. Celebrities/celetoids are created from the 'ordinary' masses and Reality TV formats are part of a systematized approach that ensures that 'urgent human concerns' either still remain unaddressed or distorted through the simplifying lens of the Reality TV paradigm.

*Lifestyle TV* – the exotic is dragged into everyday life in various simultaneously instructional and aspirational programmes dealing with topics ranging from cooking to property-buying overseas. Celebrity frequently plays an important role as seen in the rise of celebrity chefs and the prominence of recognizable presenters in exotic locales (Dunn 2006). The 'urgent human concerns' of cultural exchange and sociable eating remain avoided as travel for the vast majority grows more predictably homogeneous and fewer people than ever before actually cook at home themselves.

In cultural populism, specific differences in format and content provide the basis for the academic study of precise modes of reception and active audience interpretations. In marked contrast, critical theory argues that the most important feature of these formats is their essential similarity. Whatever apparent particularity and differences can be found, only exist to be effectively and profitably subsumed by a defining cultural climate of commodification and trivialization. The dominant, shared quality of all the various celebrity and non-celebrity, talent and non-talent-based *Banality TV* forms is the pacification of 'urgent human concerns' within the media's domineering tele-frame of formulaic predictability. For example, underlying the 'natural' and seemingly spontaneous interviews of chat shows is an underlying commercialism. Invariably the interview is linked to a plug for a recent or forthcoming project whether it be a book, movie or album. *Banality TV* also frequently involves voyeuristic, non-seductive emotional *money shot* (see below) derived from watching contestants/interviewees compete to expose themselves both figuratively and literally. The main difference between the celebrity and non-celebrity versions is largely limited to their differing ability to utilize their revelations for commercial gain. To the extent that non-celebrities can do so successfully, they may become either celetoids (the forgotten past winners of *Big Brother*-type shows) or celebrities in their own right (for example, the remembered winner of 2002's *Big Brother 3* – Jade Goody). Unpredictability does exist to the extent that it is not always possible to predict in advance who will successfully make the transition, but the defining, systematic commercial framework within which such maneuvers take place exists as a highly sophisticated form of Adorno's *culture industry*.

Illustrating Adorno's emphasis upon the rise of the general at the expense of the particular, an important aspect of Reality TV's banality stems from the fact that, in both celebrity and non-celebrity elimination programmes, the general format tends to be more important than the characters themselves. Fascination over trivial details is then normalized through the cumulative effect of further programmes consisting of edited highlights, post-programme discussions, and extended live feeds that, in the extended coverage of *Big Brother* by UK cable television channel, *E4*, includes the opportunity to watch people sleeping under duvets. *Banality TV* exemplifies McLuhan and Baudrillard's development of Adorno's persistent emphasis upon the systematic, industrialized nature of mediated culture. In their analyses, such predigested banal becomes a symptom of the way in which media *form* dominates its *content*. Thus, both Adorno and McLuhan scathingly rejected the purported differences between commodities. Adorno argued that: 'the difference between the Chrysler range and General Motors is basically illusory strikes every child with a keen interest in varieties' (Adorno and Horkheimer 1997: 123), while McLuhan claimed that the significance of industry (whether physical or cultural) is its assembly-line nature. The actual content that comes off those assembly lines is largely irrelevant: 'In terms of the ways in which the machine altered our relations to one another and to ourselves, it mattered not in the least whether it turned out cornflakes or Cadillacs' (McLuhan [1964] 1995: 23). In a similar fashion, Baudrillard's whole media theory is based upon the related contention that media fabricate non-communication in which the expression of meaningful *symbols* becomes less important than the technically efficient transmission of *signs* (as emptied-out symbols). Critical media theory's focus upon content's subjugation to form directly opposes the frequent tendency of cultural populism to substitute the description and categorization of the culture industry's products for their critical interrogation and evaluation.

## Emancipation and Empowerment: the case of the docudrama

> ... there is an inherent conservatism in the structure of such programmes and ... this conservatism has something in common with Foucault's 'spiral of power and pleasure' as it is played out in tabloid culture. Here we encounter both 'the pleasure that comes from a power that questions, monitors, watches, spies, searches out, palpates, brings to light'; as well as 'the pleasure that kindles at having to evade this power, flee from it, fool it or travesty it'.
>
> (Dovey 2000: 118)

Both Gamson (1997) and Dovey (2000) question the emancipatory potential of *Banality TV* because it tends to be premised upon a process of titillation for subsequent condemnation. This provides an immediately black and white ideological closure that would seem to leave little room for nuanced or alternative interpretations. Indeed, Dovey forcefully argues that: 'there is an astonishing concurrence between dominant ideologies of late twentieth-century capitalism and narratives of personal recovery and growth' (Dovey 2000: 121). Dovey is largely pessimistic about the potential for television to escape the commodity form but he sees at least some potential in such formats as the UK's BBC Two's *Video Nation* in the mid-1990s which provided short (two minutes on average) first-person accounts from a range of UK citizens. The strength of this format is its non-commodified, unresolved nature but its limited impact can be assessed from its tiny (and now defunct) contribution to the overall scheduling of British television. A much more significant part of the schedules, however, is taken up by the recent spate of docudrama formats that in a later evolution merged with celebrity-orientated formats.

A critical account of such programmes centres upon their innately commodified nature. The analyses of Dovey (2000) and Langer (1998) point to the way in which docudramas are constructed as portraits of the inner workings of the new service economy. Reality TV becomes a *discursive mobilization* geared towards helping viewers locate themselves amid the disorientating flows of advanced capitalism (they are an uncritical, commodified manifestation of Jameson's [1991] more radical call for new strategies of *cognitive mapping* with which to orientate oneself for resistance *not* accommodation). As in Lowenthal's previously cited analysis, the dominant frame of cultural reference in Reality TV is one of consumption. Non-celebrity docudramas, for example, frequently focus upon working life within the service industries, while conspicuous consumption is a consistently prominent theme within celebrity-based versions – in either case commodity values are foregrounded. For Langer, Reality TV serves to naturalize further the dominant meaning system of capitalism among a large swathe of middle-class society formerly relatively insulated from the vagaries of global capitalism but now vulnerable to its changeable and flux-ridden nature. Dovey's account reinforces Langer's as he points out that the frequent siting of such programmes in commercial spaces gives them the tenor of:

'a new ethnography of consumerism, leisure and aspirational desire ... In the world of docu-soap all human endeavour occurs in a zone that is enforced holiday camp, airport and mega-mall rolled into one – a zone where the aspirational desires of consumption and mass social mobility are played out.'[4]

(Dovey 2000: 140)

Docudramas seldom contain a serious argument or rational purpose. Like Barker's holiday reading, they typically consist of images and situations to be consumed quickly and uncritically. This resonates with Sontag's (1979) criticism that you cannot agree or disagree with a photograph – it is simply not in the nature of the medium's tautological explicitness. Similarly, we have also seen how Kracauer took pains to emphasize photography's privileging of contingent detail over substantive meaning. These analyses of photographic grammar serve to highlight some of the underlying factors within docudramas as illustrated by Dovey's comment about the docu-soap of life on board a luxury liner – *The Cruise*:

> we are not called upon to agree or disagree with the proposition that 'This is life cruise ship' ... There is no argument about the world being advanced here – there is just its narrativisation. Each docu-soap is its own 'spectacle of particularity'; its referencing of the public world does not extend beyond its denotation. The docu-soap is inert as public form.
>
> (2000: 151)

Dovey and Langer's criticisms can be reinterpreted as a response to the deep imbrication of television's fragmented visual grammar with the similarly decontextualized nature of the culture industry. We see here how Debord's concept of the spectacle comes together with Adorno's notion of the removal of the tension between the general and the particular to produce a deracinated 'spectacle of particularity' – particularity that can only be experienced as a spectacle divorced from any wider social meaning. The context and meaning that does exist in Reality TV formats, like commodities, comes in a highly packaged form – in this case through close editing. As we saw in Adorno's analysis of the culture industry's production of commodities, media content is made for short-term consumption so that fresh consumption can be stimulated for further profitability. Dovey highlights two crucial aspects of this approach. First, there is little for the audience to discover that is not already presented by the omniscient narrator. Secondly, the editing's constant pace and democratic focus means that all the content tends to appear of equal value – this marks a radical (but not in any political sense) departure from documentary's previous strong moral element: the demand for narrative action overrides the competing claims of any ethical frameworks or moral messages.

## Banality TV and symbolic loss

> Reality TV always flirts with disaster, both in the sense that danger, contingency, the randomness of violence, and the precariousness of life are its staples and in the sense that what it represents may prompt or demand a response that exceeds its frame ... Many natural catastrophes seem to fit perfectly within the tele-frame; sympathy and charity are the best we can do, we may as well let them be tele-mediated. But those among

> the ruins have other needs, pose other demands, raise other
> questions – if their voices can elude or exceed the tele-frame.
>
> (Nichols 1994: 18)

A consideration of Nichols's specific conception of Reality TV serves
to introduce the next chapter's discussion of the increasing merging
of entertainment and news – Langer's (1998) *Other News*. In *Blurred
Boundaries* (1994), Nichols uses the term Reality TV, in a specific
sense, to refer to the widespread conflation of previously distinct
fiction and non-fictional television formats – a blurring of the
boundaries that formerly existed between entertainment-orientated
content and journalism's traditionally more serious coverage of
current affairs. His above comment describes the way in which the
media frame tames the explosive potential of the camera hoped for
by Benjamin. Rather than 'in the midst of its debris and ruins' being
able to 'calmly and adventurously go travelling', Nichols points out
(presciently in the context of the later tragic events of Hurricane
Katrina and its disastrous aftermath) that 'those among the ruins
have other needs' beyond tele-mediation. His interpretation of the
camera's mediation of reality suggests a betrayal of Benjamin's hopes
that the camera would enable radical insights into the social
condition of the masses. Instead, the camera's ability to reveal is
co-opted by the culture industry to provide objects of stimulation for
the passive voyeurism of viewers absorbed by the tele-frame, again,
counter to Benjamin's hopes for the masses to absorb the media
rather than vice versa.

The *blurred boundaries* Nichols thus refers to in his work can be
understood as a consequence of capitalist society's remarkably adept
ability to take the grounded materiality of reality and its innate
tension between the general and the particular and reduce them to
abstract formulas and models that underpin the subsequent blurring
of social boundaries. In this context, Eagleton builds upon Marx and
Engels's evocative image that in capitalism 'all that is solid melts into
air' and Kracauer's concept of *Ratio*, to suggest that: 'Capitalism ...
for all its crass materialism, is secretly allergic to matter. No
individual object can fulfill its voracious appetite as it hunts its way
restlessly from one to the other, dissolving each of them to nothing
in doomed pursuit of its ultimate desire ... It is a culture shot
through with fantasy, idealist to its core' (Eagleton 2003: 165). In *The
Perfect Crime* (1996a), Baudrillard similarly speaks of this capitalist
ability to eviscerate particularity from reality. He writes in terms of a
murder in which no trace can be found of 'the corpse of the real'
(Baudrillard 1996a: i). The mediation of reality explicitly acknowledged in the very phrase Reality TV creates an ersatz Debordian/
Boorstinian reality in an anodyne form suitable for consumers. This
undermines Kracauer's previously cited opposition to 'dragging the

exotic into daily life rather than searching for the exotic within the quotidian' (Kracauer 1995: 311). Reality TV, despite appearing as a naturalistic guise that does not have a meta-narrative, performs its important ideological role by taming the potentially transgressive. The fact that cop shows are so popular in the Reality TV format is perhaps reflective of its own role as a policing element in culture. It creates: 'This meta-story, the *ideological reduction* [that] makes the strange *banal*' (Nichols 1994: 46; emphasis added).

According to Nichols, the central element of documentary television missing in Reality TV is 'Adherence to the principles of rhetoric that govern *the discourses of sobriety*' (Nichols 1994: 47; emphasis added). The phrase *discourses of sobriety* refers to the attempt to understand the world using factual/political resources rather than focusing upon trivial and banal constructs. We will see in the next chapter's examination of the *Other News*, and its recourse to the trivial, its conflation of current affairs with celebrity affairs and so on, that such a rational principle of rhetoric is regularly undermined in mainstream media coverage. Nichols argues that particularly striking images can momentarily exceed the enframing power of the tele-frame by managing to assume a metonymic function – even if only momentarily, an image can achieve a wider political significance over and above its nominal content. For example, he uses the case of Rodney King as an example of how his infamous beating by LAPD police, fortuitously filmed by a member of the public, could not be contained by the conventional bromides of the media. It acted as a catalyst for widespread rioting in Los Angeles because it represented a focal point for all those other unrecorded incidents of police brutality disproportionately suffered by black people in the USA.

In the following chapter we discuss the extent to which similar metonymic excess was found in the Abu Ghraib pictures, representing as they do for many people in the Islamic world an unusually explicit (in all senses of the word) view of the insouciance of American power. Unfortunately, however, the shock effect of images from events such as Abu Ghraib and the aftermath of Hurricane Katrina is often temporary. The ability to exceed the normal powerful media frame is the exception not the norm. Periodic exceedings of the tele-frame have radical political potential but that potential is vulnerable to subsequent pacification. For example, the immediate post-hurricane devastation in New Orleans clearly demonstrated the race-based socio-economic inequality of life in contemporary America, but the ultimate political fallout was relatively slight. Nichols demonstrated the predictive power of critical theory by rhetorically asking, well before the Hurricane Katrina tragedy: 'Has the shape of public response, including our own outrage, followed the contours that transformative social praxis requires, or does it spill into the Manichean, localized, and dramatic channel marked out for it by the mainstream media?' (Nichols 1994: 19). Prefiguring post-Katrina government failures in New Orleans and a subsequent inability in the rest of the USA to maintain high levels of interest in the plight of the victims, Nichols points out that: 'Public response rises and falls in relation to the pulsations and rhythms of media coverage itself' (Nichols 1994: 20). His analysis resonates with Baudrillard's cogent phrase, '*the mortal dose of publicity*' (Baudrillard 1981: 174) – simply being included in the media's frame of reference means that *your* message becomes subordinate to *their* medium (to paraphrase McLuhan) and its agenda.

Although sharing Benjamin's emphasis upon the profound qualitative changes in society that are produced by the exponential increase in the quantity of mediated output, Jameson (1998) replaces Benjamin's positive interpretation of the decline of aura with a much more negative assessment. He furthers our understanding of capitalism's powers of abstraction with his use of the term *dialectic of reification* to refer to the way in which the colonization of the cultural field by commodity values takes place at an ever deeper level but in an increasingly immaterial form: the strength of the commodification process stems from its hard-to-pin-down nature. Jameson relies upon digestive imagery to describe the Enlightenment's forces of secularization and realism as early phenomena in an ongoing historical process which:

> seizes on the properties and the subjectivities, the institutions and the forms, of an older pre-capitalist world, in order to strip them of their hierarchical or religious content ... what is dialectical about it comes as something like a leap and an overturn from quantity into quality. With the intensification of the forces of reification and their suffusion through ever greater zones of social life (including individual subjectivity), it is as though the force that generated the first realism now turns against it and devours it in its turn.
>
> (Jameson 1998: 148)

Jameson's analysis resonates not only with, once again, Marx and Engels's 'all that is solid melts into air, all that is holy is profaned', but also Benjamin and McLuhan's identification of the cultural tipping point at which the quantity of mechanically reproduced images leads to a qualitative shift in social relations.

In an additional development of this chapter's food theme (see below) it is interesting to note again the language of digestion that frequently occurs in descriptions of capitalism's ability to absorb more overtly symbolic cultural forms. For Nichols, like Jameson,

*Banality* TV is characterized by its all-consuming appetite – a generic, society-defining quality we have previously encountered in Debord's *The Society of the Spectacle*.

> Reality TV's perverse kinship with traditional documentary film, network newscasting, and ethnographic film, lies in its ability to absorb the referent. The digestive enzymes of reality TV (its distracting quality and spectacle, its dramatic story lines and self-perpetuation) break the referent down into palatable confections that do not represent an absent referent so much as cannibalize and assimilate it into a different type of substance.
>
> (Nichols 1994: 46)

Nichols is describing here a key aspect of *Banality TV* that stems directly from Adorno's account of the culture industry's ability to reduce the particular to the more easily manipulable elements of an determining general order. Without wishing to pursue the digestive metaphor in too vivid detail, *Banality TV* consumes reality and passes out the referent in an altered, deeply passive form.

The Manichaean channel Nichols refers to above, vividly describes the black and white duality that news coverage encourages at the expense of Baudrillard's call for more seductively ambiguous categories of meaning. Thus in most *Banality TV* formats, the 'goodies' are authority figures and the 'baddies' are a range of nefarious lawbreakers. The nominally more serious news *industry* invariably also proves adept at maintaining this comfortably familiar narrative framework, even when the narrative positions are reversed. Hence, on the relatively rare occasions when gross wrong-doing by institutional forces is exposed – the police now become the 'baddie' rogue elements and the victim can be an innocent member of a formerly threatening urban underclass. Such a reversal can occur: 'without necessarily changing the localized, game-like focus. *The surrounding context in which the interpretive struggle takes place – from what constitutes appropriate use of force to how crime and poverty can be eradicated ... remains untouched*' (Nichols 1994: 21; emphasis added). This represents the political manifestation of McLuhan's axiom, *the medium is the message*. The potentially explosive insights into inner-city race relations created by media events such as the Rodney King incident and Hurricane Katrina are neutralized by the media's ability to frame the story with its own particular grammar. Cultural populism and its emphasis on audience empowerment fails to confront adequately the full implications of the media's relative impermeability to interpretive strategies that will ultimately challenge the media framing process itself. No matter how superficially sophisticated such interpretations may at first appear, they are invariably circumscribed in advance by the powerfully defining structures of meaning media institutions are able to generate.

In this context of the media's framing power, *Banality TV* represents a mature development of the consequences of aura's irrevocable decline. Benjamin praised the early stages of this decline, but in its full maturity one finds much darker, more alienating aspects:

> Everything is up for grabs in a gigantic reshuffling of the stuff of everyday life. Everything, that is, is subject to interpretation by television as a story-telling machine ... The struggle for interpretive hegemony that ensues (who can make their story stick?) relocates social experience within *highly charged webs of significance* that only remain as stable as the persuasive power supporting them.
>
> (Nichols 1994: 43; emphasis added)

Here we see a close match between Nichols's 'gigantic shuffling of the stuff of everyday life' and Dovey's 'pre-digested detail of everyday life'. The critical point (in both senses) they share is a sense of the *dis*empowerment experienced by those facing the media as everyday life is processed into the media's terms. Whatever interpretive strategies audiences attempt to adopt are always reacting to this prior structural fact that interpretations are based upon the output of a story-telling *machine* rather than a pool of raw information generated as spontaneously and with as little bias as possible. *Highly charged webs of significance* is an evocative description of the social consequences of the theoretical issues addressed in Part 1. It cogently expresses not only Adorno's and Kracauer's respective focuses upon the *culture industry* and *Ratio*, but also the abstract, but nonetheless influential and pervasive nature of the whole social environment so created (à la McLuhan) in which the *society of the spectacle* (Debord) seamlessly blends the power of the image with a society-defining system of commodity production.

## Social porn and Baudrillard's seduction

> They're expected to deliver what I call, borrowing from film pornography, the 'money shot' of the talk-show text: joy, sorrow, rage, or remorse expressed in visible, bodily terms.
>
> (Grindstaff 2002: 19)

> Television talk shows represent a new pornography as they turn private affairs into public displays, make spectacles of people in order to sell commercial products, showcase deviance for our amusement, and play a deceptive game under the guise of truth ... Pornography generally involves turning people into objects and making public what is private. Talk shows do

precisely that and present a cynical, exhaustive cataloging of self-destructive behavior without benefit of comprehension or context.

(Abt and Mustazza 1997: 21)

Abt and Mustazza's above comparison of media content with pornography can be seen as a further updating of Debord's interpretation of Marx's observation that capitalism objectifies people and their social relations while perversely imputing social qualities to objects. For example, *Banality TV* bases much of its raw material upon the consumption of people's emotional lives selected disproportionately from the stratum of society pejoratively described as 'trailer-trash'. This represents a disturbing extension of capitalism's extraction of cultural surplus value from groups previously excluded from the creation of conventional economic value. Grindstaff contrasts the process of revealing undertaken by a professional actor in which his or her veridical (true) self remains secure while the acted persona is paid, with that of the daytime television participant, whose veridical self is exploited for profit and usually unpaid beyond travel expenses and a day out in a metropolitan centre: 'Producers must treat emotion – their own as well as their guests – in a routine and businesslike way, as just another element of the production process' (Grindstaff 2002: 39). In Marxism, the alienation and exploitation of the worker is a basic aspect of the capitalist production process. Now, however, not only are people exploited during their hours of work, but their work has come to include their personal lives whether that takes the form of watching *Banality TV* or being watched by it[5]. While even the most cursory glance at current media content confirms that much of it is objectifying and voyeuristic, Baudrillard's media theory provides some useful critical theoretical tools with which to go beyond merely moralistic judgements to reveal some of the underlying basic political and ideological processes at work.

In Baudrillard's work, Lowenthal's early (*then*) distinction between idols of consumption and production is radically revisited in terms of the contrasting notions of *seduction* and *production*. Baudrillard reformulates the conventional understanding of seduction and its normal sense of romance in order to illustrate the ubiquitous and pervasive cultural effects within the mediascape. In place of its romantic connotations, Baudrillard uses *seduction* as a technical term to refer to the energy involved in social exchanges that have an essentially symbolic and ambiguous nature. For example, historically, there has been a cultural tradition of men pursuing women via a series of games, gifts and general flirtation that has been met with varying degrees of success depending upon the reciprocity of the woman being so seduced. The outcome was either inherently unpredictable, or, highly predictable but still distinctly different to the culture industry's emphasis upon short-term consumption and physical stimulation. For example, in the medieval social practice of courtly love, much emotional energy was devoted to highly impractical, inevitably unrequited relationships – a young, financially weak man would typically desire a woman well beyond his own social class. An important element of the courtly love aesthetic was the way in which the complex mix of frustrated emotional energy generated by the non-consummation of this desire was frequently sublimated into various forms of artistic expression – the love songs of the spurned suitor and so on.

By stark contrast, the culture industry is predicated upon a radically different form of systematically exploited frustration. Instead of maintaining an artistically productive distance from the object of their desires, consumers' appetites are stimulated by constant and ready access. Rather than sublimating desire into symbolic expression, the culture industry repressively de-sublimates. Consumption does not provide fulfilment but rather constantly deferred satisfaction – the seductive tensions of symbolic desire are replaced with the profitability of recyclable sensations designed to aid the ready circulation of yet more commodities. The traditional notion of seduction as a mode of interaction between the sexes may be anachronistic in the light of contemporary gender politics, but Baudrillard's deliberate use of such an anachronism serves to emphasize a greater, much wider anachronism in the heavily mediated society of today – the scarcity of these ambiguous modes of interaction. Unlike symbolic cultures permeated by seductive processes, the mediascape creates a further development of the culture industry – a semiotic culture based upon the immediate satisfaction of consumer desires through the consumption of *signs* rather than *symbols*. A highly operational and functional mode of explicit revealing now dominates the mediated perspective. The link between Baudrillard and such theoretical predecessors as Kracauer, Adorno and Lowenthal, comes from their shared focus on the processes by which industrialized forms of physical production are transposed into the world of cultural representations. The profound consequence of this transposition is the pervasive colonization of cultural life by commodity values as *Banality TV*'s revelatory gaze reaches ever further into previously veiled areas of the life-world.

Baudrillard emphasizes throughout his work that the significance of this situation goes much further than the moralistic condemnation normally associated with the term *obscene*:

> From the discourse of labour to the discourse of sex ... one finds the same ultimatum, that of *pro-duction* [original emphasis] in the literal sense of the term ... To produce is to materialize by force what belongs to another order, that of the

secret and of seduction. Seduction is, at all times and all places, opposed to production. Seduction removes something from the order of the visible, while production constructs everything in full view ... Everything is to be produced, everything is to be legible, everything is to become real, visible, accountable ... This is sex as it exists in pornography, but more generally, **this is the enterprise of our culture**, whose natural condition is obscene: a culture of monstration, of demonstration, of productive monstrosity.

(Baudrillard 1990a: 34–5; emboldening added)

For Baudrillard, the *ob*-scene is not an ethically-loaded term for use in judgement over the morality of particular images. The prefix *ob* refers to the idea of *hindering* or being *against*. The *ob*-scene therefore expresses the collapse of distance in our social experience. There is no longer a scene or stage of action that we view from a distance. This collapse has occurred across society to the extent that sexual pornography is but an extreme example of a wider atmosphere of social explicitness – *social porn* – defined as the widespread cultural manifestation of excessively explicit images, not necessarily of a sexual nature (see Taylor 2007)[6]. The scene traditionally viewed upon a stage necessitates a gap between the viewer and the actor (the theatre's proscenium arch), but now that distance has imploded: 'The task of all media and information today is to produce this real, this extra real (interviews, live coverage, movies, TV-truth, etc.). There is too much of it, we fall into obscenity and pornography. As in pornography, a kind of zoom takes us too near the real, which never existed and only ever came into view *at a certain distance* (Baudrillard 1983b: 84; emphasis in original). *Banality TV* caters to an excessively *explicit* desire to see under the surface of cultural forms previously based upon social practices of seductive veiling and unveiling.

## Food porn: the raw and the cooked

[T]hese shows tend to emphasize a compelling mixture of what Levi-Strauss called, to distinguish the external facticity of nature from the social significances of culture, the raw and the cooked. Reality TV lurches between actual situations and events of startling horror, intense danger, morbid conduct, desperate need, or bizarre coincidence (the raw) and cover stories that reduce such evidence to truism or platitudes (the cooked) ... Reality TV aspires to non-friction. It reduces potential subversion and excess to a comestible glaze.

(Nichols 1994: 45)

While the previous discussion of Baudrillard's *obscene* may appear largely theoretical, practical illustrations of it are evident throughout the mediascape. This creates *social porn*'s atmosphere of ubiquitous explicitness. Pornography's *money shot* can thus be seen as merely a literal, physical climax of the mediascape's more generally sublimated need to unveil the innermost workings of the camera's target whether that proves to be a person's body or psyche. The rise of *social porn* can be most readily witnessed in the ever more bizarre format conflation and mainstreaming of Reality TV programmes about the innately explicit adult movie industry (*Porn: A Family Business, My Bare Lady, Porn Valley, Porn Week,* and so on). More significantly, however, and building upon the previously cited expressions of capitalist culture's digestive enzymes, it is also evident in areas as nominally benign as food preparation. The anthropologist Claude Levi-Strauss used the terms 'the raw' and 'the cooked' to describe the difference between the naturally existing world and that of human culture. The notion is that the act of cooking represents a symbolic transition from nature to human culture and to this extent, food preparation occupies a privileged symbolic role within society. The recent rise in popularity of TV shows based upon food preparation (and the closely related phenomenon of celebrity chefs) thus provides an interesting example of Baudrillard's distinction between aura-lacking semiotics and culturally grounded symbolism and his theory's critique of a widespread process of cultural de-symbolization.

Empirical evidence of the theoretical concept of *social porn* is provided by the practical market-based experience of *Greg Rowland Semiotics,* a company who successfully combined the rise of pornographic imagery with the idea of *Pot Noodle* as a guilty, private, pseudo-onanistic activity. In their own words:

> 'Greg Rowland Semiotics was asked to make Pot Noodle a more iconic brand. By looking at the codes of the brand, sector and product offer we devised a surprising positioning statement for Pot Noodle: "Food Porn." This directly inspired the legendary "Slag of All Snacks" communications that raised sales by 29% when on air[7]'.

Empirical evidence of this close affinity between commodity culture and pornography is further provided by Barbara Nitke, a stills photographer from the pornography industry[8] employed by the US *Food Network* to work in a television genre she labels *gastroporn*. For Nitke, both pornography and gastroporn share both an idealization and degradation of essential human activities: 'You watch porn saying, Yes I could do that,' explained Nitke. 'You dream that you're there, but you know you couldn't. The guy you're watching on the screen, his sex life is effortless. He didn't have to negotiate, entertain her, take her out to dinner. He walked in with the pizza. She was waiting and eager and hot for him' (Nitke, cited in Kaufman 2005: 57). Nitke's account illustrates how *social porn*'s images are hyper-realistic in terms of visual detail but deeply unrealistic in the sense that they are completely lacking in any more meaningful social context (the full political consequences of which are addressed in the next chapter). It is this simultaneous explicitness of depiction but lack of any symbolic content grounded in an authentically specific social context that makes social porn the most recent manifestation of the culture industry's constant attempts to profit by abstracting from the particular to the general.

In 'Debbie does salad', Kaufman (2005) describes the close fit between the filming techniques used in pornography and television cooking, pointing out how the filming of Giada, a female cook in a tight-fitting top, highlights the natural affinity between the two genres: 'this kind of caressing camera going over the food, back and forth and up and down. One of the things that makes it extremely porny is the repetition. You'll see the peach, and the camera going over those peaches again, then Giada, then the peach, then Giada, then the peach. And so this is very similar to how porn works' (Kaufman, in Gladstone 2005: n.p.).[9] Together in the *Food Network* studio, Kaufman relates how he and Nitke, watched Tyler Florence, 'a handsome, sensitive hunk' interact with a female gastroporn partner:

> a desperate housewife stared at sturdy young Tyler. Could his *arroz con pollo* quench her flaming desire? The camera zeroed in as Tyler expertly spread raw chicken breast across a cutting board. 'That is the quintessential pussy shot,' Nitke said. 'The color of it, the texture of it, the camera lingering lovingly over it.' Tyler gingerly rolled the glistening lips of chicken breast into a thick phallus, which he doused with raw egg. 'I feel a lot of love right now,' Tyler told his transfixed acolyte. 'This is a sexy dish.' ... '*This* is the pizza man,' declared Nitke. 'There's the helpless woman who can't do it for herself. In walks the cute young guy who rescues her.'
>
> (Kaufman 2005: 57; original emphasis)

Here, Nitke is vividly describing the collapsing of distance in Baudrillard's *obscene* and of which Part 1's key thinkers could only trace the early stages. In Levi-Strauss's anthropological terms of the raw and the uncooked, *gastroporn* perfectly represents *Banality TV*'s reversal of the 'cooked' into the 'raw' achieved through the removal of the barriers (Baudrillard's *scene*/stage) that create symbolic cultural meaning through *seductive* interactions. By providing such close visual detail, the camera: 'returns us to the innocence of the beasts. Here, we may watch fornication with no sense of the profane, may witness the creation of a feast with no regret that it will never be ours to taste' (Kaufman 2005: 60). There appears to be little difference in the filming techniques used in both sexual pornography and gastroporn because both genres share a technologically savvy responsiveness to the 'greedy eyes' grammar innate to the camera's optical unconscious.

The negative cultural consequences of this loss of traditional auratic experience adds an important corrective to Benjamin's optimism. *Social porn* represents the previously encountered notions of the *pseudo-event* and the *society of the spectacle* at their most symbolically deficient and tautological. Cultural populists/active audience theorists fail to see how what is apparently raw material for viewers is in fact the '*pre digested* banal detail of everyday life' to re-quote Dovey. Critical theorists, by contrast, focus upon the negative aspects of this pre digested quality and their critique is cogently captured by Kaufman's summary of the underlying ideological problem with pornography whether it be of the food or sexual variety: 'the big lie is "taste life", have a real experience, when in fact this is the most unreal experience ... "Taste life" as though by watching it you're going to actually have some sort of authentic, lifelike [experience] – not even lifelike – life itself is here, as opposed to this outrageous simulacrum that's being presented as such' (Kaufman, cited in Gladstone 2005: n.p.).

The key political implication of this situation is its resonance with Nichols's conceptualization of the *ideological reduction* of Reality TV. Voyeuristic fascination reinforces the status quo: 'The raw, the savage, the taboo and untamed require recuperation. We flirt with disgust, abhorrence, nausea, and excess seeking homeopathic cures for these very states. Reality TV provides a curative for disease through the (repetitive, tiresome) tale it tells' (Nichols 1994: 46). The culture industry's harmful effects are not to be found in tired debates about the relative merits of *high* versus *low* culture; they reside in the effect of industrialized *repetition* on the human psyche and culture whether it be at the micro-level of the camera's panning movement whether it be human sex organs or raw chicken breast, or the more macro-level repetition of *Banality TV* formats and their ever more invasive cultural presence. Dovey argues that there is a widespread media-sponsored degradation of the public sphere caused by our uncritical retreat/immersion into the graphically explicit. Pornographic movies are obviously an extreme example of this general tendency, but the frequently ludicrous nature of its skimpy plots and acting at least maintain a critical distance of amused cynicism in the viewer that may actually be less apparent in social porn: 'The ironic distances negotiated by our suspension of disbelief in the clearly fictional porn fantasy are here foreshortened through the grammar of subjective identification created by the video text[10] (Dovey 2000: 68).

The radical suggestion here is that at least in conventional pornography the viewer willingly suspends his/her belief, whereas the cultural danger of *Banality TV* is that their apparently naturalistic forms tend to suppress our critical awareness of the removal of the stage itself. Just as people are increasingly distanced from the seductive properties of a non-mediated reality, television provides its own ersatz and enervated version: 'As people cook less and less, they ogle cooking shows more and more ... Unlike home cooking, TV cooking builds to an unending succession of physical ecstasies, never a pile of dirty dishes' (Kaufman 2005: 56). A lifestyle unobtainable in the *r*eality of a commodity culture is presented as consumable in the image-only form of *R*eality TV – a neat, almost literal, trope for Adorno's previously cited quip that the culture industry requires the diner to be satisfied with the menu.

## Sensation and sociality: Big Brother and the Loft Story

> Bending over a pool of water, Narcissus quenches his thirst. His image is no longer 'other'; it is a surface that absorbs and seduces him, which he can approach but never pass beyond. For there is no beyond, just as there is no reflexive distance between him and his image. The mirror of water is not a surface of reflection, but of absorption.
>
> (Baudrillard 1990a: 67)

In some of his last work, Baudrillard's examined *Banality TV* in relation to France's version of *Big Brother* – *The Loft*. His analysis further illuminates both the contemporary fate of Benjamin's conception of distraction and McLuhan's allusion to the narcotic effects of screen culture. Rather than seeing the rise of Reality TV as evidence of the rude health of contemporary cultural life (the cultural populism model), Baudrillard sees it in terms of a 'synthetic conviviality and telegenically modified sociability' (Baudrillard 2005: 181) that has become so prominent only because there is so little left of any authentic social interaction. The repetitive qualities already discussed in relation to the homogeneity of the culture industry's products and its close alignment with pornographic camera techniques (whether pointed at people or food) are, according to Baudrillard, an essential part of the deep underlying social processes of which Reality TV is but a cultural reflection. *Banality TV* thus partakes of a general social ethos of excessive revelation that Baudrillard approaches in a similar manner to Kracauer. For example, a comparison of the following quotations provides a striking example of the continuity in themes between these *then* and *now* theorists compare the following two excerpts. The first is from Kracauer's essay '*Georg Simmel*' originally published in 1920–21:

> The more profound our experience of things is, the less it can be subsumed to its full extent under abstract concepts. Initially clothed in the image, it shines forth brightly; we should shroud it in order to possess it nude. What is most secret needs the veil of a metaphor so that it can be completely exposed.'
>
> (Kracauer 1995: 236)

The second is from Baudrillard's 2001 essay, 'Dust breeding', in which he uses the example of Catherine Millet – the author of the best-selling autobiographical account of a large number of compulsively anonymous sexual couplings – *The Sexual Life of Catherine M* – as a contemporary example of the culture industry's inability to grasp the paradox that the true nature of social reality is to be found in its shrouding. The more one seeks to reveal it in an excessively explicit and systematic fashion the further away it becomes:

> 'Think like a woman taking off her dress,' said Bataille. Yes, but the naiveté of all the Catherine Millets is to think that they are taking of their dress to get undressed, to be naked and therefore reach the naked truth, the truth of sex or of the world. If one does take off one's dress, it is to appear: not to appear naked like truth (and who can believe that truth remains truth when its veil is removed?) but to be born to the realm of appearances, to seduction which is the contrary.
>
> This modern and disenchanted view is a total misunderstanding if it considers the body to be an object waiting only to be undressed ... Especially since all cultures of the mask, the veil and ornaments say precisely the contrary: they say that the body is a metaphor and that the true objects of desire and pleasure are the signs and marks that tear it from its nudity, naturalness and 'truth,' from the integral reality of its physical being. In all places, seduction is what tears things from their truth (including their sexual truth). And if thought takes off its dress, it is not to reveal itself naked, it is not to unveil the secret of what had been hidden until then, it is to make the body appear as definitively enigmatic, definitively secret, as a pure object whose secret will never be lifted and has no need to be lifted.
>
> (Baudrillard 2005: 186)

Millet's quest for sexual fulfilment via mechanistic couplings represents a physical manifestation of the culture industry's repetitions (at a micro-level, the repetitive tracking action of the camera in the *Food*

*Network*) in which higher meaning is lost. We see here an indication of the cultural consequences of the overexposure of reality by the mechanically produced image that Benjamin began to explore optimistically as the decline of aura and which Kracauer more guardedly conceived of as the image-idea that drives away the idea and threatens the traditional artistic interpretation of a reality *permeated by cognition.*

The conceptual continuities between *then* and *now* continue further as Baudrillard also builds directly upon the comparison Benjamin makes in the '*Work of Art*' Essay between the cameraman and the surgeon. Reality TV becomes an enforcedly claustrophobic attempt (think of the tightly controlled and contained sets and compounds in which *Big Brother – The Loft* and similar programmes function) to verify the notion of *society*, when society is by its very nature a nebulous concept more likely to be destroyed than better understood by such a mode of testing. Catherine Millet's sexual exploits are of a similarly misguided nature. According to Baudrillard in the case of both Millet and the camera: 'we are in the process of dissecting – vivisecting under the scalpel of the camera ... Catherine Millet ... another kind of "vivi-sex-ion" where all the imaginary of sexuality is swept away, leaving only a protocol in the form of a limitless verification of sexual functioning, a mechanism that no longer has anything sexual about it' (Baudrillard 2005: 184). Baudrillard provides a succinctly updated version of critical theorists' objection to the culture industry and its manufactured manipulation of aura. It bears repeating that it is not a question of 'high' versus 'low' culture, it is a question of objecting to the semiotic extirpation of symbolic depth and ambiguity. The critical rejection of active audience theories is based upon a rejection of their claims to being active in any meaningful sense, constituted as they are by interactions with predigested categories of the banal.

## Conclusion

> All mass culture is adaptation ... The pre-digested quality of the product prevails, justifies itself and establishes itself all the more firmly in so far as it constantly refers to those who cannot digest anything not already pre-digested. It is baby food ... based upon the infantile compulsion towards the repetition of needs it created in the first place.
>
> (Adorno 1991: 67)

Whether on the Hot Network, E! Entertainment Television, or CBS, the splanchnic response, not the lucubrations of the intellect but the primal gut reaction – that's what hauls in the ratings. When the new president of CNN/US, Jonathan Klein, took over last November, he introduced himself to the troops with what has become the perennial 'it's about the story-telling speech'. As Van Gorden Sauter preached in the 1980s, news needs the **emo**, and executives now understand that the emo comes from the gut, the gut makes the wow, and the wow makes the money. It's not the content that matters – food, sex, or news – so much as the autonomic form.

(Kaufman 2005: 9; emphasis added)

Kaufman argues that the media disproportionately assumes an excessively *emo*tive approach. This is the basis of *social porn* and its ubiquitous and pervasive presence. It is built upon a society-wide over-dependence upon the camera-generated imagery of the *society of the spectacle* that *now* has exceeded the theoretical expectations of *then*. To the extent that cultural studies as a discipline sought to politicize culture in a fashion akin to Benjamin's hopes in his Essay for the politicization of aesthetics (to counter the Nazi aestheticization of politics) it has failed because capitalism is extremely adept at bringing all cultural forms down to the common political denominator of the commodity form. The hungry eyes of the camera merely locate food for the equally hungry maw of the culture industry – quite literally as we have seen in our discussion of *Food Network* television. Social porn is thus a combination of:

1   The innate 'greedy eyes' property of the camera
2   The complex intertwining of the camera's innate voyeurism with wider commodity values.

The theorists of Part 1 demonstrated the cultural harm caused by this development and this chapter showed that with the advent of *social porn* and *Banality TV*: 'The historical world becomes reduced to a set of simulations ... The webs of signification we build and in which we act pass into *fields of simulation that absorb us but exclude our action*. Referentiality dissolves in the non-being and nothingness of TV' (Nichols 1994: 46; emphasis added). Pre-inscribed and carefully manipulated emotional affect is made to effect what was previously still protected from commercial values by a generally accepted *discourse of sobriety* that traditionally protected the 'serious' parts of our culture. The next chapter explores in more detail the negative cognitive and political effects suffered by a society in which, true to Kracauer's fears, objects and processes permeated by cognition have given way to the image-idea.

# 8

# The politics of banality: the *ob*-scene as the *mis-en-scène*

## Introduction

> We are all quite familiar with this immense process of simulation. Non-directive interviews, call-in shows, all-out participation – the extortion of speech: 'it concerns you, you are the majority, you are what is happening.' And the probing of opinions, hearts, minds, and the unconscious to show how much 'it' speaks. The news has been invaded by this phantom content, this homeopathic transplant, this waking dream of communication ... A circular construction where one presents the audience with what it wants, an integrated circuit of perpetual solicitation. The immense energies spent in maintaining this simulacrum at arm's length, to avoid the brutal dissimulation that would occur should the reality of a radical loss of meaning become too evident.
>
> (Baudrillard 1990a: 163)

> The transpolitical is the transparency and obscenity of all structures in a destructured universe, the transparency and obscenity of change in a de-historicized universe, the transparency and obscenity of information in a universe emptied of event.
>
> (Baudrillard 1993: 25)

In the first of the above quotations, Baudrillard summarizes the focus of the previous chapter – the tautological circularity of a media system that encourages active audiences only to better disguise the underlying meaninglessness of their activity. The second quotation encapsulates the dire political consequences of such a circular system – a de-historicized and transpolitical culture once again reminiscent of Kracauer's fears. This state of affairs fatally undermines Benjamin's declared hope, at the end of his Essay, that new technologies of reproduction could create a radical politicization of aesthetics.

Baudrillard takes Benjamin's notion that with the decline of aura comes a loosening of traditional ties to space and time and pushes the concept to its illogical extreme. Non-banal political discourse becomes increasingly difficult in a mediascape premised upon an aesthetic in which, because of this loosening of ties, the decontextualized, freely floating image dominates and pervasively undermines the rational. Apart from Benjamin, this shallowness and evacuation of meaning is a central theme of the other thinkers of *then*, relating directly as it does to:

1  Kracauer's *strike against understanding*
2  Adorno's *culture industry*
3  McLuhan's *medium is the message*
4  Boorstin's *pseudo-event* and Debord's *society of the spectacle.*

This chapter builds upon these previous analyses to explore the overall political and ideological impact of the mediated image. It develops Jameson's (1991) notion of 'the cultural logic of late capitalism' as a 'waning of affect' by using Baudrillard's paradoxical notion that current mediated society suffers from images that are *too* explicit and detailed. Baudrillard's radical theory of the *implosion* of communication is opposed to Benjamin's *explosive* 'the dynamite of the tenth of second' to argue that the contemporary media is no closer *now* than it was *then* to confronting the heart of Kracauer's 'urgent human concerns' submerged as they are by a 'blizzard' of images. The superficially realist/naturalist portrayal of the everyday presented in explicit visual detail in both *Banality TV* and nominally more serious news programmes (formerly included under the term *discourses of sobriety*) are now increasingly indistinguishable. This produces an ideological representation of reality that *distracts* (in a diametrically opposed sense to that proposed by Benjamin) from the key issues of power, freedom, liberated consciousness, and so on with which critical theory concerns itself.

A *critical* examination of the West's unhealthy relationship to the mediated image is needed to uncover the true nature of the malevolence lying behind heavily mediated events (both the carefully pre-planned and the spontaneous) such as the 9/11 tragedy and the abuse of prisoners at Abu Ghraib. McLuhan ([1964] 1995) offers the myth of Narcissus as a defining metaphor for the West's problematic relationship to the screen. Influenced by McLuhan, Baudrillard suggests that the inchoate nature of the Western response to 9/11 is ultimately a result of its myopic, overly fascinated relationship to its own excessively mediated culture more than any actual power held by its perceived enemies. In this chapter, we explore how the image-sponsored strike against understanding described in previous pages has manifested itself in a geopolitical context in which the image-idea does indeed seem to have driven out the idea to the point that the US and UK governments feel able to declare war upon an abstract noun (terror). Despite being societies of the spectacle, Western governments have nevertheless struggled to compete with the Other's political use of the image. This ranges from the malevolent media savvy of Osama bin Laden's made-for-media attack of 9/11, to the *pseudo-event* staged for the world's cameras of April 2007 in which the Iranian President, Mahmoud Ahmadinejad, voluntarily released 15 captured British sailors while images from Guantanomo Bay continue to poison relations with the Islamic world. In this chapter we see that profound and generally underacknowledged political consequences result when the obscene becomes the mis-en-scène and a critical perspective is lost.

## Television's other news

the *other news* offers modes of explanation and sense-making which displace and mask the social, political and historical context in which events occur and can be made to mean. The personal and the impersonal become 'naturalized' forms of expression and intelligibility within a news discourse which deflects attention from what is perhaps a more crucial factor in explaining the conditions of mastery and its nemesis – the structures of domination and subordination.

(Langer 1998: 150; emphasis added)

What is important is the surge and volume of emotion, not its object or its subject, and it doesn't matter whether the twenty-four-hour parade of sensational effect goes nowhere except around in circles, or who sings the undying songs of love, or whether the revelation of divine celebrity takes the form of Madonna, next week's serial killer, or the president of the United States.

(Lapham 2001: ix)

A major strength of critical media theory is its ability to undermine conventional accounts with what Žižek refers to as *The Parallax View* (2006). In addition to the conventionally recognized barriers to democratic expression that exist within the mediascape, critical theory enables us to see that at a deep-rooted, structural level, it is characterized by *explicitness without understanding* – the alignment of commodity values and media technologies allows the medium to dominate the message. The *Other News* provides an extremely useful example of this ideological role played by the media. It expands upon our previous analysis of celebrity and *Banality TV* to show how their combined effects are felt in the steady diminishment of reason-based public discourse. Langer (1998) defines television's *Other News* as news content that does not fit Nichols's previously discussed sober discourses of politics, economics, foreign affairs and other important social issues: 'the news story and the advertisement are collapsed together through a language mobilized from billboards, newspaper entertainment pages, fan magazines and television commercials. Hyperbole and exuberance are the keynotes' (Langer 1998: 57). Resistance to this situation by those within the media itself is the exception that proves the rule[1].

The previous analysis of the *culture industry thesis* demonstrated how systematic processes and effects form a rationalized (in terms of pure consumptive efficiency) kernel to our otherwise largely irrational and emotive consumption of commodities. Similarly, in the developed culture industry of the contemporary mediascape, politics assumes a new hue akin to the previously encountered *emo*. In a media-sponsored abandonment of sober discourses, debate containing conceptual depth is now *systematically* replaced by a complex amalgamation of more innately superficial, surface-level modes of discourse based upon personality, celebrity, the spectacle, *pseudo-events*, and so on. This means that in the place of traditional categories of discriminating thought and reason, the mediated public sphere is now dominated by amorphous and intangible associations. The mere fact that images are presented of a person or an event *now* provides a new form of de-symbolized aura in which tautological justification (for example, celebrities/brands are well known/recognizable because they are well known/recognizable) is largely immune to critical evaluation by media commentators and cultural populists subscribing to the values of that tautological environment.

The rise of the *Other News* and a general cultural environment of the *obscene* has its roots in Kracauer's identification of contingency as a dominant value within the mass ornament and is a key factor in the betrayal of Benjamin's early optimistic hopes for distraction. According to Langer, the *Other News* helps to create a 'regulated latitude of ideological positions' (Langer 1998: 51). Any potential for the creation of a system more open to radical and less predictably structured meaning is undermined by the way in which the existing dominant and subordinate meaning systems are reinforced by the seeming naturalness of the tele-frame and its circumscribing effect. A new false consciousness for the media age is created in two main forms:

1  The masses are presented with an elitist celebrity order to which they can both aspire and defer in a predominantly passive mode.

2   A regime of 'common-sense' media values (see Barthes 1973 [1957]) is created. This is based upon the self-evident nature of images in the face of which the audience, once again, adopts a largely passive and accommodative response. Even the most imaginative interpretations do not tend to question the validity of the tele-frame itself.

The tele-frame's meaning system is not imposed upon people; rather, as previously pointed out, it works in a less overtly hierarchical and historically exploitative manner than the privileges traditionally enjoyed by elites. Its common-sense quality encourages an uncritical acceptance of the media's content and produces various layers of tautological communication so that:

1   The photographable is what is photographed
2   The celebrity is well known for being well known
3   The branded good has value because it is a brand
4   The reporting of the *Other News* is important because it is reported.

Celebrities contribute to the production of a commonsensical false consciousness through the ease with which, in stark contrast to the majority of consumers, they circulate in their elite social realm and personify the commodity form. They illustrate our repeated recourse to Marx's observation that within capitalism commodities circulate in a manner akin to social relations while human relations within the rest of us non-celebrities are increasingly objectified and static.

The *Other News*' deceptively natural, cyclical, formulaic nature creates 'a metaphysical system which poses causal relations as fluctuating between grand cycles of external recurrence (the more things change ... )' (Langer 1998: 154) – an ideology of repetitive normality. Langer argues that the main ideological impact of the *Other News* is the essentially conservative message this gives the public through its 'drama of fatalism'. This conservatism implicitly suggests that one should be glad with one's lot because life could be much worse compared with the private/natural disasters that are presented for viewing. In addition, the ongoing diet the *Other News* provides of the personal tribulations of celebrities exposed by the media demonstrates how their fame is hard won and, therefore, although individual celebrities may be censured, the institution of celebrity itself is not. In such a context, inequality and other key social problems become much easier to define as accidents of fate rather than as the result of the particular actions of historical and economic actors/actions – and this is where the usually subtle ideological functioning of the mediascape becomes most obvious and close to what Marx originally meant by his notion of false consciousness.

## Explicitness without understanding: social porn, Monica Lewinsky and current *affairs*

> The visual is *essentially* pornographic, which is to say that it has its end in rapt, mindless fascination; thinking about its attributes becomes an adjunct to that, if it is unwilling to betray its object; while the most austere films necessarily draw their energy from the attempt to repress their own excess (rather than the more thankless effort to discipline the viewer). Pornographic films are thus only the potentiation of films in general, which ask us to stare at the world as though it were a naked body.
>
> (Jameson 1993: 1)

The theoretical accounts previously discussed (for example, McLuhan and Baudrillard's) emphasized the dumb, narcotic fascination engendered by the media's screens. Above, Jameson radically interprets this as an innate property of the camera. In *Banality TV*, the concept of ordinariness does the same type of ideological work (albeit less dramatically) that body-based sentiment does in pornography. In both cases, the reality of the immediate is given precedence over contemplative thought so that: 'The genre ... is a kind of machine for producing ordinariness, where ordinariness is associated with emotion (the body) and expertness with reason (the mind), the former a signifier of the private world of personal relations, the latter a signifier of the larger universe of social relations' (Grindstaff 2002: 21). Such is the democratic nature of ubiquitous celebrity, that sophisticated interpretive skills become devalued. The predominantly conversationally based and personalized content of *Banality TV* and daily news programmes (and the increasing similarities of the two formats) inhibits conceptual complexity while their provocative content finds itself naturally aligned with the accommodating grammar of television: 'they orchestrate emotional encounters on television in order to capitalize on the visual immediacy of the medium' (Grindstaff 2002: 59).

The net result of all the processes encountered in the previous chapters is the creation of a cultural climate in which the self-referential realm of 'news' has more to do with the internal needs of the mediascape than it manages to relate to the dispassionate reporting of events that could be more squarely located within the realm of 'serious' news. Thought that is critical of the dominant tele-frame is made more difficult by formats whose *raison d'être* is sensationalism and an excessive dependency upon images. That *Banality TV* mitigates against serious debate of abstract issues is hardly surprising given its obvious purpose as an entertainment vehicle and its subsequent structural dependence upon the decontextualized and overtly dramatic. What is much more disturbing is the extent to which the conventional meaning of *current affairs* has seamlessly merged with the sexual connotations of that term. Nominally serious and entertainment-based formats are now increasingly indistinguishable with television becoming:

> a machine for making the money shot. How else to explain the incessant news coverage of President Clinton's affair with Monica Lewinsky? Not since the coverage of John Wayne Bobbit have I heard so much public discussion about a man's penis. There were moments when the biggest difference between Larry King Live and Jerry Springer was the fact that all the guests on King's show were white men with perfect teeth.
>
> (Grindstaff 2002: 250)

It is critical media theory's consistent re-emphasis of the implications of McLuhan's axiom – *the medium is the message* – that illuminates the ironical situation whereby explicit subject matter obfuscates politically informed thought because, as Jameson contends, film promotes a pornographic attitude to the world around us.

McGrath's description of the ideological work carried out by the naturalist television dramas of the 1970s is still remarkably pertinent to today's mediascape and this growing conflation of the *discourses of sobriety* with *Banality TV*:

> Naturalism contains everything within a closed system of relationships. Every statement is mediated through the situation of the character speaking. Mediated to the point of triviality ... In terms of presenting a picture of society, it can only reveal a small cluster of subjective consciousness, rarely anything more ... it encapsulates the status quo, ossifies dynamics of society into a moment of perception, crystallizes the realities of existence into a paradigm, but excludes what it refers to.
>
> (McGrath 1977, cited in Dovey 2000: 152)

McGrath's statement is important for the succinct way it summarizes some of this book's key themes. In particular, it points to McLuhan's account of the unconscious, narcotic infiltration of the medium's effects as it presents its content to the audience (as in his previously cited image of the burglar using a juicy steak to steal from under the nose of the watchdog of the mind) and Baudrillard's emphasis upon the overwhelming nature of the absorption and fascination engendered by the screen. McGrath's description of the early precursor to Reality TV sums up the paradoxical phenomenon of *explicitness without understanding* – the media's frame circumscribes social experience into a closed self-contained system and *as it does so, excludes the very thing it represents*. The cultural forms created by this process have profound political implications of a type that cultural populism's misplaced optimism prevents it from seeing. It is too wedded to understanding media content from within its own closed system and terms rather than, as critical theory does, questioning the desirability and justification of the very system itself.

Baudrillard's work represents perhaps the most trenchant culmination of McLuhan's *the medium is the message* sentiment: 'It is not as vehicles of content, but in their very form and very operation, that media induce a social relation ... The media are not co-efficients, but effectors of ideology ... The mass media are anti-mediatory and intransitive. They fabricate non-communication' (Baudrillard 1972: 169[2]). With the advent of more sophisticated media than were available for Benjamin's analysis, we can see the further evolution of his notion of distraction and Jameson's description of 'rapt, mindless fascination'. The result for Baudrillard is 'an abyss of language, an abyss of linguistic seduction, a radically different operation that absorbs rather than produces meaning. The sarcophagus of linguistics was tightly sealed, and fell upon the shroud of the signifier' (Baudrillard 1990a: 57). In his penultimate book before his death Baudrillard described Reality TV in a manner that evokes Adorno and Kracauer's assessment of the culture industry, as well as succinctly describing the atmosphere of a contemporary mediascape in which *Banality TV* has colonized sober discourse to produce: 'a mirror of platitudes ... life that has already been rigged by all the dominant models' (Baudrillard 2005: 181).

## The visually inspired decline of the public sphere

> Closer in character to poetry than prose, the electronic media employ a simplified vocabulary adjusted to the demands of a thirty-second television commercial (no compound sentences, words of one or two syllables, parable in place of argument), and *they depend for their effect on the substitution of the part for the whole*. The gaunt face of a Rwandan child stands surrogate for the continent of Africa, a helicopter shot of an Iowa cornfield expresses the boundless store of American virtue.
>
> (Lapham 2001: viii; emphasis mine)

> He does not violate the old truth-morality. Rather, like the news maker, he evades it. It is not only advertising which has become a tissue of contrivance and illusion. Rather, it is the whole world. The ambiguities and illusions of advertising are only symptoms. Advertising events are no less or more unreal than all other pseudo-events.
>
> (Boorstin [1961] 1992: 214)

The above two quotations forcefully express a perceived alignment between factual news coverage and commercial advertising. Television *now* portrays the 'strike against understanding' of which Kracauer (and more inadvertently Benjamin) identified *then* in its vestigial, photographic form. The quantitative increase in images produces a profoundly qualitative change which Lapham describes in terms of the (il)logical extension of photography's 'greedy eyes' tendency in the coverage of important issues. The damaging social consequence is that reasoned argument is increasingly replaced by a vaguely associative form of images. Part of photography's iconic appeal is the misleading way it appears not to mediate: a photograph is its own content, or, as McQuire puts it, 'a medium in which the signifier effaced itself before the force of the signified' (McQuire 1998: 30[3]). Despite this apparent neutrality, photography's particular form creates what Sontag describes as a democracy of images that reduces everything to the same banal quality of the photographable[4] – a tendency Benjamin tried to imbue with radical potential but which this book's approach has consistently questioned. Television news provides a technologically more sophisticated version of the same essential technological grammar that underlies photography, but with much greater ideological effects. It uses repetitive individual iconic representations (for example, sepia photographs/early film to portray historical events) for the representation of otherwise complex situations. Langer uses the term *condensation symbols* to describe Lapham's notion of a metonymic function which contrasts with Nichols's concept of metonymic moments that momentarily succeed in escaping the tele-frame. In this instance, familiar images create a visual shorthand of instant, uncritical recognition.

The ideological impact occurs when, through the familiarity bred by such symbols, the audience tends to forget that the representation of whole events by iconic images only *purports* to represent the full conceptual complexity. As Lapham puts it above: 'they depend for their effect on the substitution of the part for the whole'[5]. Just as we tend through familiarity to forget (or choose to acknowledge initially and then subsequently overlook) the extent to which various celebrities are famous merely for being famous, so iconic representations are included in news coverage under the guise of adding to our understanding of an event when in fact they oversimplify it. As with critical theory's rejection of the overly optimistic claims made for popular culture by active audience researchers, Langer argues that with respect to television news there is a real danger that defenders of its democratic visual form are indulging in a form of *complacent relativism* defined as 'a misplaced and depoliticized valorisation of "the everyday"' (Langer 1998: 24). Uncritical acceptance of TV news' over-reliance upon images rather than concepts means that

this 'depoliticized valorisation of the "everyday"' smoothly complements the pervasive predigested banality of everyday life presented
in more overtly entertainment-orientated forms of television.

An eagerness to defend the way in which the television news
'shows it the way it is' misses the value-laden structure that in fact
underlies such a seemingly self-evident natural form. For example,
news reporting of the 2007 Israeli military operation in Southern
Lebanon illustrates the only superficially neutral nature of this
mediated process:

> On the front page of another issue of the [New York] *Times* was
> the stock tragic Arab refugee shot of a distraught Lebanese
> woman in an abaya holding a terrified child. I tell you what the
> *Times* is not going to run. They're not going to run a big
> colour photo above the fold on the front page of a pretty,
> light-skinned young Lebanese woman in Prada shoes, Diesel
> jeans and a Dolce & Gabbana blouse with an arm blown off or
> half her face missing. The media have been selling this war like
> a sporting event: 'Hizbullah fire 105 rockets into Haifa and
> northern Israel, killing four and wounding 18, while the Israelis
> struck Sidon and Tyre, launching 48 bombing sorties against
> suspected Hizbullah positions with "some reports of civilian
> casualities".' The audience becomes addicted to narratives,
> digestible narratives. No news organisation is going to meet its
> quarterly market projections by shoving political and moral
> quandaries down the throats of its audiences[6].

This reliance upon images that speak for themselves, combined with
circulation-driven sensitivity to market share, exhibits the same basic
qualities as celebrity production. Boorstin's above conflation of the
newsmaker with the advertiser indicates points to a cultural alignment of commercial and technological grammars. The combined
effect of these quantitative and qualitative effects produces a media-
facilitated form of cultural extinction: public discourse is irreparably
colonized by the values of appearance rather than substance –
Debord's notion that the dominant capitalist social value has
changed from one of 'having' into one of 'appearing'. Above, both
Boorstin and Lapham highlight a deeply disturbing process whereby
the reporting of non-commodified, unemotive or non-*pseudo-events*
become, to paraphrase Benjamin, as rare as an orchid in the land of
a mediascape that is self-referential but not self-reflexive. Images and
formulas cross-reference each other only in a repetitive, unquestion-
ing mode of circulation. Critical self-awareness in the media becomes
subordinate to the way in which it prefers: 'to spectacularize the
symptoms of crisis and commentary, rather than risk the possibility
of indicting themselves as contributing culprits' (Goldman and
Papson 1998: 10). On rare, particularly traumatic occasions as

Nichols previously pointed out, this unreflexive self-referential insularity of the media may be temporarily exposed. One stark example was provided by the contrast in the levels of coverage devoted to the death of Princess Diana and the amount of analysis of the media's own crucial contributory role in that death.

Visuality's influence over rational discourse is consistently reflected in more subtle but cumulatively important ways at the highest levels of US political life. The Congressional 9/11 Commission suggested that President Bush's failure to read his President's Daily Briefing documents may have contributed to the failure to prevent the tragedy. President Bush's apparent lack of comfort with the written word provides a useful trope for the wider audience of television news[7]. As Sidney Blumenthal, the journalist and former senior adviser to Bill Clinton, recounts:

> Bush ... does not read his President's Daily Briefs, but has them orally summarised every morning by the CIA director ... 'I know he doesn't read,' one former Bush national security council staffer told me. Several other former NSC staffers corroborated this. It seems highly unlikely that he read the national intelligence estimate on WMD before the Iraq war that consigned contrary evidence that undermined the case to footnotes and fine print. Nor is there any evidence that he read the State Department's 17-volume report, The Future of Iraq, warning of nearly all the postwar pitfalls.
>
> (Blumenthal 2004: n.p.)

Without wishing to succumb to the media's tendency to personalize issues (which was criticized in the previous examination of celebrity), the dire consequences that resulted from President Bush's lack of attention to written accounts in both the case of 9/11 and the subsequent second Gulf campaign highlight in dramatic form the risks that accompany the mass media's deconceptualization of the public sphere. President Bush's failure to read the relevant pre-Gulf conflict reports encapsulates in microcosm our wider society's failure to read complex political situations properly. *Discourses of sobriety* make way for an over-dependence upon the image with profoundly negative geopolitical implications.

## Geo-politics and the death of sober discourse

Of all nations in the world, the United States was built in nobody's image. It was the land of the unexpected, of unbounded hope, of ideals, of quest for an unknown perfection. It is all the more unfitting that we should offer ourselves in images. And all the more fitting that the images which we

make wittingly or unwittingly to sell America to the world
should come back to haunt and curse us. Perhaps, instead of
announcing ourselves by our shadows and our idols, we would
do better to try to share with others the quest which has been
America.

(Boorstin [1961] 1992: 245–6; emphasis added)

Written at the height of the Cold War and although originally
referring to Communism, Boorstin's above words are now painfully
relevant to the gulf that exists most significantly not just as a
geographical area to which troops are periodically dispatched but as
an alarming gap in cultural misunderstanding between Western and
Islamic sensitivities. This book's analysis of the media's over-
dependence upon images to the exclusion of more rational thought
implies crucial social consequences much greater than merely an
elitist perception of a loss of quality in the realm of culture. Boorstin
feared that America's over-reliance upon images would come back to
haunt it. In a terrible fashion, the events of 9/11 confirmed his fear
and the continued, shallow image-based nature of the subsequent
media coverage merely served to reinforce the import of his words.
Writing a full 40 years before the World Trade Center (WTC)
terrorist incident, Boorstin foresaw this manner in which images
displace more substantive values and ideals to America's own detri-
ment. His criticism of America's obsession with image over substance
accurately sensed the visual form of Osama Bin Laden's murderous
backlash in which he chose the heavily symbolic and visually striking
WTC towers for his act of destruction carefully designed to be
consumed as a media event[8].

On 11th September 2001, Osama Bin Laden returned the Hollywood disaster movie to its homeland. He gained maximum media
impact by using visual terms deliberately designed to fit into the
functional categories of a semiotic communicational order ruled by
images and designed for the generation and manipulation of
uncritical emotion – the *emo*. This was demonstrated by the way in
which Ground Zero and its emergency workers quickly became
emotive icons. As such, the attack represents a perverse
re-engineering of the West's perceived over-dependence upon images
by someone, who in Boorstin's terms, represents a champion of
ideals (however distorted) over images and an otherwise natural
critic of the shallow values contained within *pseudo-events* of which
9/11 was such a tragic example[9]. Despite the very real effects
experienced by its victims and those New Yorkers in the immediate
vicinity and aftermath, the rest of the USA experienced the WTC
attack as an excessive Hollywood-style privileging of the image – to
the extent that the release of several films was postponed because of
their perceived similarity to actual events. Hollywood producers were

even consulted by US intelligence services for their views as to the likely nature of further attacks and its influence continued to be a constant factor in the post-9/11 political response. Ronald Reagan's *Star Wars* sounding Cold War 'Empire of Evil' was replaced by an 'Axis of Evil' often discussed in colloquial terms borrowed liberally from the Western film genre.

The media thus played a major role in constructing not only the public's perceptions of the tragic events of 9/11 but also the conditions necessary for the maintenance of an alarming conceptual deficit in which discussion of possible causes was overruled by a rush to produce a military response (the war on terror). Rather than dwelling upon the causes of previously simmering and then overtly violent anti-American discontent, US television and media coverage of the tragedy was immediately, and thereafter persistently, dominated by the constant repetition of iconic images and soundbites. There was repeated, stand-alone footage of the second plane crashing, while camera crews camped at the dramatically sounding Ground Zero provided constant (but largely unchanging) visual updates from the smoldering wreckage. Blanket coverage at Ground Zero was quickly supplemented with images of world leaders expressing sorrow, and shortly afterwards celebrity-based benefit concerts involving a surfeit of emotion-laden soft-focus close-ups and candle-strewn sets. Detailed considerations of the tragedy's historical and political context were displaced illustrating the US media's pathological over-reliance upon images and sentiment.

Both US and UK coverage of the 9/11 terrorist act was dominated by a spate of human interest interviews with emergency workers, survivors, and relatives of the deceased still hoping against the available evidence that their loved-ones were still alive. Emotionally vampiric interviews familiar to regular viewers of disasters around the world were mixed with stentorian but ultimately vacuous commentary, similar in tone and placatory, uncritical purpose to the commentary that accompanied Princess Diana's death and mass floral response. In both media events, 'why?' was a frequently uttered question only in the sense of a lament rather than a critical observation. Despite the constant coverage, there was no significant attempt to address the question in a structured and non-emotional fashion because the media's self-serving interpretation of the 'new mood' of the country deemed this to be appropriate. In the case of Princess Diana's death, the underlying complicity of the television anchors with the paparazzi directly involved in the actual accident meant that the reasons behind the 'why' could not be examined too closely. In the case of 9/11, irrespective of any potential political pressure, the US media naturally avoided the deeper aspects of the 'why' question because the formats it uses are particularly ill-equipped to deal with it.

A more sustained attempt to answer the question would inevitably raise the question of the practical causes of the worldwide resentment felt towards the USA and much more practically inconvenient issues such as the Central Intelligence Agency's (CIA's) large-scale and well-documented initial funding of both Bin Laden and Saddam Hussein. These are the type of important political issues that, as we have seen throughout this book, effectively become non-questions in a media predicated upon fragmented images and decontextualized discourse. Thus, in a manner that Bin Laden probably factored into his calculations, the media turned him into 'public enemy number one' or in terms of this book an *anti*-celebrity, a move that effectively insulates him from more nuanced critical analysis. One vivid example of the media's tendency to create an atmosphere of non-neutral banality that occludes meaningful discourse was provided during the first weeks of the second Gulf campaign when a large number of complaints were logged by the US Defence Department's press office. These complaints related, not to any substantive issues relating to the conduct of the war, but instead to the dress-sense and garish clothes worn by Victoria Clarke, the colour-blind Assistant Secretary of Defence for Public Affairs[10]. In the context of a military campaign in which civilian deaths are not known to the nearest hundred thousand, even critical theory appears ill-equipped to tackle the full banality of *Banality TV*.

## The Gulf conflicts

Žižek (2002) delineates two major post-9/11 options open to America: 'it can either further fortify its sphere from which it watches world tragedies via a TV screen' or it can 'finally risk stepping through the fantasmatic screen that separates it from the Outside World, accepting its arrival in the Real World' (Žižek 2002: 49). The second Gulf conflict can be seen as an acting out of the former option rather than the latter. Despite heated debates and huge mass public demonstrations over the two Gulf conflicts, the biggest shifts in the British and American publics' perceptions occurred through a series of vivid, defining images at various crucial stages. Baudrillard's analytical approach illustrates the value of critical media theory's concepts to understand more fully the ideological nature of such images. His speculations upon the *hyper-reality* of the conflicts usefully explain the actual *grounded* impact of the hyper-operationalism of the Allied military techniques. In contrast, the purportedly 'critical' debates of the mainstream media during the first Gulf conflict centred upon questions related to the media themselves such as the limited access to the war action provided by the US military's pool system and the alleged censorship of journalists. Much bigger questions were left unasked such as the reasons why images of oil-polluted birds were given equal (if not greater) billing on Western television screens to pictures of dead Iraqi soldiers and the fact that in 1998 CNN was advertising for the next expected war as if part of its next season's television schedules (Merrin 2005: 91).

In the face of this mainstream media prudishness about asking questions that fundamentally interrogate the tele-frame, Baudrillard's critical media theory doggedly describes the profound social harm caused by the disintegration of the *symbolic* and its systematic replacement with its etiolated semiotic substitute – the *sign*. In keeping with this book's account of the culture industry and *Ratio* from *then*, he poignantly describes how unpredictable social processes have *now* become supplanted by pre-encoded, predictable models for both actual military engagement and its reception on the screens back home. At a macro-level, the historical unpredictability of war is replaced by a result we know in advance due to massive inequalities in technological weaponry, and at a micro-level, confrontation with the enemy takes place in a form that is so heavily mediated that it produced 'the most horrifying [non-]images of unilaterality as, over seventy miles of trenches, front-line Iraqi soldiers were bulldozed and buried alive. Already *dead in advance* before the American forces they were not worth engaging, only burying' (Merrin 2005: 88). In terms of the media's reporting of the conflicts, the decontextualized/depersonalized portrayal of Iraqis through night-vision missile guidance sights and the additional mediation of these images through the formulaic segments of prime time news programmes provide a particularly tragic illustration of Benjamin's previously cited criticism of the Futurists' perverse enjoyment of war and the notion that 'mankind could become an object of contemplation for itself' (Essay: Epilogue). Particularly in media coverage of the first Gulf conflict, death of fellow human beings was reduced to a digitally neon version of *Candid Camera* so that: 'In [this] hyperrealization of experience and simultaneous distancing from the symbolic reality of its effects, nowhere does Baudrillard's comment, the more closely the real is pursued "the greater does the real absence from the world grow" find more horrific support' (Merrin 2005: 92).

Undue optimism was at its media-sponsored peak during the fall of Baghdad and the Ozymandias-like toppling of Saddam Hussein's statue. This incident contained a forewarning of the cultural misunderstandings to come when a US soldier momentarily draped the

Stars and Stripes around the statue's face. Merrin's interpretation of the incident is a good example of the manner with which critical media theory like Baudrillard's extends Debord's *pseudo-event* to reach the parts of the mediascape other theories simply cannot:

> With Saddam's disappearance, all that was left was a non-event produced and framed for our consumption as the definitive and predictable sign of the regime's end. The self-liberation of the Iraqis could not be accomplished: when it became clear that they could not quickly pull the statue down the American military stepped in to finish the job. The Iraqis did not understand the primacy of the western audience, the time constraints even of rolling news, and the networks' fear of a drifting audience and their need to deliver that 'Kennedy' moment ('where were you?' … 'watching television'). So the Iraqis were excluded from this act, in an implosion of media and military with the event that neutralized and short-circuited the people's efforts, replacing them with that demanded, semiotic image of the statue's fall. Believing that they were the centre and meaning of the act, the Iraqis did not see that they were only the extras, providing local colour and a guarantee of authenticity and legitimacy for the western audience for whom the event really occurred.
>
> (Merrin 2005: 109)

Such examples, forcefully communicate the misleading significance afforded to individual images and events by the media and the profound consequences this has had upon political discourse in the West's *discourses of sobriety*.

## Punishing Lynndie England and Saving Private Lynch

Lynndie England was the US army reservist who gained worldwide notoriety with the publication of various photographs from Abu Ghraib showing the abuse of Iraqi prisoners, one of which infamously showed her holding a dog leash around an inmate's neck. Coincidentally, Ms England came from the same US State, West Virginia, as another famous female US soldier, Jessica Lynch. Both women vividly illustrate the flip-sides of the same rhetorical coin – excessively mediated representations. In the visually metonymic codes of the tele-frame, one provided shorthand for US heroism and one for its brutality. Lynndie England's parents experienced at first hand the image-led nature of the media's account of the conflict as a whole and the consistency with which images are processed within the tele-frame whether good or bad:

Ms England's mother, Terrie, told the Baltimore Sun newspaper: 'It's all over the news, but we're not hearing anything new. They just keep showing the pictures. How many times do I have to see those pictures?' ... 'Just like what happened with that Lynch girl, this is getting blown out of proportion,' Ms England's father said. 'But in a negative way rather than a positive way'.

(Buncombe 2004: n.p.)

The invasive reach of Hollywood and the culture industry's influence into the previous sober discourse of non-entertainment was further exemplified by the domination of the front pages and morning news bulletins of the US media on 2 April 2003 by the story of a daring rescue by US soldiers of an injured 19-year-old female colleague that was filmed at the army's invitation. It was presented by one anchorman with the words 'It's just like a movie but it happened in real life' and covered throughout the media with the tag line: *Saving Private Lynch*. The 'rescue' of Private Lynch, was presented by US television channels in explicitly Hollywood terms and just like *Saving Private Ryan* it promoted profoundly misleading impressions.[11]

The media-constructed *Saving Private Lynch* centred upon a feel-good message that continued to follow the tele-frame of *pseudo-events* with further mediation that included a televised press conference for Private Lynch's subsequent home-coming. This *emo*-based reporting unsurprisingly failed to discuss various aspects of her rescue that had initially given her the status of a heroine and were subsequently found to be false. Excluded facts included: Iraqi doctors had unsuccessfully attempted to return her to US troops who had turned them back with gun fire; her injuries stemmed from a traffic accident rather than actual combat; and, perhaps most disturbingly, there were no enemy troops near her at the time of her 'rescue' – US troops were aware of this and acted out a camera-friendly 'daring' rescue operation for the cameras and reporters that accompanied them (Potter 2003). By the time a discourse of sober analysis could be applied, the *emo*tive, affective associations to be made between one soldier's fate and a Hollywood blockbuster had already achieved their substantial ideological effects[12]. To this extent, critical accounts of the media tend to operate under conditions of 'catch-up' – critical voices do arise (including those of Private Lynch herself [see Helmore 2003]), but they are innately ill-suited to match the much more shallow but much speedier nature of the uncritical commentary that tends to substitute banal real-time descriptions for more considered conceptual analysis.

## Abu Ghraib

In Britain, the distraction from the deeper significance of the Abu Ghraib photographs came in the form of a debate over whether similar pictures of British troops abusing Iraqi prisoners elsewhere were fake or not. In May 2004, Piers Morgan the editor of the UK's *Daily Mirror* tabloid newspaper left his post when the photographs he printed were proved to be false. It is interesting to note that as doubts were being raised about their veracity, debate was at least taking place as to whether they were still accurate representations of real events not originally photographed. In this particular instance, although the issue of authenticity dominated proceedings, possibly fake pictures nevertheless did allow deeper discussion about the sorts of abuse that were taking place. The furore caused by The *Daily Mirror* pictures provided an interesting example of Bracewell's assessment of the contemporary status of the image where: ' "authenticity" is the hallmark of truth, and hence the gauge of social value ... *there is now the sense that authenticity itself can be sculpted to suggest veracity as an image, in which truth remains ambiguous*' (Bracewell 2002: 66; emphasis added).

In the *Ecstasy of Communication* (1988) among other works, Baudrillard develops the theme of modern communication's tendency towards uncontrollable circulation. The roots of this uncontrollable circulation can be found in Sontag's (1979) earlier examination of photography's defining status as the ground-breaking technology of the image where she asserts that: 'Photographs document sequences of consumption carried on outside the view of family, friends, neighbours.' (Sontag 1979: 9). The lack of values with which to judge the appropriateness of the image is for Sontag an intrinsic part of the conceptually reductive nature of the technology. She argues that: 'there is an aggression implicit in every use of the camera' and that it is responsible for 'an ever increasing spread of that mentality which looks at the world as a set of potential photographs' (1979: 7). Specifically in the light of Abu Ghraib, Sontag points out that, although 'trophy' pictures have been taken in many previous military and social conflicts, these particular photographs:

> ... reflect a shift in the use of pictures – less objects to be saved than evanescent messages to be disseminated, circulated ... now the soldiers themselves are all photographers – recording their war, their fun, their observations of what they find picturesque, their atrocities – and swapping images among themselves, and emailing them around the globe ... since the pictures were meant to be circulated and seen by many people, it was all fun.

And this idea of fun is, alas, more and more – contrary to what Mr Bush is telling the world – part of the 'true nature and heart of America'.

(Sontag 2004: 3)

Although they would seem unlikely bedfellows, Baudrillard's notion of *the ecstasy of communication* was implicitly acknowledged by Donald Rumsfeld who complained that it was much harder nowadays to control the information sent back home by soldiers serving overseas. Unlike conventional letters in which the censors can black out the offending parts, Rumsfeld bemoaned the fact that US soldiers were 'running around with digital cameras and taking these unbelievable photographs and then passing them off, against the law, to the media, to our surprise' (cited in Sontag 2004: 5). Rumsfeld's complaint provides a practical politician's insight to complement Baudrillard's theoretical account of a society in which signs circulate for their own sake and which gave rise to the trophy-seeking behaviour of the Abu Ghraib photographers which so dramatically undermined the Coalition's attempts to brand itself as *Occupation-Lite.*

The images of prisoner abuse reflected the West's ongoing narcissistic obsession with the screen and it is perhaps this unhealthy obsession which fuels much of the misguided nature of its neo-Orientalism (Said [1979] 2003). A culture premised upon the tautological circulation of signs thus struggles to understand one in which symbols are privileged over signs – as illustrated in October 2005 by the controversy caused by the Danish newspaper *Jyllands-Posten's* printing of cartoons of the Prophet Mohammad. A keen awareness of this process arguably marks the malevolent acuity of Bin Laden. He is the latest in a string of iconic Islamic hate-figures that previously included the Ayatollah Khomeni, and who share the status of being bracketed within a discourse of evil[13]. Bin Laden fulfils the role portrayed in Baudrillard's work of the Manichean demiurge who creates the evil illusions against which God and goodness avail themselves. The biggest danger for the West, however, is that Bin Laden and others play this role self-consciously. They know which buttons to press in order to produce effects that go right to the core of the West's own deeply embedded *social porn,* of which Abu Ghraib was but a particularly shocking example. An alarming implication of this chapter's analysis is that the media's role in facilitating America's increasingly myopic separation from the Islamic Other has been incorporated as an integral part of the terrorists' game plan.

## Conclusion

> Accustomed to live in a world of pseudo-events, celebrities, dissolving forms, and shadowy but overshadowing images, we mistake our shadows for ourselves. To us they seem more real than the reality ... Our technique seems direct only because in our daily lives the pseudo-event always seems destined to dominate the natural facts. We no longer even recognise that our technique is indirect, that we have committed ourselves to managing shadows. We can live in our world of illusions. Although we find it hard to imagine, other peoples still live in the world of dreams. We live in a world of our making. Can we conjure others to live there too? We love the image, and believe it. But will they?
>
> (Boorstin [1961] 1992: 249)

> they don't draw careful distinctions between democracy as a system of government and democracy as a form of entertainment ... The automatous machinery of the electronic media makes a ceaseless and sometimes joyful noise, but to whom does it speak, and in what language? And why – behind the splendid twinkling of the whirligig façade – is the silence so loud?
>
> (Lapham 2001: xii)

The events analysed in this chapter suggest that the answer to Boorstin's above rhetorical question is 'no'. Similarly, Lapham usefully summarizes our contention (contained within the notion of *social porn*) that the pervasive reach of the culture industry into the traditional realm of *the discourses of sobriety* has profoundly negative political consequences that Benjamin severely underestimates in his Essay. The obsessively repetitive attention paid by the media to *pseudo-events* obscures the deeper social issues of which they are only reflections. Although the media's obsession with celebrity lives and deaths appears relatively benign, this chapter has demonstrated the much more serious geopolitical effects from the strike against understanding fostered by the contemporary *society of the spectacle*'s *Ratio* and reflected in such *pseudo-events* as the 9/11 tragedy and the toppling of Saddam Hussein's statue in the centre of Baghdad. Against audience-empowerment theorists, no matter how forceful or persuasive they are in purely critical terms, counter-hegemonic readings of such media products as *Saving Private Lynch* struggle to compete with the pre-primed nature of the values seamlessly communicated by the sophisticated tele-frame of the contemporary culture industry. Even if the manufactured drama of Private Lynch's rescue had been true, it is more than simply churlish to point out that various insidiously cynical pre-programmed responses are necessary from news producers and consumers alike in order for the story of one rescued soldier to be privileged over the fate of hundreds of thousands of less fortunate civilians. In the prior case of Afghanistan, similarly distorted priorities led to the media's disproportionate reporting on the fate of Marjorie . . . the lion from Kabul zoo.

In his *Contributions to Analytical Psychology* (1928), Jung argued that an individual's psychology could be profoundly, albeit unwittingly, influenced by an underpinning dependency of the wider society (cited in McLuhan [1964] 1995: 21). He used the example of the average Roman citizen who was inevitably infected by a general social atmosphere permeated by slavery and claimed the individual is powerless to resist such an influence. Innis ([1951] 2003) and McLuhan ([1964] 1995) used a similar argument to describe the cultural impact of media technologies through history. This chapter suggests that social porn now permeates media discourse in the West and the *Jerry Springer* nature of the Abu Ghraib photographs points to the validity of Jung's analysis. The *social porn* of the image is a fertile resource from which Bin Laden and others base their media-savvy strategies. The true malevolent ingenuity of Bin Laden's 9/11 outrage thus resides in his knowing incorporation of the West's inability to see beyond its own Narcissus-like fixations. For example, Osama Bin Laden's image is now readily familiar to all but a tiny proportion of Western populations but a similarly tiny proportion of people are likely to be aware of the full geopolitical context from which Bin Laden sprang. There is, for example, no significant public discussion of the historical parallels and links that can be made between his acts and the Royal House of Saud's uneasy yet perennially intertwined relationship with the Ikhwan bedouin fighters and the Wahabi fundamentalist strand of Islam. The USA was traumatized, yet fundamentally unenlightened, by the shocking yet constantly repeated images of the twin towers being hit. Unaccompanied by significant efforts to understand, mere repetition of the images reflected the fundamentally distorted perspective of a society increasingly incapable of thinking outside the self-referential media realm alluded to throughout this book.

# Conclusion

## Myths and the media: Medusa

We have learned in school the story of the Gorgon Medusa whose face, with its huge teeth and protruding tongue, was so horrible that the sheer sight of it turned men and beasts into stone. When Athena instigated Perseus to slay the monster, she therefore warned him never to look at the face itself but only at its mirror reflection in the polished shield she had given him. Following her advice, Perseus cut off Medusa's head with the sickle which Hermes had contributed to his equipment. The moral of the myth is, of course, that we do not, and cannot, see actual horrors because they paralyze us with blinding fear; and that we shall know what they look like only by watching images of them which reproduce their true appearance. These images have nothing in common with the artist's imaginative rendering of an unseen dread but are in the nature of mirror reflections. *Now of all the existing media the cinema alone holds up a mirror to nature. Hence our dependence upon it for the reflection of happenings which would petrify us were we to encounter them in real life. The film screen is Athena's polished shield.*

(Kracauer 1965: 305; emphasis added)

Kracauer uses the Medusa myth to make a clear distinction between 'the artist's imaginative rendering of an unseen dread' and 'mirror reflections'. The traditional role of the artist of *then* (Benjamin's notion of art's contemplation-inducing qualities and Kracauer's characterization of an art 'permeated by cognition') is *now* supplanted by the mirror reflections of sophisticated modern media technologies. Kracauer sees film's empowering potential in the way it produces images that: 'beckon the spectator to take them in and thus incorporate into his memory the real face of things too dreadful to be beheld in reality' (1960: 306). Like Benjamin's hope that the masses would absorb media images, rather than being absorbed by traditional art forms, for Kracauer too, there is the hope that the spectator is in control of the process. The ability to view such images as those that came out of the liberation of the Nazi death camps means that: 'we redeem horror from its invisibility behind the veils of panic and imagination. And this experience is liberating in as much as it removes a most powerful taboo' (1960: 306). The taboo that Kracauer refers to is the threat of inhibition in the face of direct experience. The film screen, acting as a modern embodiment of Athena's polished shield, allows the spectator to view events from one stage removed. In a similar fashion to the mis-guided nature of Benjamin's optimistic belief in distraction as an empowering feature of mass culture, the hopes Kracauer rested upon the screen appear, with historical hindsight to be misplaced. They sit rather uneasily with his own analysis of the way in which, in practice, *Ratio* rips away the veils of cultural symbolism. In the preceding chapters, Baudrillard's analysis has suggested that the media-sponsored removal of taboo has proceeded to such an extent that the traditional notion of the obscene associated with taboo is now replaced with the *obscene*, the stage-less immediacy of an optical unconscious effectively lacking any social constraints.

Experience of today's mediascape points to both the essential accuracy of Benjamin and Kracauer's early analyses of the basic mediated processes of mass culture but also the betrayal of their hopes that these would ultimately prove empowering. Rather than allowing us to enjoy the benefits of a technologized Athen's shield:

> The voyeuristic gaze threatens to overwhelm the narrative structure of the conventional documentary. The video clip is more reality fetish than evidence, as it is replayed over and over, slowed down, grabbed, processed, de- and re-constructed for our entertainment and horror. The video clip here stands for a reality (of horror) that cannot be known but which must at the same time be contained.
>
> (Dovey 2000: 59)

The media's efficient containment of otherwise inhibitory tendencies comes at the cost of a McLuhanite auto-amputation. We extend our ability to manage reality, but we lose some of our ability to know it with the depth offered by less technological forms of narrative. Film has its own inherent properties so that, according to Kracauer: 'the question arises whether it makes sense at all to seek the meaning of horror images in their underlying intentions or uncertain effects' (Kracauer 1960: 305). This resonates with McLuhan's *the medium is the message*. The crucial point is that a situation soon arises in which: 'The mirror reflections of horror are an end in themselves' (Kracauer 1960: 306). This is a key element of a critical understand-ing of the media. The detailed discussion of media content typical of various forms of cultural populism is guilty of missing the bigger picture. As McLuhan argued, the form in which content is presented is its true cultural effect. It is worth remembering that it is only a few lines after his famous aphorism that McLuhan, as previously cited, suggests that in terms of the machine's social impact: 'it mattered not in the least whether it turned out cornflakes or Cadillacs' ([1964] 1995: 7–8). This is also the political import of

Adorno and Debord's critical analyses. Adorno's culture industry outpaces the hopes held by Benjamin as it applies mechanical production to cultural life with the exponentially systematic extirpation of the particular and its replacement with the general. Similarly, Debord describes an image-based society in which the spectacle becomes a generalizing frame of reference before which we as mass spectators are invariably numb.

## Myths and the media: Narcissus

> The Greek myth of Narcissus is directly concerned with a fact of human experience, as the word Narcissus indicates. It is from the Greek word narcosis, or numbness. The youth Narcissus mistook his own reflection in the water for another person. This extension of himself by mirror numbed his perceptions until he became the servomechanism of his own extended or repeated image. The nymph Echo tried to win his love with fragments of his own speech, but in vain. He was numb. He had adapted to his extension of himself and had become a closed system.
>
> (McLuhan 1995 [1964]: 41)

In contrast to Kracauer's use of the Medusa myth, McLuhan uses the figure of Narcissus to illustrate the dangerously seductive properties of the new space of non-inhibited experience afforded by media technologies. In his interpretation the media have a numbing effect upon their users to which they are generally oblivious. A common misunderstanding of the Narcissus story is that he fell in love with his reflection knowing that it was an image of himself. It is this reading of the myth that gives us the modern sense of the adjective 'narcissistic' as meaning the love of oneself. According to McLuhan, however, this misunderstanding detracts from the significance the myth has for our experience of media technologies. Mass-media society risks suffering the mythical fate of Narcissus in its reliance upon its own diverse range of narcotic reflections. Narcissus was unaware that the reflected face was his own: he became obsessively fascinated with an image for its own sake. This is the seductive power that McLuhan highlighted in a manner that echoes (appropriately in this context) Kracauer's assertion that the mirror reflections risk becoming an end in themselves: 'the power of the image to beget image, and of technology to reproduce itself via human intervention, is utterly in excess of our power to control the psychic and social consequences ... the medium creates an environment that is as indelible as it is lethal' (McLuhan, cited in Moos 1997: 90).

Despite his widespread reputation as a keen advocate of media technologies the above quotations show how sensitive McLuhan was to their culturally damaging qualities – damage that occurs independently of society's wishes. He frequently identified many negative cultural aspects to their adoption with such unequivocal statements as: 'Most media ... are pure poison – TV, for example, has all the effects of LSD. I don't think we should allow this to happen' (McLuhan, in Moos 1997: 72) and the equally blunt, but seldomly highlighted comments such as:

> If TV was simply eliminated from the United States scene, it would be a very good thing ... TV, in a highly visual culture, drives us inward in depth into a totally nonvisual universe of involvement. It is destroying our entire political, educational, social, institutional life. TV will dissolve the entire fabric of society in a short time. If you understood its dynamics, you would choose to eliminate it as soon as possible.
>
> (McLuhan, in Moos 1997: 77–8)

McLuhan argued that any technology creates a level of auto-amputative numbness but he placed particular emphasis upon the particular strength of the media's *autoamputative* power instead of the empowering possibilities Benjamin foresaw in the camera's explosive power. In Benjamin's analysis the traditional artwork absorbed the viewer in contrast to the masses who absorb the reproduced work, for McLuhan and Baudrillard, the distance from which contemplation took place in traditional culture no longer exists. In our particularly advanced age of mechanical reproduction, we suffer from the same overpowering fascination with surfaces as Narcissus but our reflective (not reflexive) surfaces are significantly more absorbing than a mere pond. Baudrillard's analysis returns us to the critical potential implicit within McLuhan and his account of the transformative nature of the media notwithstanding his standard reputation as an optimistic endorser of the global village. In both McLuhan and Baudrillard's work Benjamin's positive interpretation of *distraction* and its purportedly liberating possibilities is undermined and replaced with a much more prosaic reality of a culture built upon pre-encoded messages intended for tautological transmission rather than symbolic exchange.

## The ideology of one-dimensionality

> private space has been invaded and whittled down by technological reality. Mass production and mass distribution claim the *entire* individual, and industrial psychology has long since ceased to be confined to the factory. The manifold processes of introjection seem to be ossified in almost mechanical reactions.

> The result is, not adjustment but *mimesis*: an immediate identi-
> fication of the individual with *his* society, and through it, with
> the society as a whole.
>
> (Marcuse 1968: 10; emphases in original)

> Information counts upon curiosity as the attitude with which
> the viewer approaches the product. The indiscretion formerly
> the prerogative of the most wretched of journalists has become
> part of the very essence of official culture. The information
> communicated by mass culture constantly winks at us.
>
> (Adorno 1991: 83)

The cultural impact of the *Other News* resides not only in the
significant proportion of all news programming it takes up, but
perhaps more importantly the more subtle, qualitative impact it
achieves through the close juxtaposition of its form and tone, and
the blurred boundaries this causes with the *discourses of sobriety*. The
*Other News* cultivates among its viewers a tendency towards either
dramatic or emotional identification (combined in the *emo*) rather
than critical thought and this ideological component is more
powerful for being implicit and low key. This is an important
paradox (which is additionally implicit in this book's more general
analysis about celebrity/trivia culture as a whole) – its deeply
ideological function tends to occur without due recognition that it is
ideological: 'ideology ... so produces and constructs the real as to
cast the shadow of its absence over the perception of its presence ...
the real is by necessity empirically imperceptible [in] the capitalist
mode of production' (Eagleton, cited in Mitchell 1992: 170).

*Banality TV* and the *Other News* undermine rational discourse but
do so while appearing to constitute either just 'harmless fun' or with
the active collaboration of its audiences, and so purportedly immune
from the charge of being manipulative. In this manner, cultural
populism's accommodative interpretations of the contemporary tele-
frame adopts the same erroneous approach that classical political
economy adopts to the commodity form. The latter is 'interested
only in contents concealed behind the commodity-form, which is
why it cannot explain the true secret, not the secret *behind* the form
but *the secret of this form itself*' (Žižek 1989: 16; emphasis in original).
The subtle effectiveness of contemporary forms of false consciousness thus derives from their essentially non-coercive nature. The
critical theorists of *then* would perhaps struggle to apply their
ideological analysis of the culture industry to such overt expressions
of manipulation as T.V.'s *Big Brother* with its blatant recuperation of
Orwell's critical inspiration to the point that: 'the formula of
cynicism is no longer the classic Marxian "they do not know it, but
they are doing it"; it is "they know very well what they are doing, yet
they are doing it"' (Žižek 1994: 8).

A crucial ideological aspect of the culture industry typically overlooked by cultural populists is thus the manner in which ideology is created, not by the difficult task of persuading a potentially resistant and cynical person, but by the *de facto* success to be achieved by constant exposure to systemic repetitions that produce their own qualitative effect. To illustrate this point Žižek uses the example of the various symbolic practices associated with religion (baptism, confession, communion, and so on). Our conventional understanding is that these practices reflect and embody a prior belief, but Žižek argues this underestimates the actual belief-generating power of the acts themselves *irrespective* of any prior belief, so that such symbols:

> far from being a mere secondary externalization of the inner belief, stand for the very mechanisms that generate it. When Althusser repeats, after Pascal: 'Act as if you believe, pray, kneel down, and you shall believe, faith will arrive by itself', he delineates an intricate reflective mechanism of retroactive 'auto-poetic' foundation that far exceeds the reductionist assertion of the dependence of inner belief on external behaviour. That is to say, the implicit logic of his argument is: kneel down and you shall believe that you knelt down because of your belief – that is, your following the ritual is an expression/effect of your inner belief; in short, the 'external' ritual performatively generates its own ideological foundation.
>
> (Žižek 1994: 12–13)

This book has demonstrated the theoretical roots of a critical theory that sets itself apart from cultural populism by being sensitive to this ideological component. It is not enough to believe that you are consuming the culture industry's content in an ironic or empowering fashion, the fact that you are consuming generates its own non-autonomous forms of belief – irrespective of your intentions.

## The *perversion* of cultural populism

> everything now is aestheticized: politics is aestheticized in the spectacle, sex in advertising and porn, and all kinds of activity conventionally referred to as culture – a sort of all-pervasive media-and-advertising-led semiologization: 'culture degree Xerox'
>
> (Baudrillard 1993: 9)

> Reality TV may be as sensational as it wishes, it may be as seemingly decentered, ahistorical, and futureless as it chooses, but ... it is never critical of the hierarchy perpetuated by its own form ... Reality TV can be as heterogenous, dispersive,

self-conscious, and reflexive as all get out, but it never calls our
own position as virtual participant and actual consumer into
question.

(Nichols 1994: 59)

Baudrillard and Nichols highlight above the betrayal of Benjamin's
hopes for the politicization of aesthetics by means of technologies of
mechanical reproduction voiced in his Essay. The all-inclusive reach
into culture produces a 'culture degree Xerox' that generally avoids
critique by nature of its pervasive ubiquity. Žižek uses the psychoanalytical category of *perversion* as a technical (rather than a judgemental term) to describe, not acts of sexual deviancy, but, rather, an
excessive reliance upon rules or structures. The notion can usefully
be applied to cultural populism. It is perverted for the manner with
which it uncritically reinforces the media's tendency towards ideological reduction. Despite the polysemic riches afforded by *Banality
TV* and its diverse targets, its ideological content remains homoge-
neously part of the culture industry. *Banality TV* and its associated
formats become a diversionary tactic to avoid dealing with genuine
social problems and their complex causes: 'Unpredictability, uncertainty, contingency: they loom as symptoms of incomprehension
masquerading behind an aesthetics of sensation' (Nichols 1994: 59).
Thus, any radical potential to be found within Benjamin's *distraction*
and Kracauer's belief in the eventual unveiling of *Ratio*'s inadequa-
cies are co-opted back into the *society of the spectacle*.

Cultural populism sacrifices any notion of a critical edge for a
celebratory engagement with such contingency and its excitingly
random manifestations (although such nominal randomness appears
in predictable, formulaic packages/formats). In contrast, critical
theory refuses to interpret such representations of contingency as
evidence of ongoing interpretive struggle. Instead, it interprets them
as examples of an *ex post* justification/fig-leaf for a struggle that in
reality is profoundly unequal. Cultural populism's emphasis upon the
significance of interpretative activity fails to give adequate weight to
the disproportionately systemic nature of the commodifying influences upon this interpretive process. To re-emphasize Nichols's
previously cited point, social experience becomes *relocated* within
*highly charged webs of significance*. Traditional forms of social experience are thus liquidated as Benjamin did indeed recognize, but in a
manner vulnerable to systemic commodification to an extent he did
not foresee.

The ideological result is that rather than seeking to understand
the complexity of contemporary capitalist society, its politics are
reduced in cultural populism to the perverted fetishization of
*Banality TV*'s narrative structures. Nichols shares with Langer (1998)
the belief that the rise of these new formats serves an ideological

purpose – an *ideological reduction,* or, as Langer terms it, a *discursive mobilization.* Global capitalism brings new levels of uncertainty and social flux for formerly stable elements – especially previously secure groups like the middle class. *Banality TV* becomes a tool of ideological containment that translates this otherwise threatening outside world of economic migrants, job instability and the relativization of previously strong social institutions such as the Church, into more easily consumable (if no more ultimately understandable) visual packages. In this manner, the inner-city ghettos from which more young black men go to prison than college are transformed from a material indictment of society's failings to the source of a whole range of Reality programming. They provide a suitably dramatic urban backdrop for witnessing the reassuring (albeit piecemeal) reassertion of the authorities' control. The contingency Kracauer and others emphasize as an intrinsic feature of the photographic image's content is allied within Reality TV's presentation of a correspondingly contingent society. The result is that instead of the mass media providing an authentic forum for substantive political debate over such uncomfortable social facts as the very existence of ghettos, it is the contingent immediacy of the images from the urban jungle in various docudrama formats which means that 'an aesthetics of sensation underlies reality TV' (Nichols 1994: 59). It is claimed that postmodernity shatters traditional meta-narratives (Lyotard 1979); in this process of fragmentation Reality TV contributes the 'construction of an endless "now"', 'its preference for the chronicle, the random and the unforeseen over the order and cohesion of historiography' (Nichols 1994: 59)'

For Nichols, the critical tradition of documentary film opens up 'questions of magnitude. Reality TV privileges social events that have their political content leached from them due to the mass media's preference for simplistic morality plays. As we have indicated with our example of inner-city ghettos, Reality TV does not do questions of magnitude. For example (building further upon the notion of the self-referential circuit): 'Celebrating the conviction of two LAPD officers for beating Rodney King in 1991 "ends" the story, on the episodic level, but does nothing to address the social conditions that underpin it structurally' (Nichols 1994: 60). The effect of Reality TV/*Other News*/Cult of Celebrity is to reduce big political questions to the status of the personal/ity. Any strongly felt outrage at the time of a particular spectacle is quickly channelled into the next. This creates: 'a reactive politics that may mirror, in disturbing ways, the very forms of absorption and distraction that should be among its primary targets' (1994: 60). Once again we can see how Benjamin's hopes for distraction have been betrayed by its sanitized incorporation into the frame of the mediascape.

## The problem with distraction

> Let Proust have his madeleines. We have ads. Some of my
> students are embarassed ... that cultural junk food is what they
> share ... Yet it is precisely the recognition of jingles and brand
> names, precisely what high culturists abhor, that links us as a
> culture. More than anything else this paper-thin familiarity is
> what gives Adcult its incredible reach and equally incredible
> shallowness. It is a culture without memory and hence without
> depth.
>
> (Twitchell 1996: 7)

Benjamin chose to be optimistic about the kind of distraction that
more critical commentators such as Duhammel saw in terms of a
theft of thought 'I can no longer think what I want to think. My
thoughts have been replaced by moving images' (cited in Benjamin,
Essay: Section XIV). For Benjamin, distraction educates humanity *en
masse* bypassing the hierarchies encoded in traditional knowledge,
and therein resides its emancipatory potential. Similarly, cinema
imposes shock, but in training the sensorium of viewers it provides
them with a means of representing an environment of shock, of
mastering it. But beyond this rather vague formulation, Benjamin
fails to fully develop the concept of distraction – especially its
potentially negative cultural implications. Despite the differences
between Benjamin and the Frankfurt School's much more negative
assessments, both approaches do recognize the dialectic of technologically facilitated social developments and the profound cultural
change they induce. In Benjamin's Essay, the new media technologies of his time provided the vehicle for the undermining of
traditional, oppressive social forms. In contrast, Fascism represented
the non-dialectical reification of tradition. It sought to use tradition
in a mythic, totalizing and oppressive manner. In this context,
Benjamin's optimistic interpretation of media effects can be viewed
as being inevitably affected by a desire to find counterweights to
Fascism's malign use of aura. This laudable aim however, blinded
Benjamin to the manner in which the dialectical process generated
not only new modes of mass reception, but also correspondingly
novel modes of mass subordination – *friendly fascism*.

   Adorno's reservations about Benjamin's theories are recorded in
their correspondence, and prefigure his own culture industry thesis.
Adorno accused the Essay of various forms of romanticism, arguing
that: 'I do not find your concept of distraction convincing – if only
for the simple reason that in a communist society work will no
longer be organized in such a way that people will no longer be so
tired and stultified that they need distraction' (Adorno, cited in
Jameson 1980: 123). Gilloch neatly summarizes the characteristic
bluntness with which he supplemented this critique:

For Adorno, distraction ... is simply an index of capitalist domination; it is not linked with genuine enjoyment and pleasure, but signifies only the demise of the subject's capacity for real happiness; it is devoid of critical potential ... distraction is a symptom of, not a solution to prevailing conditions ... Far from ... engaging in the 'tactile appropriation' of artworks, the distracted audience is a consequence of the monotonous, mind-numbing routine of mechanized labour under capitalism. Distraction in the cinema is merely the corollary of alienation and exploitation in the factory and the boredom, apathy and atrophied sensibilities of the modern city ... Distraction involves only a weary satisfaction with the banalities of the 'culture industry' ... 'The laughter of the audience at a cinema ... is anything but good and revolutionary; instead, it is full of the worst sadism'.

(Gilloch 2002: 192–3)

Adorno argues that this misguided faith in distraction has its roots in another romantic assumption: that the media of mechanical reproduction are intrinsically progressive. But for Adorno the opposition Benjamin erected between the auratic work of art and the output of the media of mass reproduction is invalid. Adorno saw 'true' art in terms of *autonomous work*, an autonomy largely absent in the products of the new media. Thus, in failing to incorporate this quality of autonomy in his analysis of the traditional work of art, Benjamin overestimates the so-called 'art of the masses' while ignoring the radical innovation of purportedly elitist high art. Adorno argues for a re-examination of *high art* that would do full justice to its emancipatory content. Similarly he notes that cinema (the repository of Benjamin's highest hopes as we have seen), when produced for mass entertainment, contrives to minimize the very techniques that gave Benjamin such hope: 'When I spent a day in the studios of Neubabelsberg ... what impressed me most was how *little* montage and all the advanced techniques that you emphasize are actually used: rather, reality is everywhere *constructed* with an infantile mimetism and then photographed' (Adorno, cited in Jameson 1980: 124; emphasis in original).

Benjamin's identification of traditional aura's diminishment ('like water pumped out of a sinking ship') can be reinterpreted in practice as a pumping out of the grounds necessary for even the possibility of producing truly critical understandings. Tradition is replaced by the tautological predictability of the culture industry. For Adorno, Benjamin's characterization of tradition as reactive, and mass culture as progressive, is an insufficiently dialectical polarization of the situation. It rests upon 'the anarchistic romanticism of blind confidence in the spontaneous power of the proletariat in the historical process – a process which is itself a product of bourgeois society' (Adorno in Jameson 1980: 123). In his contrasting account of the culture industry, the autonomous work of art and the mass art of mechanical reproduction do not exist as historically successive periods. Rather, they are inextricably intertwined: 'Both are torn halves of an integral freedom, to which however they do not add up' (Adorno in Jameson 1980: 123). Benjamin posits a succession, in which the auratic artwork immured in repressive social values, is replaced by the art of technological reproduction and emancipatory potential. Opposing this, Adorno argues that there are elements of traditional art, in particular its indifference to profit principle, whose continued survival gives high art its radical social value. However, since the latter cannot communicate with the masses, its impact is necessarily limited. Thus for Adorno high and popular culture both contain progressive elements and factors that preclude their full realization – the components of a genuinely emancipated culture are scattered across these divergent forms.

The overt ideology of fascism that so troubled Benjamin now reappears as a subtler form of ideology in the guise of the pseudo-satisfaction of consumption. The 'omnipresence of the stereotype imposed by technical skill' (Adorno, in Duttmann 2000: 40; also cited in Chapter 2) is a serviceable summary of Hollywood's commodified output. Within the logic of the culture industry thesis, the predominant vehicle for Jameson's 'further intensification of the forces of reification' are these means of promulgating the increasingly pervasive influence of the commodity ethos. Moreover, its spread is abetted by the adroit co-optation of any resistance that arises to it. This can be seen in the way in which aesthetic forms that initially arise as a form of resistance (such as that of modernism) have become co-opted as a mainstay of contemporary advertising – as Jameson notes 'our entire system of commodity production and consumption today is based on those older, once anti-social modernist forms' (Jameson 1998: 149). In recent decades this process has grown ever more exacting and vigilant, stalling any potential empowering dialectical response to the remorseless reification of the contemporary mediascape that might have originally been identified in Benjamin's analysis. The recuperative power of the commodity form *now* typically continues to frustrate attempts to challenge the totalizing logic embodied in the culture industry thesis *then*. For example, the urban fashion of alienated African American youth originally based upon an aesthetic reaction to profound social inequality is quickly packaged and marketed as a 'look' or a 'sound' to be consumed in the shopping malls of the white suburbs[1]. Unlike Benjamin, the inherent properties of media technologies can be seen as a vital factor in generating this rapacious appetite for new, only nominally radical, cultural forms to commodify.

## The ob-scene as media critique

> We no longer partake of the drama of alienation, but are in the ecstasy of communication. And this ecstasy is obscene. Obscene is that which illuminates the gaze, the image and every representation. Obscenity is not confined to sexuality, because today there is a pornography of information and communica-tion, a pornography of circuits and networks, of functions and objects in their legibility, availability, regulation, forced signifi-cation, capacity to perform, connection, polyvalence, their free expression. It is no longer the obscenity of the hidden, the repressed, the obscure, but that of the visible, all-too-visible, the more visible than visible; it is the obscenity of that which no longer contains a secret and is entirely soluble in information and communication.
>
> (Baudrillard 1988: 22)

Because he tends to be perversely mis-labelled as a postmodern celebrator of the mediated world, a seriously under-acknowledged feature of Baudrillard's work is its traditionally critical nature. In clear opposition to Benjamin's celebration of the decline of aura, Baudrillard defends symbolic exchange in the face of the contempo-rary semiotic order. Implicitly in his work, Benjamin's *decline of aura* and the rise of *distraction* as well as McLuhan's notion of *auto-amputation* are used to argue that, in unprecedentedly sophisticated ways, the alignment of media technologies and commodity values *now* fatally undermines the symbolic grounds upon which authenti-cally free human interactions rest. Baudrillard's account of the implosion of the traditional social stage implicitly draws upon the thinkers explored in Part 1. His *obscene* can thus be read in terms of:

1 Benjamin's account of the rise of an optical unconscious that cuts through traditional, non-mediated modes of seeing
2 Kracauer's notion of truth being found in what is veiled rather than what is revealed
3 McLuhan's conception of *implosion*
4 Adorno's assertion that the culture industry is frequently explicit in terms of its willingness to unveil spectacle-friendly aspects of reality for profit but much more coy about dealing with deeper human issues. The culture industry is unwilling to deal with the uncommodifiable seductive properties of the symbolic.
5 Boorstin and Debord's argument that excessive visuality creates the objectifying dominance of the *pseudo-event* and the *society of the spectacle* respectively.

The particular contribution of Baudrillard's critical theory is the way he combines the above points in a sustained demonstration of how a high level of explicit visual information does not bring us closer to reality, but in fact carries us further away into a realm of simulation. Kracauer located the origins of this tendency in the innate properties of photography and made a distinction between a true understanding of history and the merely technically correct visual representation encountered in a photograph: 'This history omits all characteristics and determinations that do not relate in a significant sense to the truth intended by *a liberated consciousness* ... In a photograph, a person's history is buried as if under a layer of snow' (Kracauer 1995: 51; emphasis added). The direct corollary of Kracauer's analysis is that the knowledge we do derive from the media's revealing depiction of reality is not a liberated one.

Kracauer's *Ratio* described how the culture industry creates a systemic ersatz replacement for reality in the form of the *mass ornament*. His terms prefigure later conceptions of *hyperreality* and developments such as *Banality TV*. For Baudrillard, the *hyperreal*, defined as that which is more real than the real itself, is marked by the absence or increasing irrelevance of an original model upon which the imitation is based. In the phenomenon of Irish theme bars, for example, semiotic levels of Irishness exceed that to be found in Ireland[2]. This reduction of the full ambiguity and complexity of reality and a certain quality of excessiveness contained within media representations is what Kracauer described in pre-Baudrillardian terms when he suggests that: 'The desolation of *Ratio* is complete only when it removes its mask and hurls itself into the void of random abstractions that no longer mimic higher determinations, and when it renounces *seductive* consonances and desires itself even as a concept' (Kracauer 1995: 180; emphases added). The previous imitation of reality is replaced by a realm of 'random abstractions'. In this manner, *Banality TV* programmes suffer from format inflation. Thus, once talent shows based upon a process of eviction evolved to include celebrities, the variations upon the theme being almost endless – celebrities compete in contexts ranging from a jungle (*I'm a Celebrity – Get Me Out of Here!*) to various sorts of competition, in dance (*Strictly Come Dancing, Dancing With the Stars*), ice-skating (*Strictly Ice Dancing*), circus acts (*Cirque de Celebrite, Celebrity Circus*), weight loss (*Celebrity Fit Club*), and so on). The predictable format becomes increasingly independent of any 'higher determinations'. Culturally grounded symbolic values are replaced by the ready-made commodified categories of the culture industry.

Kracauer's argument that *Ratio* renounces 'seductive consonances' is a direct forbearer of Adorno's systemic, operationalized culture industry and reappears in Baudrillard's notion of *seduction*. Prior to mass-media society, sexuality was perhaps the most intimate and private aspect of social experience. For Baudrillard, the fate that befalls sexuality in a mediated culture, is indicative of a general process of industrialized revelation that takes Kracauer's *then* concept of *Ratio* to an exponentially new level – a *now* pervaded by 'a pornography of circuits and networks'. In contrast to cultural populism, Baudrillard, like Adorno before him, argues that the breadth of available polysemic interpretations belies their essentially uniform nature. The range is indeed wide as he recognizes in his claim that American television constitutes 'the living incarnation of the ludic' (Baudrillard 1990a: 150). However, such interpretations are of limited liberatory value because: 'They are no longer objects of libidinal investment; for they are made selectively available within a range of choices – with leisure itself now appearing, relative to work, as just another channel on the screen of time' (1990a: 158). This argument is reminiscent of two important features of Adorno's culture industry argument: the increasing incursion of work into the previously distinct and insulated personal leisure time; and his previously cited dismissal of purported differences between commodities.

The peculiarly *absorbed* nature of the fascination that the media engenders has been recognized by all the key theorists under consideration in this volume. For Baudrillard, like Adorno before him, the mediascape's promotion of fascination represents a social sphere emptied out of the more enchanted and seductive properties present in a symbol-rich non-mediated society. Mass-media society is an etiolated, pervasively commodified realm of semiotic signs that are manipulated systematically by a culture industry that has at its disposal ever more sophisticated techniques:

> All this belongs to the ludic realm where one encounters a cold seduction – the narcissistic spell of electronic and information systems, the cold attraction of the terminals and mediums that we have become, surrounded as we are by consoles, isolated and seduced by their manipulation ... This is the modern meaning play, the 'ludic' sense, connoting the suppleness and polyvalence of combinations. Understood in this sense, 'play,' its very possibility, is at the basis of the metastability of systems. It has nothing to do with play as a dual or agonistic relation; it is the cold seduction that governs the spheres of information and communication. And it is in this cold seduction that the social and its representations are now wearing themselves thin.
> (Baudrillard 1990a: 162)

Using McLuhanite notions (narcosis, hot and cold) but with distinctly more critical intent, Baudrillard suggests that a 'choice' between commodities that are essentially the same replaces the warm seductive properties of a culture based upon symbolic exchange. From this radical critical perspective, mass-media society of the *now* involves the cold seduction of semiotic codes. The skill with which consumers can manipulate such codes, is not grounds to be positive. It is defended by cultural populists/active audience theorists as displacement activity in an attempt to compensate for the codes' ultimate lack of critical non-commodified substance.

It is this basic disagreement that continues to fuel the parallel theorizations of cultural populism and critical theory. In recent Deleuzian-inspired variants of cultural populism, the concept of *flow of desire* is used to interpret positively the cold seductions of the culture industry.

> From one angle, RTV [Reality TV] is a nightmarish cybernetic dystopia. But the control society is not simply the latest notion in a line of pessimistic scenarios. These new conditions create both new intolerables and new potentials: Antidotes 'can be tracked down only in what for the moment appears to be poison' (Virno, 2004). In the control societies, it is 'not a question of worrying or hoping for the best, but of finding new weapons' (Deleuze, 1990/1995: p. 178). Although RTV seeks to transform the world into an experiment, it is also impossible to contain all impulses into the game dynamic. Rather than lament the loss of the interiorized subject, we look to dividual practices of fluctuation and collaboration for new possibilities. If capital, via control societies, 'interweaves' reality and television, then this interweaving can be undone and the threads reworked to make new meshworks (Dyer-Witheford, 1999, p. 71). Producing desubjectified flows does not guarantee their containment (as containment belongs to disciplinary society's techniques); their very fluctuation can become new sites for alternatives. This means there is ambivalence at the heart of the absorption (Virno, 2004, p. 84).
>
> (Bratich 2006: 77–8)

In opposition to such consistently misguided optimism, this book reasserts the unambivalently negative aspects of the distracted absorption promoted by *Banality TV.*

## Conclusion: aura, the pornographic and prudish, and the case of Picasso's *Guernica*

> Our present political order is based upon the non-being of human deprivation. What we need to replace it with is a political order which is also based upon non-being – but non-being as an awareness of human frailty and unfounded-

ness ... Tragedy reminds us of how hard it is, in confronting non-being, not to undo ourselves in the process. How can one look upon that horror and live? At the same time, it reminds us that a way of life which lacks the courage to make this traumatic encounter finally lacks the strength to survive. Only through encountering this failure can it flourish.

(Eagleton 2003: 221)

Previous chapters have demonstrated the extent to which the *society of the spectacle* is grounded in sensation and an over-dependence upon the image. This serves to exclude people and issues from the tele-frame as previously argued by Nichols in his description of the decline in the *discourses of sobriety*. Both Nichols and Eagleton's analyses fundamentally question Kracauer's positive interpretation of the Medusa myth. They problematize Kracauer's hope that film will 'redeem horror from its invisibility behind the veils of panic and imagination'. Instead of the media functioning as an empowering modern version of Athena's shield, it serves as a barrier that prevents us from traumatic encounters with the realities of human existence – replacing them with the manufactured *R*ealities of *Banality TV* in which our encounters with human deprivation are continuously deferred and filtered by the use of spectacle for grounding *emo*-driven sensations. Eagleton cites Adorno's remark that: 'There is tenderness only in the coarsest demand: that no-one should go hungry any more' (Eagleton 2003. 174). He points out that in the Judeo-Christian tradition the term *anawim* refers to the wretched beloved of God, arguing: 'The dispossessed are a living sign of the truth that the only enduring power is one anchored in an acknowledgement of failure. Any power which fails to recognise this fact will be enfeebled in a different sense, fearfully defending itself against the victims of its own arrogance' (Eagleton 2003: 176). It is the world's starving *anawim* that are systematically excluded in a *society of the spectacle* grounded in sensation rather than sensitivity, and it is the failure of our mediated culture to acknowledge failure that lies behind the West's fear that, as Boorstin foresaw and 9/11 so tragically demonstrated, our images will come back to haunt us.

Even in Benjamin's optimistic interpretation of the camera's new mode of distraction, he is aware of the danger of the rise of the semiotic over the symbolic. It is worth repeating a final time the final lines of the epilogue to his Essay. He so eloquently describes the negative trends we can see more clearly *now* with the advent of Banality TV: 'Humankind, which in Homer's time was an object of contemplation for itself. Its self-alienation has reached such a degree that it can experience its own destruction as an aesthetic pleasure of the highest order' (Essay: Epilogue). In his 2001 essay '*Dust breeding*', Baudrillard cites Benjamin's lines in full (Baudrillard 2005: 184) demonstrating the critical continuities in this book's choice of theorists from *then* and *now.* Benjamin's seminal account of the significance of reproductive media technologies, rejoices in their explosively revolutionary nature – 'Then came the film and burst this prison-world asunder by the dynamite of the tenth of a second' – to the point that 'in the midst of far-flung ruins and debris' he enjoins us to 'calmly and adventurously go travelling' (Essay: Section XIII). We reserve the right to put on our intellectual hard-hats and point out that we still need to find a better home than either a cave or the ruins and debris of a culture dominated by the spectacle.

Despite this book's consistently pessimistic and critical interpretation of today's mass-media society there is still hope to be found in Adorno's assertion that the culture industry is 'pornographic but prudish while true art is ascetic but unashamed' (Adorno and Horkheimer 1997: 140). This goes directly to the theme of the *obscene.* A culture based upon mechanically reproduced explicitness is prepared to exhibit and unveil everything at a surface level (the pornographic) but needs to censor the ambiguous and the seductive (it has a prudish attitude to high art and idealistic concepts autonomous from commercial values). On 5 February, 2003 at the United Nations (UN) Headquarters in New York there was an emblematic demonstration of critical theory's continued relevance to today's mediascape. The US Secretary of State, Colin Powell, spoke at a press conference as part of a concerted diplomatic effort by the US and the UK to obtain UN backing for an invasion of Iraq. In the hall where the press conference took place normally hangs a large tapestry – a reproduction of Pablo Picasso's famous anti-war painting – *Guernica.* For the press conference, the tapestry was covered by a blue curtain veiling the evocative scenes depicted in Picasso's artwork. While Benjamin hoped to see the greater politicization of aesthetics, events at the UN that day illustrated the continued aesthetic manipulation of politics. Two competing arguments were put forward to explain this veiling. One was that a plain blue backing was much more suitable as a neutral background for the television cameras. To the extent that this book is unashamedly pessimistic, critical media theory can point to this effective censoring of Picasso's message not by heavy-handed authoritarianism, but by the no less effective removal of a powerful political aura due to the media's technical requirements and innate grammar. The other reason suggested for the veiling was that US diplomats requested the action to avoid the incongruity of discussing an impending military action under this powerful anti-war symbol. If this was the true reason, critical theory offers optimism and hope to the extent that, in the midst of media-sponsored obscenity, there is still a need to veil and politicians can still be made to feel shame.

# Notes

## Chapter outlines

1 Reality TV is used throughout this book with a capitalized R in order to highlight its essentially manufactured, faux-reality quality. For useful overviews of the Reality TV phenomenon see Hill (2005), Holmes and Jermyn (2004), Kilbourn (2003), Murray and Ouellette (2004) and Biressi and Nunn (2004).

## Introduction

1 For a discussion of the complex relationship between the immaterial qualities of media technologies and their profoundly physical effects see our previous work *Digital Matters: The Culture and Theory of the Matrix* (Harris and Taylor 2005).
2 See Lash (2002) for an example of this theoretical embracing of immanence and for a critical response see Taylor (2006).
3 For useful recent overviews of these fields see Lacey (2002), Ross (2003) and Staiger (2005).
4 See McGuigan (1992) for a full discussion of this topic.
5 Barker and Brooks develop this theme further in *Knowing Audiences* (1998) where they link Judge Dredd fans with the Utopianism of the Chiliasts as initially explored in Karl Mannheim's *Ideology and Utopia*.
6 Mentioned in Adorno and Horkheimer's *Dialectic of Enlightenment* (2002), Scylla and Charybdis are two Greek mythological sea creatures that represent a classical source for the colloquial expressions 'between a rock and a hard place' or 'between the Devil and the deep blue sea'.

## Chapter 1

1 All references to Benjamin's Essay are made to sections of the Essay rather than page numbers, on the assumption that the majority of readers will be referring to such web-based resources as http://bid.berkeley.edu/bidclass/readings/benjamin.html
2 See Harris and Taylor (2005) for a book-length treatment of the issue of im/materiality in a technological world.

3  For example see 'TV time and catastrophe, or *beyond the pleasure principle* of television' in Mellencamp (1990).
4  For a detailed analysis of this merging of economic and cultural realms see Marshall Berman's *All That is Solid Melts into Air: The Experience of Modernity* (1983).
5  Meek provides the following interesting interpretations of the phenomenon of mass television mourning:

> Community would henceforth be symbolised through the cinematic spectacle of the return of the dead. In a parody of what Bataille and his colleagues saw as the principle of expenditure in the ancient festivals, film becomes the primary mediator with the spirit world. With television, mourning becomes electronic at new global levels.
>
> (*Meek 1998: n.p.*)

> The crowd of the unmourned who have always threatened to play havoc in the world of the living and were therefore given free reign at predetermined, culturally sanctioned periods of archaic festival, now co-exist in the purgatorial present of television.
>
> (*Meek 1998: n.p.*)

# Chapter 2

1  Disenchantment is a concept originally developed by the German sociologist Max Weber and refers to the manner in which as modernity progresses more and more of our lives become dominated by systemic structures that promote various forms of rationality but which leave less and less room for more traditionally spontaneous cultural forms and their qualities of ambiguity and unpredictability (a theme explored in Part 2's detailed account of contemporary media trends). The 'disenchantment of the world' is a phrase that Weber uses in *The Protestant Ethic and the Spirit of Capitalism* ([1930] 2001) to describe the cultural effects of rapid modernization with its new technologies and bureaucratic structures.
2  Kracauer's description owes something to Simmel's concepts of *neurasthenia, Chokerlebnis* and new *blasé* mental attitudes that urban dwellers need to adopt as a survival strategy with which to deal with the qualitatively new social conditions created by mass living.
3  See Harris and Taylor (2005, ch.4) for a full discussion of photography's role within a wider commodity culture.

# Chapter 3

1  Adorno and Horkheimer, *Dialectic of Enlightenment* (1997), although the majority of references are drawn from this translation, a number are taken from the new translation, *Dialectic of Enlightenment: Philosophical Fragments* (2002).

2  For example, in terms of the status of the arts in mass media society see Rosenberg and White's *Mass Culture: The Popular Arts in American* (1957), and their *Mass Culture Revisited* (1971).

3  See for instance 'On the fetish character in music and the regression of listening' (Adorno 1991: 26–52).

4  Baudrillard's various works suggest that contemporary consumer society is irredeemably commodified to the extent that artistic and aesthetic meaning is fatally flawed. He explores the society-defining overarching nature of the commodity in such early work as *The System of Objects* (1996b) (first published in 1968) and *The Consumer Society* (1998) (first published in 1970), while in his later work he explicitly addresses the implications of such a system for art, for example, *Art and Artefact* (1997) and *The Conspiracy of Art* (2005).

# Chapter 4

1  See Ewen (1996, 1999, 2001) and Ewen and Ewen (1992).

2  This notion of fear reappears in Baudrillard's reinterpretation of Durkheim's collective effervescence. The fear to be had in collective rituals has been replaced by the thrills to be derived from the operational categories of the culture industry (see Merrin 2005).

3  This tradition finds its earliest expression in Kapp's *Grundlinien einer Philosophie der Technik* ([1877] 1978) who argues for telegraph cables as extension of nerve fibres, plates as hands and so on, Marx likewise talks of cyclopean organs that reproduce the motive action of the human worker. However, one of the earliest and most profound meditations on this theme is to be found in Butler's *Erewhon* ([1872] 1970), a text known to McLuhan, as revealed by his allusion to man as the reproductive organs of the machine world. McLuhan thus argues that the writing and the word is an extension of the eye, the wheel and the road the extension of the foot, and electronics as an extension of the nervous system, technology thus become a global body, uniting humanity en masse (literally, 'in a body'). Media abstract, replicate and extend various sensory process and modalities, so that they become not simply methods of perceiving the environment but elements of the environment itself. Humanity here becomes, in Freud's memorable phrase, 'a prosthetic god'.

4   McLuhan was aware of the provisional nature of his reading of television, and that a shift in technology could render them redundant. He responded to the possibility of television becoming a 'hot', or high-definition, image by asserting that a television image that attained the informational density of cinematic image, would no longer be television but a new medium – an issue that has become increasingly relevant with the advent of high-definition, large and widescreen, home cinema set-ups.

## Chapter 5

1   The passages cited here are taken from Freddy Perlman and John Supak's translation, *The Society of the Spectacle* (Debord 1977), which is widely available online. References refer to the text's numbered sections (N), which remain constant across various translations.
2   And later again by Jameson (1998) with his concept of the *dialectic of reification*.
3   In some of the latest theoretical accounts of such developments this process is referred to as bio-politics as seen in the work of Hardt and Negri (2000, 2005), Poster (2006) and Jenkins (2006a, 2006b).
4   Paradoxically, this is evident even in his films, from his earliest experiments which refuted cinema's visuality by subjecting its audience to hour-long monologues accompanying a blank screen, to his later film which delivered a commentary on images that heaped contempt on them, and on their audience.
5   *Gresham's Law* is a concept in economics whereby upon the introduction of counterfeit money, people will tend to hoard legitimate currency and try to spend the false money. The overall effect is that the counterfeit money becomes a greater proportion of the overall money in circulation as the good money is withdrawn and hoarded.
6   'Preface to the third French edition', *The Society of the Spectacle*, trans. David Nicholson-Smith (Debord 1994).

## Chapter 6

1   For more general overviews of celebrity see Evans and Hesmondhalgh (2005) and Turner (2004).
2   *Pop Idol*-type programmes provide a topical illustration of this process. Various niche alternatives (rock, heavy metal, 'bad' boy/girl singer and so on) are presented to viewers as genuine evidence of the musical choice on offer, when in fact, they are often geared to maximize the demographic appeal and hence

marketability of the programme. It is this underlying matrix of commodified values, not authentic musical considerations that ultimately determines the success of the contestants. The sophistication and extent of the market differentiation employed is illustrated by the frequent success of 'innocent' young boys performing songs deemed to be old-fashioned. In the guise of breaking the mould of viewers' expectations, they all too predictably appeal to older viewers for whom they have been chosen.

3 'Through this process individuals unconsciously adopted the values of alienated culture, so that they unwittingly subscribed to a degraded version of humanity' (Rojek 2001: 34).

4 Furthermore, any potential role for celebrity figures as an embodiment of anti-traditional social resistance tends to be quickly packaged as a cultural commodity. This process can work both upwards and downwards in so far as it reduces punks to the visual content of London tourist postcards and elevates such previously counter-cultural figures as Mick Jagger to the British Knighthood (June 2002) or Johnny Rotten to the Reality TV programme *I'm A Celebrity – Get Me Out of Here!* (January 2004).

5 Potlatch refers to the practice among the rich in some indigenous tribes of burning all their possessions in a dramatic cultural reversal of the Western capitalist notion of *conspicuous consumption*.

6 See Rojek (2001: 91, 92), especially such comments as 'We are drawn to celebrities for a variety of reasons. These can only be concretely established through empirical investigation' (2001: 92). Such sentiments indicate an *a priori* resistance to the theoretically based approach of the culture industry thesis.

7 In the sixteenth century, Etienne de LaBoetie introduced the notion of *voluntary servitude* (*servitude volontaire*). Whereas for Boetie people, by laziness, do not adequately appropriate their freedom, for Spinoza, people even fight for their slavery, as if it were their salvation. In an essay at the end of Pauline Reage's erotic classic, *The Story of O*, Jean Paulhan relates how in 1838 a group of newly freed West Indian slaves massacred their former owner and his family for not taking them back into bondage.

8 Although, given the rise of product placement, commercial tie-ins, and so on, this less obviously commercialized aspect of movies is perhaps debateable.

9 As Lowenthal (1961) suggests in his essay 'The little shop girls go to the movies' and Adorno writes in 'The culture industry: enlightenment as mass deception' (Adorno and Horkheimer 1997).

## Chapter 7

1  A recent newspaper feature article describes this phenomenon as 'Brilliantly Boring' and describes various websites and television programmes devoted to presenting non-events such as cheese maturing in real time as dumbly fascinating *pseudo-events*. See Burkeman and Topping (2007).
2  See Coleman (2003, 2006, forthcoming).
3  See Hemmens (2007).
4  Dovey's description of this zone resonates with J.G. Ballard's fictional representations in such works as *Cocaine Nights* (1996) and *Super-Cannes* (2001).
5  For an extended treatment of this idea see Andrejevic (2004).
6  The ubiquitous mainstream reach of porn is illustrated by the recent success of porn stars into previous family-orientated formats: 'Rachel Ray, whose undeniable porniness has landed her her own magazine – *Every Day with Rachel Ray* – to be published by that renowned purveyor of raunch – *Reader's Digest*. The dominion of the enteric brain has propelled porn from the social ghetto to social diffusion just as it has propelled Jenna Jameson to US magazine and cooking shows from Boston public television to the big time' (Kaufman 2005: 60).
7  See www.semiotic.co.uk/potnoodle.html
8  Nitke has published a mainstream coffee-table book of her porn-set stills entitled *Kiss of Fire*.
9  Taken from an interview entitled *Pornucopia* with Brooke Gladstone, 7 October 2005; see www.onthemedia.org/transcripts/transcripts_100705_porn.html
10 The inward looking nature of voyeurism in the contemporary mediascape has culminated in the commercial success of DIY/amateur porn and fictionally portrayed in Irvine Welsh's *Porno* (2002).

## Chapter 8

1  This was demonstrated by the furore created by Mika Brzezinski, a US television news presenter who objected on air to the morning bulletin's lead story about Paris Hilton's previous night's appearance on the *Larry King Show* (Harris 2007).
2  Cited in Mitchell (1987: 203).
3  See Chapter 4 of Harris and Taylor (2005) for a detailed discussion of this quality of photography.
4  In Sontag's *On Photography* (1979) she quotes Edward Weston's photographing of toilet bowls and their equation with Greek marble statues. In *Digital Matters: Theory and Culture of the Matrix*

we cite Don Delillo and Italo Calvino's fictional expressions of the 'madness' this democracy of images can tend to create in those seeking to capture on film their surroundings – see Harris and Taylor (2005: 90–9).

5 This is a toned down but thereby more insidious version of photography's previously cited normalization of toilet bowls as an object of aesthetic contemplation – see previous note.

6 August Kleinzahler Diary – *London Review of Books*, 17 August 2006, p. 35.

7 The linguistically challenged nature of the Bush administration has been analysed in detail in Miller's *The Bush Dyslexicon: Observations on a National Disorder* (2001) and a more overtly satirical account of Donald Rumsfeld's incoherent public utterances re-presented in the form of poems and haikus in Seely's *Pieces of Intelligence: The Existential Poetry of Donald H. Rumsfeld* (2003).

8 The event was addressed from the perspective of critical media theory in Baudrillard's *The Spirit of Terrorism* (2002) and Žižek's *Welcome to the Desert of the Real* (2002).

9 Baudrillard develops this idea further in *The Spirit of Terrorism* (2002), in which the destruction of the Twin Towers is explained in terms of his theory's distinction between cultures based on symbolic and semiotic exchange.

10 See Gary Younge (2003) and judging from survey evidence, despite (or perhaps ironically because of) the extensive nature of the media's coverage of the second Gulf conflict, basic factual issues have failed to survive: 'According to a New York Times/ CBS survey, 42% of the American public believes that Saddam Hussein is directly responsible for the September 11 attacks on the World Trade Centre and the Pentagon. And an ABC news poll says that 55% of Americans believe that Saddam Hussein directly supports al-Qaida' (Roy 2003: n.p.).

11 For example see Curtis White's (2003) entertaining critique of the negative representations of intellectuals in Spielberg's *Saving Private Ryan*.

12 A similar process occurred with the false story of Iraqi soldiers pulling Kuwaiti babies from incubators in the previous Gulf conflict based upon the emotional (but coached by a US public relations firm) testimony of a 15-year-old Kuwaiti girl initially known only by her first name of Nayirah, but who was later discovered to be the daughter of a Kuwaiti Emir keen to help encourage US public opinion to support military involvement. See www.prwatch.org/books/tsigfy10.html (accessed 28 June 2007). In this context, Naomi Klein (2003) illustrates the nature of the media's ideological manipulations by comparing the

unequal media treatment given to Private Lynch and Rachel Corrie – a US peace activist killed by the Israeli army on 16 March 2003.
13 See Baudrillard's 'Whatever happened to evil?' chapter in Baudrillard (1993) for a full discussion of this theme.

## Conclusion

1  It is interesting to note in this regard that the style of wearing jeans pulled low down past the hips along with unlaced sneakers stemmed from the fact that inmates have their belts and shoe-laces removed upon entering prison. The symbolic protest against the social order signified by the subsequent adoption of this style by socially alienated black ghetto youths, however, is fatally undermined once it becomes just another commodified 'look'.
2  The (il)logical extension of this process is one in which Irish bars in Ireland itself begin to adapt their own content to reflect the 'reality' of Irish theme bars elsewhere in the world. This illustrates what Baudrillard means with his notion that in the simulacra the model begins to dictate terms and conditions to the prior reality.

# Bibliography

Abercrombie, N. and Longhurst, B. (1998) *Audiences*. London: Sage.

Abt, V. and Mustazza, L. (1997) *Coming after Oprah: Cultural Fallout in the Age of the TV Talk Show*. Bowling Green, OH: Bowling Green State University Press.

Adorno, T.W. (1991) *The Culture Industry: Selected Essays on Mass Culture*. Ed. J.M. Bernstein. London and New York: Routledge.

Adorno, T.W. (1992) *Negative Dialectics*. Trans. E.B. Ashton. New York: Continuum.

Adorno, T.W. (1994) Analytic study of the NBC 'Music Appreciation Hour' *The Musical Quarterly*, 78(2): 325–77.

Adorno, T.W. (1998) *Critical Models: Interventions and Catchwords*. (Ed and trans. H.W. Pickford. New York: Columbia University Press.

Adorno, T.W. and Horkheimer, M. (1997) *Dialectic of Enlightenment*. Trans. J. Cumming. London: Verso Books.

Adorno, T.W. and Horkheimer, M. (2002) *Dialectic of Enlightenment: Philosophical Fragments*. Trans. E. Jephcott. Palo Alto, CA: Stanford University Press.

Alasuutari, P. (ed.) (1999) *Rethinking the Media Audience*. London: Sage.

Andrejevic, M. (2004) *Reality TV: The Work of Being Watched*. Oxford: Rowman & Littlefield.

Ang, I. (1985) *Watching 'Dallas'*. London: Methuen.

Ballard, J.G. (1996) *Cocaine Nights*. London: Flamingo.

Ballard, J.G. (2001) *Super-Cannes*. London: Flamingo.

Banet-Weiser, S. and Portwood-Stacer, L. (2006) 'I Just want to be me again!' Beauty pageants, reality television and post-feminism, *Feminist Theory*, 7(2): 255–72.

Barker, M. (1998) 'Critique: audiences "R" us' in R. Dickinson, R. Harindranath and O. Linné (eds.) *Approaches to Audiences: A Reader*. London: Arnold.

Barker, M. and Brooks, K. (1998) *Knowing Audiences: 'Judge Dredd' – its Friends, Fans, and Foes.* Luton: University of Luton Press.

Barker, M. and Brooks, K. (1998) 'On looking into Bourdieu's black box' in R. Dickinson, R. Harindranath and O. Liné (eds.) *Approaches to Audiences: A Reader.* London: Arnold.

Barthes, R. (1973 [1957]) *Mythologies.* London: Paladin Books.

Barthes, R. (1982) *Camera Lucida.* New York: Hill and Wang.

Baudrillard, J. (1981) *For a Critique of the Political Economy of the Sign.* New York: Telos Press.

Baudrillard, J. (1983a) *Simulations.* New York: Semiotext(e).

Baudrillard, J. (1983b) *In the Shadow of the Silent Majorities.* New York: Semiotext(e).

Baudrillard, J. (1988) *Ecstasy of Communication.* New York: Semiotext(e).

Baudrillard, J. (1990a) *Seduction.* London: MacMillan.

Baudrillard, J. (1990b) *Fatal Strategies.* London: Pluto Press.

Baudrillard, J. (1993) *The Transparency of Evil: Essays on Extreme Phenomena.* London: Verso.

Baudrillard, J. (1996a) *The Perfect Crime.* London: Verso.

Baudrillard, J. (1996b) *The System of Objects.* London: Verso.

Baudrillard, J. (1997) *Art and Artefact.* Ed. N. Zurbrugg. London: Sage.

Baudrillard, J. (1998) *The Consumer Society.* London: Sage.

Baudrillard, J. (2002) *The Spirit of Terrorism.* London: Verso.

Baudrillard, J. (2005) *The Conspiracy of Art.* Cambridge, MA: MIT Press.

Benjamin, W. (1973) *Illuminations.* Trans. H. Zohn. London: Fontana.

Benjamin, W. (1985a) *Charles Baudelaire: A Lyric Poet in the Era of High Capitalism.* Trans. H. Zohn. London: Verso.

Benjamin, W. (1985b) *One Way Street and Other Writings.* Trans E. Jephcott and K. Shorter. London: Verso.

Berman, M. (1983) *All That is Solid Melts into Air: The Experience of Modernity.* London: Verso Books.

Biressi, A. and Nunn, H. (2004) *Reality TV: Realism and Revelation.* London: Wallflower Press.

Blair, D. (2007) Geldof and Bono blast G8 for betraying Africa, *Telegraph Online*, 10 June.
www.telegraph.co.uk/news/main.jhtml?xml=/news/2007/06/09/wgeight109.xml. (accessed 28 June 2007).

Blumenthal, S. (2004) Hear no evil, read no evil, speak drivel, *The Guardian*, 15 April.

Bonner, F. (2003) *Ordinary Television*. London: Sage.

Boorstin, D. ([1961] 1992) *The Image: A Guide to Pseudo-Events in America*. New York: Vintage.

Bracewell, M. (2002) *The Nineties: When Surface Was Depth*. London: Flamingo.

Bratich, J. (2006) 'Nothing is left alone for too long': reality programming and control society subjects, *Journal of Communication Inquiry*, 30(1): 65–83.

Brunsdon, C., Johnson, C., Moseley, R. and Wheatley, H. (2001) Factual entertainment on British television, *European Journal of Cultural Studies*, 4(1): 29–62.

Brunsdon, C. (2003) Lifestyling Britain: the 8–9 slot on British television, *International Journal of Cultural Studies*, 6(1): 5–23.

Buncombe, A. (2004) The couple at the centre of a scandal that horrified the world, *Independent*, 7 May. http://news.independent.co.uk/world/middle_east/article59323.ece (accessed 28 June 2007).

Burkeman, O. and Topping, A. (2007) Brilliantly boring, *The Guardian Online*, 3 April. www.guardian.co.uk/g2/story/0,,2048707,00.html (accessed 28 June 2007).

Butler, S. ([1872]1970) *Erewhon*. London: Penguin.

Carey, J. (1989) *Communication as Culture: Essays on Media and Society*. London: Routledge.

Coleman, S. (2003) A Tale of Two Houses: The House of Commons, the Big Brother House and the people at home. London: Hansard Society.

Coleman, S. (2006) How the other half votes: Big Brother viewers and the 2005 British General Election campaign, *International Journal of Cultural Studies*, 9(4): 457–79.

Coleman, S. (forthcoming) Beyond the West(minster) wing: the depiction of politics and politicians in British soap operas, *Television and New Media*.

Couldry, N. (2000) *The Place of Media Power: Pilgrims and Witnesses of the Media Age*. London: Routledge.

Couldry, N. (2003) *Media Rituals: A Critical Approach*. London: Routledge.

Cronenberg, D. (1983) *Videodrome*. Universal Pictures.

Debord, G. (1977) *The Society of the Spectacle*. Trans F, Perlman and J. Supak. Detroit, MI: Black and Red.

Debord, G. (1991) *Comments on the Society of the Spectacle*. Trans. M. Imrie. London: Verso Books.

Debord, G. (1994) *The Society of the Spectacle*. Trans. D. Nicholson-Smith. Cambridge, MA: Zone Books.

Deleuze, G. (1995) Postscript on control societies, in *Negotiations*. Trans. M. Joughin. New York: Columbia University Press (Original work published 1990).

Dickinson, R., Harindranath, R. and Linné, O. (eds) (1998) *Approaches to Audiences: A Reader*. London: Arnold.

Dovey, J. (2000) *Freakshow: First Person Media and Factual Television*. London: Pluto Press.

Dunn, D. (2006) Singular encounters: mediating the tourist destination in British television holiday programmes, *Tourist Studies*, 6(1): 37–58.

Duttmann, A.G. (2000) Tradition and destruction: Walter Benjamin's politics of language, in A. Benjamin and P. Osborne (eds) *Destruction & Experience*. Manchester: Clinamen Press.

Dyer-Witheford, N. (1999) *Cyber-Marx: Cycles and Struggles in High Technology Capitalism*. Urbana, IL: University of Illinois Press.

Eagleton, T. (2003) *After Theory*. London: Allen Lane.

Espinas, A. (1897) *Les Origines de la Technologie*. Paris: F. Alcon.

Evans, J. and Hesmondhalgh, D. (eds.) (2005) *Understanding Media: Inside Celebrity*. Maidenhead: Open University Press.

Ewen, S. (1996) *PR! A Social History of Spin*. New York: Basic Books.

Ewen, S. (1999) *All Consuming Images: The Politics of Style in Contemporary Culture*. New York: Basic Books.

Ewen, S. (2001) *Captains of Consciousness: Advertising and the Social Roots of the Consumer Culture*. New York: Basic Books.

Ewen, S. and Ewen, E. (1992) *Channels of Desire: Mass Images and the Shaping of American Consciousness*. Minneapolis, MN: University of Minnesota Press.

Fiske, J. (1987) *Television Culture*. London: Routledge.

Fiske, J. (1989a) *Understanding Popular Culture*. London: Routledge.

Fiske, J. (1989b) *Reading the Popular*. London: Unwin Hyman.

Fiske, J. (1993) *Power Plays Power Works*. London: Verso.

Fiske, J. (1996) *Media Matters: Race and Gender in U.S. Politics*. Minneapolis, MN: University of Minnesota Press.

Gamson, J. (1994) *Claims to Fame: Celebrity in Contemporary America*. Berkeley, CA: University of California Press.

Gamson, J. (1997) *Claims to Fame: Celebrity in Contemporary America.* Los Angeles, CA: University of California Press.

Genesko, G. (1999) *McLuhan and Baudrillard: The Masters of Implosion.* London: Routledge.

Giles, D. (2002) Keeping the public in their place: audience participation in lifestyle television programming, *Discourse & Society*, 13(5): 603–28.

Gilloch, G. (2002) *Walter Benjamin: Critical Constellations.* Cambridge: Polity.

Goldman, R. and Papson, S. (1996) *Sign Wars: The Cluttered Landscape of Advertising.* London: Guildford Press.

Goldman, R. and Papson, S. (1998) *Nike Culture: The Sign of the Swoosh.* London: Sage.

Gottdiener, M. (2001) *The Theming of America: American Dreams, Media Fantasies, and Themed Environments.* Boulder, CO: West View Press.

Grindstaff, L. (2002) *The Money Shot: Trash, Class, and the Making of TV Talk Shows.* Chicago, IL: University of Chicago Press.

Gritten, D. (2002) *Fame: Stripping Celebrity Bare.* London: Allen Lane.

*The Guardian* (1999) Woodstock wars: junk food prices turn mood. www.guardian.co.uk/international/story/0,3604,282927,00.html (accessed 28 June 2007).

Hannigan, J. (1998) *Fantasy City: Pleasure and Profit in the Postmodern Metropolis.* London: Routledge.

Hansen, M. (1987) Benjamin, cinema and experience: 'The Blue Flower in the Land of Technology', *New German Critique*, 40: 179–224.

Hansen, M. (1991) Decentric perspectives: Kracauer's early writings on film and mass culture, *New German Critique*, 54: 47–76.

Hardt, M. and Negri, A. (2000) *Empire.* Cambridge, MA: Harvard University Press.

Hardt, M. and Negri, A. (2005) *Multitude: War and Democracy in the Age of Empire.* London: Penguin.

Harris, J. Ll. and Taylor, P.A. (2005) *Digital Matters: Theory and Culture of the Matrix.* London: Routledge.

Harris, P. (2007) Why I said no to Paris Hilton mania, *The Observer*, 1 July. www.guardian.co.uk/usa/story/0,,2115818,00.html. (accessed 1 July 2007).

Held, D. (1980) *Introduction to Critical Theory: Horkheimer to Habermas.* London: Hutchinson.

Helmore, E. (2003) Private Jessica says President is misusing her 'heroism', *The Observer.* http://observer.guardian.co.uk/ international/ story/0,6903,1081186,00.html. (accessed 28 June 2007).

Hemmens, W. (2007) 'Reality TV hunt for students', *The Guardian* http://education.guardian.co.uk/higher/news/story/ 0,,2050271,00.html (accessed 28 June 2007).

Hermes, J. (1999) Media figures in identity construction, in P. Alasuutari (ed.) *Rethinking the Media Audience.* London: Sage.

Hill, A. (2005) *Reality TV: Audiences and Popular Factual Television.* London: Routledge.

Holmes, S. and Jermyn, D. (eds.) (2004) *Understanding Reality Television.* London: Routledge.

Hussey, A. (2001) *The Game of War: The Life and Death of Guy Debord.* London: Jonathan Cape.

Inglis, F. (1990) *Media Theory: An Introduction.* Oxford: Blackwell.

Innis, H. ([1951] 2003) *The Bias of Communication.* Buffalo: University of Toronto Press.

Jameson, F. (ed). (1980) *Aesthetics and Politics.* London: Verso.

Jameson, F. (1991) *Postmodernism or, The Cultural Logic of Late Capitalism.* Durham, NC: Duke University Press.

Jameson, F. (1993) *Signatures of the Visible.* London: Routledge.

Jameson, F. (1998) *The Cultural Turn: Selected Writings on the Postmodern, 1983–1998.* London: Verso.

Jenkins, H. (2006a) *Fans, Bloggers, and Gamers: Exploring Participatory Culture.* New York: New York University Press.

Jenkins, H. (2006b) *Convergence Culture: Where Old and New Media Collide.* New York: New York University Press.

Jung, C.G. (1928) *Contributions to Analytical Psychology. New York: Harcourt, Brace and Co.*

Kapp, E. ([1877] 1978) *Grundlinien einer Philosophie der Technik.* 2nd edn. Düsseldorf: Stern.

Katz, E., Liebes, T., Peters, J.D. and Orloft, A. (et al) (2002) *Canonic Texts in Media Research.* Cambridge: Polity Press.

Kaufman, F. (2005) 'Debbie does salad: the Food Network at the frontiers of pornography, *Harpers Magazine,* October: 60.

Kilbourn, R. (2003) *Staging the Real: Factual Programming in the Age of Big Brother.* Manchester: Manchester University Press.

Kittler, F.A. (1990) *Discourse Networks 1800/1900.* Stanford, CA: Stanford University Press.

Kittler, F.A. (1997) *Literature Media, Information Systems*. Amsterdam: Overseas Publishers Association.

Kittler, F.A. (1999) *Gramophone, Film, Typewriter*. Stanford, CA: Stanford University Press.

Klein, N. (2003) On rescuing Private Lynch and forgetting Rachel Corrie, *The Guardian Online* 22 May. www.guardian.co.uk/israel/comment/0,10551,961025,00.html (accessed 28 June 2007).

Knab, K. (ed.) (1981) *The Situationist International Anthology*. Berkeley, CA: Bureau of Public Secrets.

Koch, G. (2000) Cosmos in film: on the concept of space in Walter Benjamin's 'Work of art' essay, in A. Benjamin and P. Osborne (eds.) *Destruction & Experience*. Manchester: Clinamen Press.

Kompare, D. (2004) Extraordinarily ordinary: the Osbournes as 'An American Family', in S. Murray and L. Ouellette (eds.) *Reality TV: Remaking Television Culture*. New York: New York University Press.

Koss, J. (1997) Hooked on Kracauer, *Assemblage*, 31: 80–9.

Kracauer, S. (1960) *Theory of Film: The Redemption of Physical Reality*. New York: Oxford University Press.

Kracauer, S. (1965) *Theory of Film: The Redemption of Physical Reality*. New York: Galaxy.

Kracauer, S. (1995) *The Mass Ornament: The Weimar Essays*. Cambridge, MA: Harvard University Press.

Kracauer, S. (2000) *From Caligari to Hitler: A Psychological History of the German Cinema*. Princeton, NJ: Princeton University Press.

Kroker, A. (1984) *Technology and the Canadian Mind: Innis/McLuhan/Grant*. Montreal: New World Perspectives.

Lacey, N. (2002) *Media Institutions and Audiences. Key Concepts in Media Studies*. Basingstoke: Palgrave Macmillan.

Langer, J. (1998) *Tabloid Television: Popular Journalism and the 'Other News'*. London: Routledge.

Lapham, L. (2001) *Lights, Camera, Democracy! Selected Essays*. New York: AtRandom.com Books.

Lash, S. (2002) *Critique of Information*. London: Sage.

Livingstone, S. and Lunt, P. (1994) *Talk on Television: Audience Participation and Public Debate*. London: Routledge.

Lorenzo-Dus, N. (2006) Buying and selling: mediating persuasion in British property shows, *Media, Culture & Society*, 28(5): 739–61.

Lowenthal, L. (1961) *Literature, Popular Culture, & Society*. Palo Alto, CA: Pacific Books.

Lyotard, J. F. (1979) *The Postmodern Condition: A Report on Knowledge*. Manchester: Manchester University Press.

Marcuse, H. (1968) *One Dimensional Man*. Boston, MA: Beacon Books.

Marcuse, H. (2002[1964]) *One Dimensional Man: Studies in the Ideology of Advanced Industrial Society*. London: Routledge.

Marshall, D. (1997) *Celebrity and Power: Fame in Contemporary Culture*. Minneapolis, MN: University of Minnesota Press.

Marx, K. ([1887] 1983) *Capital: A Critique of Political Economy*, Vol 1. London: Lawrence & Wishart.

Marx, K. (1988) *Economic and Philosophic Manuscripts of 1844*. Trans. M. Milligan. (Buffalo, NY: Prometheus Books).

McDonough, T. (2004) *Guy Debord and the Situationist International: Texts and Documents*. Cambridge, MA.: MIT Press.

McGuigan, J. (1992) *Cultural Populism*. London: Routledge.

McLaughlin, T. (1996) *Street Smarts and Critical Theory: Listening to the Vernacular*. Madison, WI: University of Wisconsin Press.

McLuhan, M. (1951) *The Mechanical Bride: A Folklore of Industrial Man*. New York: Vanguard Press.

McLuhan, M. (1962) *The Gutenberg Galaxy: The Making of Typographic Man*. Buffalo: University of Toronto Press.

McLuhan, M. ([1964] 1995) *Understanding Media: The Extensions of Man*. London: Routledge.

McLuhan, M. (1997) 'Notes on Burroughs', in M. Moos (ed.) *Media Research: Technology, Art, Communication*. Amsterdam: Overseas Publishers Association.

McQuire, S. (1998) *Visions of Modernity: Representation, Memory, Time and Space in the Age of the Camera*. London: Sage.

Meek, A. (1998) "Benjamin, the televisual and the 'fascistic subject'." www.latrobe.edu.au/screeningthepast/firstrelease/fir998/AMfr4e.htm (accessed 28 June 2007).

Mellencamp, P. (ed.) (1990) *Logics of Television: Essays in Cultural Criticism*. London: BFI Publishing.

Merrifield, A. (2005) *Guy Debord*. London: Reaktion Books.

Merrin, W. (2005) *Baudrillard and the Media*. Cambridge: Polity.

Miller, M.C. (2001) *The Bush Dyslexicon: Observations on a National Disorder*. New York: W.W. Norton.

Mitchell, W.J. (1992) *The Reconfigured Eye: Visual Truth in the Post-photographic Era*. Cambridge, MA: MIT Press.

Mitchell, W.J.T. (1987) *Iconology: Image, Text, Ideology*. Chicago, IL: University of Chicago Press.

Moos, M. (ed.) (1997) *Media Research: Technology, Art, Communication.* Amsterdam: Overseas Publishers Association.

Morley, D. (1986) *Family Television.* London: Comedia.

Murray, S. and Ouellette L. (eds.) (2004). *Reality TV: Remaking Television Culture.* New York: New York University Press.

Nichols, B. (1994) *Blurred Boundaries: Questions of Meaning in Contemporary Culture.* Bloomington, IN: Indiana University Press.

O'Neil, J. (1991) *Plato's Cave: Desire, Power, and the Specular Functions of the Media.* NJ: Ablex Norwood.

Palmer, G. (2004) 'The New You': class and transformation in lifestyle television, in S. Holmes and D. Jermyn (eds.) *Understanding Reality Television.* London: Routledge.

Palmer, G. (2005) The undead: life on the D-list, *Westminster Papers in Communication and Culture,* 2(2): 37–53.

Palmer, G. (2006) Coming together: thedatingchannel.com and the future of television, *Journal of Media Practice,* 7(2): 109–21.

Palmer, G. (2007) An American fairytale: extreme makeover: home edition, in D. Heller (ed.) *Makeover Television Revisited.* London: Tauris Press.

Plato (1955) *The Republic.* London: Penguin.

Poster, M. (1990) *The Mode of Information.* Cambridge: Polity.

Poster, M. (2006) *Information Please: Culture and Politics in the Age of Digital Machines.* Durham, NC: Duke University Press.

Potter, M. (2003) The real saving of Private Lynch, *The Toronto Star,* 4 May. www.commondreams.org/headlines03/0504-05.htm (accessed 28 June 2007).

Radway, J. (1984) *Reading the Romance: Women, Patriarchy and Popular Literature.* Chapel Hill, NC: University of North Carolina Press.

Rojek, C. (2001) *Celebrity.* London: Reaktion Books.

Rosenberg, B. and White, D.M. (eds.) (1957) *Mass Culture: The Popular Arts in America.* Toronto: Collier-Macmillan.

Rosenberg, B. and White, D.M. (eds) (1971) *Mass Culture Revisited.* New York: Van Nostren Reinhold: New York.

Ross, K. (2003) *Media and Audiences. New Perspectives.* London: Open University Press.

Roy, A. (2003) Mesopotamia. Babylon. The Tigris and Euphrates, *The Guardian Online,* 2 April. http://books.guardian.co.uk/writersoniraq/story/0,,927994,00.html (accessed 28 June 2007).

Said, E. ([1979] 2003) *Orientalism.* London: Penguin.

Scanell, P. (1996) *Radio, Television and Modern Life.* Oxford: Blackwell.

Seabrook, J. (2000) *Nobrow: The Culture of Marketing, The Marketing of Culture.* London: Methuen.

Seely, H. (2003) *Pieces of Intelligence: The Existential Poetry of Donald H. Rumsfeld.* New York: Free Press.

Sontag, S. (1979) *On Photography.* London: Penguin.

Sontag, S. (2004) What have we done? *Guardian,* 23 May, G2 Section.

Sorkin, M. (ed.) (1992) *Variations on a Theme Park.* New York: Hill and Wang.

Staiger, J. (2005) *Media Reception Studies.* New York: New York University Press.

Stevenson, N. (2002) *Understanding Media Cultures: Social Theory and Mass Communication.* London: Sage.

Taylor, L. (2002) From ways of life to lifestyle: the 'ordinari-ization' of British gardening lifestyle television, *European Journal of Communication,* 17(4): 479–93.

Taylor, P.A. (2006) Putting the critique back into 'A Critique of Information', *Information, Communication & Society,* 9.5, November: 553–71.

Taylor, P.A. (2007) The pornographic barbarism of the self-reflecting sign, *International Journal of Baudrillard Studies,* 4(1). www.ubishops.ca/BaudrillardStudies/vol4_1/taylor.htm (accessed 1 July 2007).

Thompson, J. (1995) *The Media and Modernity: A Social Theory of the Media.* Cambridge: Polity.

Turner, G. (2004) *Understanding Celebrity.* London: Sage.

Twitchell, J. (1996) *ADcultUSA: The Triumph of Advertising in American Culture.* New York: Columbia University Press.

Virno, P. (2004) *A Grammar of the Multitude.* Los Angeles, CA: Semiotext(e).

Weber, M. (1968) The routinization of charisma, in G. Roth and C. Wittich (eds.) *Economy and Society.* New York: Bedminister Press.

Weber, M. (2001[1930]) The Protestant Ethic and the Spirit of Capitalism. London: Routledge.

Welsh, I. (2002) *Porno.* London: Vintage.

White, C. (2003) *The Middle Mind: Why Americans Don't Think for Themselves.* San Francisco, CA: HarperCollins.

Williams, R. (1974) *Television: Technology and Cultural Form.* London: Fontana.

Winn, M. (1977) *The Plug-In Drug.* London: Penguin.

Winner, L. (1977) *Autonomous Technology: Technics-out-of-control as a Theme for Political Thought.* Cambridge, MA: MIT Press.

Witkin, R. (2002) *Adorno on Popular Culture.* London: Routledge.

Witte, K. (1975) Introduction to Siegfried Kracauer's 'The Mass Ornament', *New German Critique*, 5: 59–66.

Younge, G. (2003) "What *is* she wearing?" *The Guardian*, 2 April G2 Section.

Žižek, S. (1989) *The Sublime Object of Ideology.* London: Verso.

Žižek, S. (ed.) (1994) *Mapping Ideology.* London: Verso.

Žižek, S. (2002) *Welcome to the Desert of the Real.* London: Verso.

Žižek, S. (2006) *The Parallax View.* London: MIT Press.

# Index

abstraction 47, 57, 115
  society dominated by 51
Abt, Vicki 149, 167
Abu Ghraib prison 163
  abuse of Iraqi prisoners at 192, 194–5,
    197
  mediation of events at 178
achieved celebrity 140
acoustic space 88–9
admiring identification 152
Adorno, Theodor Ludwig Wiesengrund
    [1903–69] 25–7, 34, 40, 47, 51, 60–84,
    99, 120, 135, 138, 142, 158–159, 161,
    166, 168, 175, 200, 206–9, 211
advertising 87, 123, 148–9, 184
advertising campaigns 70
aesthecization of politics
  fascism characterized as 53
aesthetic
  creation of new 29
aesthetic production 17
aesthetic sensibility 77
aesthetic terrorism 109
aesthetics
  politicization of 53
Afghanistan 197
Africa
  effect of radio on 100
African American youth
  urban fashion of 208
aggression
  implicit in use of camera 46
Ahmadinejad, President Mahmoud 179
alienation 115, 119–20
  drama of 209
allegorical signs 47
alphabetization
  effects of 91
Althusser, Louis Pierre [1918–90] 203
ambiguous transparency 148
*American Idol* 72, 75, 143
anawim 213
Andrews, Julie 11
angst 65
anti-landmine campaign 146
architecture 35
art
  after advent of technological repro-
    duction 30

analysis of 70
as exhibition 20
as ritual 20
changing exhibition quality of 21
commercial considerations in 72
de-localization of 23
evolution of 21
fascism and 28
historical formation and function of
    18
mechanical reproduction 20–21
mediatization of 17
politicization of 27
religious veneration and 21
art *see also* high art; low art
artist
  traditional role of 198
artistic reproductions
  quantitative increase of 21
ascribed celebrity 140
Athena's Shield 213
attributed celebrity 140
audience empowerment 6, 9
audience investment 138
audiences
  co-option of 143
  empowerment of 144
aufhebgen 111
aura
  cinema and 152
  decline of 23, 139, 209
  definition of 18–9
  destruction of 41
  in art 21
  loss of 145
  manipulation of political purposes 29
  photography and 43
  playing with 149–51
  political implications of decline in
    27–34
  release from 63
aura of authenticity 149
aural culture 95
auratic art
  traditional 35
auratic concentration
  shift to reproductive distraction 35
authenticity
  aura of 149

# A CRITICAL AND CULTURAL THEORY READER

Second Edition

**Edited by Anthony Easthope and Kate McGowan**

Praise for the first edition

*"The selection is judicious and valuably supplemented by thorough commentaries that contextualise and clarify the debates and issues and the importance of each excerpt. Though today there may be many readers in and around cultural and media studies, Easthope and McGowan's remains vital..."*

*Times Higher Educational Supplement*

This Reader introduces the key readings in critical and cultural theory. It guides students through the tradition of thought, from Saussure's early writings on language to contemporary commentary on world events by theorists such as Baudrillard and Žižek. The readings are grouped according to six thematic sections: Semiology; Ideology; Subjectivity; Difference; Gender and Race; and Postmodernism.

The second and expanded edition of this highly successful Reader reflects the growing diversity of the field.

- Featuring thirteen new essays, including essays by Homi Bhabha, Simone de Beauvoir, Franz Fanon and Judith Butler
- With a general introduction as well as useful introductions to each of the thematic sections
- Including summaries of each of the extracts - invaluable for students and lecturers.

Key reading for areas of study including cultural studies, critical theory, literature, linguistics, English, media studies, communication studies, cultural history, sociology, gender studies, visual arts, film and architecture.

**Essays by:** Louis Althusser, Roland Barthes, Jean Baudrillard, Homi K. Bhabha, Judith Butler, Hélène Cixous, Simone de Beauvoir, Ferdinand de Saussure, Jacques Derrida, Umberto Eco, Frederick Engels, Franz Fanon, Michel Foucault, Sigmund Freud, Julia Kristeva, Jacques Lacan, Jean-François Lyotard, Colin MacCabe, Pierre Macherey, Karl Marx, Kobena Mercer, Laura Mulvey, Rajeswari Sunder Rajan, Edward Said, Slavoj Žižek.

**Contents:** *Section 1: Semiology - Section 2: Ideology - Section 3: Subjectivity - Section 4: Difference - Section 5: Gender - Summaries - Biographies - References - Index.*

2004   304pp

978-0-335-21355-9  (Paperback)   978-0-335-21356-6  (Hardback)

# KEY ISSUES IN CRITICAL AND CULTURAL THEORY

Kate McGowan

*"... the ideal book for students of cultural theory and one that is sensitively attuned to the political challenges of our times. Whether explaining dialectical materialism or the lyrics of Oasis and The Arctic Monkeys, Kate McGowan is an enlightening and entertaining guide."*

*Professor Stephen Regan, Durham University*

From a man with electric underpants, to the indelible mark of 9/11 in a global cultural imaginary, Kate McGowan addresses the questions of cultural meaning and value which confront us all today. The book explores the often complex paradigms of critical thinking and discusses the possibilities of engaging and critiquing the cultural values that relate to our present.

Dealing directly with the issues entailed in cultural analysis, the book avoids simply looking at the eminent authors or movements in critical and cultural theory, and instead focuses on why studying culture matters to us today:

- What are the 'proper' objects of cultural study?
- What makes something 'art'?
- What can critical and cultural theory contribute to contemporary debates about ethics?
- What possibilities are opened up by theories of 'otherness' in thinking about the stranger or outsider in today's society?
- How does a culture contest its own values - in relation to race, gender, class, sexuality and a variety of faiths and abilities?

*Key Issues in Critical and Cultural Theory* is key reading for students studying humanities, and for those with an interest in culture, aesthetics, ethics and philosophy who want to understand how these affect the world.

**Contents:** *Acknowledgements - Introduction - Textuality and Signification - Aesthetics - Ethics - Alterity - The Real - The Inhuman - Conclusion - Glossary - Notes - Bibliography.*

2007   176pp
978-0-335-21803-5  (Paperback)    978-0-335-21804-2  (Hardback)